Instant Legal Forms:

Ready–to–Use Documents
for Almost Any Occasion

Ralph E. Troisi

LIBERTY HOUSE®

First Edition • First Printing

Copyright © 1989 by Ralph E. Troisi. Reproduction or publication of the content in any manner except by photocopying for personal use, without express permission of the publisher, is prohibited. The publisher takes no responsibility for the use of any of the materials or methods described in this book, or for the products thereof. Printed in the United States of America. LIBERTY HOUSE books are published by LIBERTY HOUSE, a division of TAB BOOKS Inc. Its trademark, consisting of the words "LIBERTY HOUSE" and the portrayal of Benjamin Franklin, is registered in the United States Patent and Copyright Office.

Library of Congress Cataloging-in-Publication Data

Troisi, Ralph E.
Instant legal forms : ready-to-use documents for almost any occasion / by Ralph E. Troisi.
p.   cm.
Includes index.
ISBN 0-8306-3028-7 (pbk.)
1. Forms (Law)—United States—Popular works.   I. Title.
KF170.T76   1988
347.73'055—dc19
[347.30755]
88-28210
CIP

TAB BOOKS Inc. offers software for sale. For information and a catalog, please contact TAB Software Department, Blue Ridge Summit, PA 17294-0850.

Questions regarding the content of this book should be addressed to:

Reader Inquiry Branch
TAB BOOKS Inc.
Blue Ridge Summit, PA 17294-0214

Edited by Carl H. Silverman

Contents

1   Receipt   1

A receipt is a document which acknowledges the receiving of money or property. The person who gives someone else money or property keeps the receipt as proof that he or she gave the money or property to the other person.

Typical receipts include a general receipt, receipt for payment in full, receipt for payment on an account, receipt for money paid for someone else, receipt for rent, and receipt for a salary.

2   Consent to Release Information and Records   9

A consent to release information and records is a document in which the person signing the consent gives permission to someone else to release information and records to the person signing the consent, or to another person. Hospitals, schools, doctors, banks, and other institutions and persons have a duty of confidentiality to patients, students, and depositors. That duty prevents them from releasing information or records without the consent of the patient, student, or depositor.

3   Request for Credit Information and Request for Explanation of Denial of a Credit Application   19

A request for credit information is a document which asks a credit agency or other creditor for information that the agency or creditor has in its file on the person signing the request. You can use a request for credit information when a bank or other lender denies your application for credit based on information obtained from a credit agency or creditor. If the lender denies the application because of information obtained from a credit agency, the lender will tell you the name and address of the credit agency. You send a request for credit information to the credit agency to find out what information in the agency's file caused the lender to deny your credit application.

A request for explanation of denial of a credit application is a document which asks a bank or other lender to explain why the lender denied your credit application. When a lender denies your credit application, the lender will tell you whether or not the denial was based on information obtained from a credit agency or from someone other than a credit agency. If the information came from a credit agency, you send the request for credit information described above to the credit agency to find out what information in the agency's file caused the lender to deny your credit application. If the information came from someone other than a credit agency, the lender will not necessarily tell you the name and address of the information source. You send a request for explanation of denial of a credit application to the lender to discover the source of the information that led to the denial of credit. You then contact that source to discover and possibly correct the information that led to the denial of credit.

4   Affidavit   35

An affidavit is a document in which a person makes a statement and swears to the truth of that statement in front of a person authorized to give oaths, usually a notary public. Since an affidavit is a sworn statement made upon oath, it is similar to a statement made by a witness in a trial. The person who makes an affidavit could be guilty of perjury if he or she knowingly makes a false statement in the affidavit.

5   Will and Affidavit of Witnesses to Will   41

A will is a document that contains a person's instructions for his or her property and other affairs after death. It may include a *codicil*, which is an addition to a will signed after the original will was signed. A will may include an affidavit of the testator or testatrix (the person making the will), and of the witnesses to the will. In the affidavit, the witnesses swear that they saw the person who made the will sign the will in their presence, and that he or she appeared to be of sound mind. The testator or testatrix swears he or she signed his or her will voluntarily. A will is valid even if there is no affidavit of the testator or testatrix and the witnesses. But if an affidavit is not signed and it becomes necessary to probate the will, whoever is managing the estate may have to locate the witnesses, which could delay completion of the probate.

6   Joint Ownership Agreement to Avoid Probate   63

Probate is the court process of managing a deceased person's affairs. It begins when someone petitions a probate court to admit a deceased person's will to probate, or to open a probate for someone who died without a will. Probate takes time and costs money. Sometimes probate is necessary, but often it can and should be avoided. One way to avoid probate is to own all your property jointly with right of survivorship with one or more other people. When one joint owner dies, ownership of the property automatically belongs to the surviving joint owner.

7   Living Will   91

A living will is a document that expresses your desire to be allowed to die a natural death. Medical technology enables doctors and hospitals to keep people alive by artificial means. If you do not want to be kept alive by artificial means, a living will directs your doctors, family, and others not to keep you alive by these means.

8   Residential Rental Agreement   115

A rental agreement is an agreement in which the owner of property gives a renter the temporary use of the owner's property for a fee. In a residential rental agreement an owner, called a *landlord*, allows a renter to use a house owned by the landlord as the renter's home.

and other insurance coverage, and other terms of the agreement between the parties.

Preface

In an ideal world, everyone would be able to afford an attorney to handle their legal affairs. Attorneys would work quickly and charge fair prices for their work. They would write documents that everyone could understand.

We do not live in an ideal world. Attorneys tend to prepare documents that only other attorneys can understand, and many people fear and distrust attorneys—so they either neglect legal matters or try to handle them without an attorney.

I wrote this book to explain, in plain English, commonly used legal documents. I wanted to help people—especially those who could not afford an attorney—prepare simple legal documents themselves, rather than have them neglect their legal affairs. I wanted to explain which documents non-lawyers could prepare, and which they could not prepare. For documents in the latter category, this book provides information to help the reader use an attorney wisely.

How to Use This Book

This book explains commonly used legal documents. It will help you lend money; buy, sell, or rent a car, house, or other property; obtain information and records; write a will; avoid probate; avoid artificial life-support systems; protect yourself in dealing with home improvement and other contractors; appoint someone to handle your affairs in case you become disabled; and much more.

This book gives you forms for common legal documents and step-by-step instructions to fill out those forms. It not only includes blank forms for you to photocopy, but it also provides sample documents so you can see how completed forms should look. The samples are explained simply and thoroughly.

The forms in this book are for use in simple, straightforward situations. If your situation is not simple, you should consult an attorney. Reading this book will prepare you to talk with an attorney about your situation.

GENERAL INSTRUCTIONS

The following general instructions apply to all the forms in this book:

Typewriter or Pen   You may use a typewriter, or print with nonerasable ink, when completing the forms in this book.

Size of Paper   You may use letter- or legal-size paper for any legal document, except where noted. You may use other sizes for most documents, but if you intend to record a document at your county recorder's office, you should only use letter- or legal-size paper. Some recorder's offices will refuse to record odd-shaped documents.

Changes in Documents   You should not make any changes in a will, living will, deed, assignment, or power of attorney. If you need to make any changes in these documents, prepare a new document. If you need to make minor changes in a receipt, consent, rental agreement, or other form in this book not mentioned above, you can do so as long as all the parties who sign the form also initial the changes. Do not go overboard in making changes in a form. If the changes are more than a few minor ones, prepare a new document.

Remaining Blanks   The forms in this book contain blank lines in which you fill in the information necessary to complete the forms. You will not always use all of these blank lines. Mark a large, wide "X" through any unused portions of these lines. Doing so prevents someone from adding information in the blanks which changes the terms of the document.

Initialing of Multipage Forms   Some of the forms in this book are more than one page long. For those forms, all of the parties who sign the form should initial each page of the form. Witnesses and notaries do not have to initial each page, only the parties do, although the form is valid even if the parties do not do this. Initialing each page of a form makes it harder for someone to insert a new phony page into the form which changes the terms of the document.

Notarization   Certain documents have to be witnessed and/or notarized to be legally valid, such as living wills, wills, affidavits, powers of attorney, assignments, and deeds. Some documents do not have to be witnessed or notarized to be valid, such as residential and personal property rental agreements, bids and contracts with independent contractors, promissory notes, and other documents.

Even though some documents do not have to be witnessed and/or notarized, some county recorder's offices will not record a document unless it is notarized. Some institutions will not honor certain documents, such as consents to release information, unless they are notarized. In order to make the forms in this book more useful to you, witness and/or notary sections are provided for all documents where witnesses and/or notaries are required, for all documents which you might want to record, and for all documents where having the documents witnessed and/or notarized will help convince institutions to honor the documents.

Losing a Document   If you lose the original of a document and you did not record the original at your county recorder's office, you should prepare a new document. If you recorded the original at your county recorder's office, you do not need to prepare another original. The recorded copy is legal proof of the contents and signing of the document.

States, Commonwealths, Parishes, and the District of Columbia   In the blank forms in this book, all fifty states are referred to as "states," even though Pennsylvania, Virginia, Massachusetts, and Kentucky are really commonwealths. Where blank forms refer to "State" you can delete "State" and put "Commonwealth" in those four states. In the District of Columbia, you can delete references to "County of," and replace "State of" with "District of Columbia." In Louisiana, delete "County" and put "Parish."

DOCUMENTS NOT INCLUDED IN THIS BOOK

The following documents are commonly used legal documents for which this book does not provide forms:

Trusts   A trust names a person, called a *trustee*, to manage property for the benefit of another, called a *beneficiary*. The person who creates a trust is the *trustor*. The trustor and the trustee can be the same person.

Trusts have many uses. You can use trusts to reduce taxes or to avoid probate. (Probate is the process of managing a deceased person's affairs through a court.) You can use trusts to appoint a capable person or institution to manage the property of someone who is not capable of managing his or her own property.

Chapters 5 and 6 explain using trusts to avoid probate and to reduce taxes. This book does not provide forms for trusts. Trust agreements, and the documents that accompany trust agreements, are normally too complex for non-lawyers to prepare.

Real Estate Contracts, Mortgages, and Trust Deeds   Real estate contracts, mortgages, and trust deeds are three documents that are used to finance the purchase of real estate. All three documents provide that if a buyer does not make the required payments, the seller or lending institution can take back the property that was sold to the buyer.

A seller can use a real estate contract when a buyer cannot obtain financing from a bank. Banks and other lending institutions use trust deeds or mortgages to finance property.

Trust deeds and mortgages differ from real estate contracts in several ways. One important difference is that, with trust deeds and mortgages, title to the property passes to the buyer at the time of the sale. The buyer gets a deed to the property at the time of the sale, even though the buyer still owes money for the property. In a real estate contract the seller does not give the buyer a deed (title) until the buyer pays the seller all the money the buyer owes for the property.

This book does not include forms for real estate contracts, mortgages, and trust deeds because real estate law differs among all 50 states and among counties and cities within each state. For that reason, sellers and buyers of real estate should consult local professionals.

Listing, Earnest Money, and Escrow Agreements   Listing agreements, earnest money agreements, and escrow agreements are documents that are used for the sale and purchase of real estate.

A *listing agreement* is an agreement between a seller and a real estate broker. In a listing agreement, the seller agrees that if the broker sells the seller's property, the seller will pay the broker a commission for the sale.

An *earnest money agreement*, sometimes called an *offer to purchase*, is an agreement between a seller and buyer of real estate. It includes the essential terms of the sale of the property. It provides that the buyer will obtain a loan from a bank or other institution to buy the property, or provides that the seller and buyer will prepare a real estate contract to finalize the sale of the property.

From the buyer's point of view, the purpose of an earnest money agreement is to keep the seller from selling the property to someone else while the buyer tries to obtain a loan for the property. From the seller's point of view, the purpose of an earnest money agreement is to bind the buyer to buying the property. If the seller and buyer meet all the conditions in the earnest money agreement and the buyer does not buy the property, the seller can keep the money that the buyer gave the seller when the earnest money agreement was signed. That money is called *earnest money*.

Escrow is a method used to complete, or close, a real estate sale. An *escrow agent* is a middle person between a seller and buyer of property. An escrow agent holds the buyer's down payment and all the signed contracts, mortgages, or trust deeds for the property until the seller and buyer meet all the conditions of the sale. Once all the conditions have been met, the escrow agent records the real estate documents at the recorder's office in the county where the real property is located. After recording the documents, the escrow agent disburses the entire sales amount to the seller if the buyer obtained full bank financing for the property, or disburses the buyer's down-payment if the buyer is not paying the entire sales amount at closing. The escrow agent gives the seller and buyer copies of all the important documents involved in the sale.

This book does not include forms for listing agreements, earnest money agreements, and escrow agreements because of the differences in real estate laws among different states, counties, and cities.

Chapter 1

Receipt

A receipt is a written document that acknowledges the receiving of money or property. The person who receives the money or property signs and dates the receipt. The person who gives the money or property keeps the receipt as proof that he or she gave the money or property to the receiver. You should always ask for a receipt so that the receiver cannot later deny that you gave him or her the money or property.

Receipts are more useful when you give cash or property than when you give a check. After a check is endorsed and cashed, it will eventually come back to you and serve as proof that you paid the other person.

TYPES OF RECEIPTS

Receipts vary in their description of why someone is giving the property or money to someone else. For example, a receipt can explain that the property given is payment in full of all money or property owed by the giver to the receiver. If the receiver accepts the money or property as payment in full, the receiver cannot claim later that the giver owes the receiver more money or property.

All receipts must include the following:

- what is given
- who is giving
- who is receiving
- when and where the receiving occurs
- date the receiver signed the receipt
- signature of the receiver

The next section of this chapter provides sample receipts and explanations of the samples for the following types of receipts:

- general receipt
- receipt for payment in full
- receipt for payment on an account
- receipt for money paid for someone else
- receipt for rent
- receipt for a salary

The receipts discussed in this chapter are simple receipts. Receipts are usually short and simple, but they can be complex, especially those involving real estate. If you need a receipt for the purchase of real estate or a receipt for a large sum of money with numerous conditions, have an attorney prepare the receipt.

Sample General Receipt (FIG. 1-1)

The sample general receipt contains all the information that a receipt must contain. It describes what is given, who is giving, who is receiving, when and where the receiving occurs, and it is signed and dated by the receiver. It does not explain why Edward L. Harris gave the money to John M. Jones or if any balance remains after the payment, but it does not have to in order to be a valid receipt. Such an explanation, however, is wise to include on a receipt.

Fig. 1-1. General Receipt (Sample)

General Receipt

This written document acknowledges that on February 2, 1989, at 222 Third Street, Waynecastle, Pennsylvania, 17294, John M. Jones, whose address is 222 Third Street, Waynecastle, Pennsylvania, 17294, received Two Hundred Dollars ($200.00) from Edward L. Harris, whose address is 333 Fourth Street, Waynecastle, Pennsylvania, 17294.

Dated: 2/02/89

_____
John M. Jones

© 1989 by Ralph E. Troisi

Sample Payment-in-Full Receipt (FIG. 1-2)

The sample payment-in-full receipt contains the same information as the general receipt, but adds a clause explaining that the $200.00 is all the money that Edward L. Harris owes John M. Jones. If there were a dispute later as to how much money Harris owed Jones, this receipt would resolve the dispute. If Jones accepts the $200.00 and signs this receipt, he cannot recover any more money from Harris. For that reason, before signing such a receipt, Jones should be sure that $200.00 is all that Harris owes him.

Sample Payment-on-Account Receipt (FIG. 1-3)

The sample payment-on-account receipt explains that the $200.00 should be applied to a specific account that Edward L. Harris has with John M. Jones. If Harris has more than one account with Jones or if Jones represents a company that has thousands of accounts, the receipt avoids any confusion as to which account should be credited with the payment. The sample describes the balance that remains to be paid after Harris makes this payment. This avoids any confusion as to how much he owes after making the payment.

Be careful in accepting a partial payment of a debt from another person. By accepting a partial payment, you may give up the right to dispute the amount of money that is owed you or other terms of the agreement with the person making the payment.

Fig. 1-2. Receipt for Payment in Full (Sample)

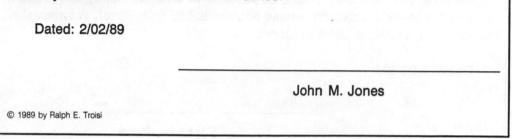

Receipt For Payment in Full

This written document acknowledges that on February 2, 1989, at 222 Third Street, Waynecastle, Pennsylvania, 17294, John M. Jones, whose address is 222 Third Street, Waynecastle, Pennsylvania, 17294, received Two Hundred Dollars ($200.00) from Edward L. Harris, whose address is 333 Fourth Street, Waynecastle, Pennsylvania, 17294, as payment in full of all money or property owed by Edward L. Harris to John M. Jones.

Dated: 2/02/89

_____
John M. Jones

© 1989 by Ralph E. Troisi

Fig. 1-3. Receipt for Payment on Account (Sample)

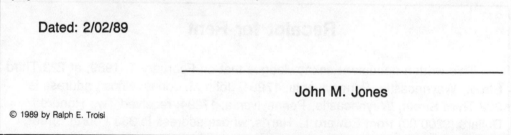

Receipt for Payment on Account

This written document acknowledges that on February 2, 1989, at 222 Third Street, Waynecastle, Pennsylvania, 17294, John M. Jones, whose address is 222 Third Street, Waynescastle, Pennsylvania, 17294, received Two Hundred Dollars ($200.00) from Edward L. Harris, whose address is 333 Fourth Street, Waynecastle, Pennsylvania, 17294, as a payment on Edward L. Harris's Account No. 425623. There remains owing on Account No. 425623 after the payment received herein, the sum of $2,200.00.

Dated: 2/02/89

_____
John M. Jones

© 1989 by Ralph E. Troisi

If a dispute arises as to the amount of money owed or as to other terms of an agreement, the parties to the agreement should resolve the dispute before partial payments are made. If there is a dispute as to the balance owed, the parties can resolve the dispute by signing a written statement agreeing that the balance owed is a specific amount of money. If there is a dispute as to other terms of an agreement, the parties can resolve the dispute by signing a written statement agreeing to a resolution of the dispute. If the parties cannot resolve these disputes in this way, each of the parties should consult an attorney before partial payments are made or accepted.

Sample Receipt for Money Paid for Someone Else (FIG. 1-4)

The sample receipt for money paid for someone else explains that the giver, Edward L. Harris, is giving the receiver, John M. Jones, $200.00 on behalf of someone else, Frederick J. Johnson. Since payment-in-full language is used, if Jones accepts the $200.00 and signs the receipt, Jones could not claim later that Johnson owes him more than $200.00.

Fig. 1-4. Receipt for Money Paid for Someone Else (Sample)

Receipt for Money Paid for Someone Else

This written document acknowledges that on February 2, 1989, at 222 Third Street, Waynecastle, Pennsylvania, 17294, John M. Jones, whose address is 222 Third Street, Waynecastle, Pennsylvania, 17294, received Two Hundred Dollars ($200.00) from Edward L. Harris, whose address is 333 Fourth Street, Waynecastle, Pennsylvania, 17294, as payment in full of all money and property owed by Frederick J. Johnson, whose address is 555 Fifth Street, Waynecastle, Pennsylvania, 17294, to John M. Jones.

Dated: 2/02/89

_____

John M. Jones

Sample Receipt for Rent (FIG. 1-5)

The sample rent receipt explains that the $200.00 is the rent Edward L. Harris owes John M. Jones for February 1989 for property located at 333 Fourth Street. If Harris pays his rent in cash, this receipt may be the only proof that he paid his rent for that month.

Fig. 1-5. Receipt for Payment of Rent (Sample)

Receipt for Rent

This written document acknowledges that on February 2, 1989, at 222 Third Street, Waynecastle, Pennsylvania, 17294, John M. Jones, whose address is 222 Third Street, Waynecastle, Pennsylvania, 17294, received Two Hundred Dollars ($200.00) from Edward L. Harris, whose address is 333 Fourth Street, Waynecastle, Pennsylvania, 17294, as one month's rent on 333 Fourth Street, Waynecastle, Pennsylvania, 17294, for the month of February 1, 1989 through February 28, 1989.

Dated: 2/02/89

_____

John M. Jones

Sample Receipt for a Salary (FIG. 1-6)

The sample salary receipt explains that the $200.00 is the salary that Edward L. Harris owes John M. Jones for gardening services in January, 1989. It avoids any dispute as to whether, when, why, or how much Harris paid Jones.

Fig. 1-6. Receipt for a Salary (Sample)

Receipt for a Salary

This written document acknowledges that on February 2, 1989, at 222 Third Street, Waynecastle, Pennsylvania, 17294, John M. Jones, whose address is 222 Third Street, Waynecastle, Pennsylvania, 17294, received Two Hundred Dollars ($200.00) from Edward L. Harris, whose address is 333 Fourth Street, Waynecastle, Pennsylvania, 17294, as payment of John M. Jones's salary for gardening services rendered to Edward L. Harris from January 1, 1989 through January 31, 1989.

Dated: 2/02/89

_____

John M. Jones

Instructions for Blank Receipt (FIG. 1-7)

Figure 1-7 is a blank receipt. The form has blank spaces with a number under each space. Before filling in any of the blanks, make several photocopies of the form. Use one copy as a work copy, one as an original, and the rest as future work copies or originals. Fill out the work copy first and be sure it is correct, then type or print in the blanks on your original.

The following numbered instructions match the numbers under the blanks in the form:

(1) Enter the date that the money or property is received.

(2) Enter the address where the money or property is received.

(3) Enter the full name(s) of the person(s), company(s), or organization(s) that received the money or property. If someone received the money or property for a company, organization, or other person, first list the name of the person who received the money or property, then list the name of the company, organization, or person on whose behalf the signer received the property.

(4) Enter the address(es) of the person(s), company(s), or organization(s) that received the money or property. If someone received the money or property for a company, organization, or for another person, first list the address of the person who received the money or property, then list the address of the company, organization, or person on whose behalf the signer received the money or property.

(5) Enter a full and accurate description of the money or property that was received. If money was received, type or print the amount of money in words and in numbers. Put the numbers in the parentheses. If property is received, put "none" in the parentheses. If property is received, include any title number, serial number, model number, make (such as Honda, Ford, Chevrolet, etc.), year of manufacture, or other information that will make it clear beyond any doubt what property is being referred to.

(6) Enter the full name(s) of the person(s), company(s), or organization(s) that gave the money or property.

(7) Enter the address(es) of the person(s), company(s), or organization(s) that gave the money or property.

(8) If you want to describe the reason why the money or property is given, you should do so in this blank. For example, if the money or property is payment in full of all sums owed by the giver to the receiver, or is a payment on an account, a payment for someone else, a rent payment, or a salary payment, explain each by including the wording contained in the samples earlier in this chapter. If the money or property is being given for some reason not explained in one of the samples, include an explanation of the reason why the money or property is being given. Remember, a receipt should explain whether a payment is a partial payment or a payment in full of all sums owed by the person making the payment. If the payment is a partial payment, a receipt should state, in this blank, the balance owed after the payment is made. If you do not want to describe the reason why the money or property is given, put "not applicable" in this blank.

(9) Enter the date the money or property is received, which should be the same date that the receipt is signed by the receiver(s).

(10) The receiver(s) should sign his, her, or their full name(s) here. If the receiver is receiving the money or property on behalf of a company or organization, the receiver should sign here and indicate that he or she is signing on behalf of the company or organization. For example, the president of a corporation would sign, "Acme Tools, Inc., by: John M. Jones, President". As another example, an employee of a corporation would sign, "Acme Tools, Inc., by: John L. Williams, Shipping Clerk".

After the receipt is signed, the person giving the money or property should keep the original receipt as proof that he or she gave the property or money to the receiver, and the receiver should keep a copy of the receipt for his or her records.

Fig. 1-7. Receipt (Blank). *Page 1 of 1*   **7**

Receipt

This written document acknowledges that on _____,
                                            (1)

at _____
                        (2)

_____,

_____
                        (3)

_____,

whose address(es) is/are _____
                                        (4)

_____

_____,

received _____
                        (5)

_____

_____

_____

_____

($ _____) from _____
        (6)   (6)

_____

_____,

whose address(es) is/are _____
                                        (7)

_____,

as _____
                (8)

_____

_____

_____

Dated: _____
                (9)

_____   _____
                (10)

Chapter 2

Consent to Release Information and Records

A consent to release information and records is a document in which a person gives someone else permission to release information and records to the person signing the consent, or to another person.

Hospitals, schools, doctors, banks, and other institutions and persons often have a duty of confidentiality to patients, students, and depositors. That duty prevents them from releasing information or records concerning a patient, student, or depositor to another person without the consent of that patient, student, or depositor.

Attorneys use consents to obtain information related to lawsuits filed by their clients. Doctors and other medical people use these consents to obtain information about a patient that will help the doctor diagnose or treat a patient. Insurance companies use these consents to obtain information regarding property damage or injuries involved in a claim. A job applicant can use these consents to obtain school or other records needed for a job application.

Sample Consent (FIG. 2-1)

Figure 2-1 is a sample consent to release information and records. The sample includes the following information that all consents to release information and records should include:

- The name and address of the person giving the consent (the signer). Sometimes the person giving the consent is consenting to the release of information or records about someone else. For example, the person giving the consent could be the parent of a child who was a patient or student. If the person signing the consent is signing for someone else, the consent should describe the relationship between those two people.

- Words of consent and authority. A consent must state that the signer consents to and authorizes the release of information and records.

- The name and address of the person or institution who has the information or records. In many institutions, there is a "custodian of records," who is in charge of keeping all the records of the institution. In most institutions, there is also an "administrator," who is in charge of the entire institution. A consent should authorize both the custodian of records and the administrator of an institution to release the information and records. If the signer is trying to obtain records and information from a doctor or other individual, the consent should include the name and address of that individual.

- A description of what information or documents the signer of the consent wants released. The sample gives consent to release all information and records regarding the signer, including information from a specific hospitalization. If the signer only wants certain information or records released, the consent should explain that. For instance, a consent could provide, ". . . to release any and all information and records related to my hospitalization in St. James Hospital from June 4, 1989 to June 6, 1989 only. This consent is limited to information and records related to that hospitalization." As another example, a consent could provide, ". . . to release any and all information and records from the 1986-87 school year. This consent is limited to information and records related to that school year only."

- The name and address of the person or persons to whom the signer wants the information or records given. With consents for use by attorneys, insurance companies, employers, or schools, a consent should allow employees of these people or institutions to obtain the information.

- A release from liability for providing the information or records. Institutions and people will release information and records more willingly if a consent says that the signer relieves the institution or person from any legal liability for releasing the information or records.

- The date and place where the consent is signed. *Where* the consent is signed affects which state's laws govern the consent. *When* the consent is signed is important because many institutions require that such consents be signed within six months, or even 90 days, of presentation of the consent. For this reason, consents should be as current as possible.

- The signature of the person giving the consent. If the signer is consenting to the release of information regarding another person, such as a child, the signer should sign as the parent of the child.

- The signatures of two witnesses and a notarization. Some states require consents to be witnessed and notarized. Not all states require this. Witnessing and notarizing a consent adds formality to the consent, and will help convince the hospital, institution, or other person who has the information or records that the consent is valid. Neither of the witnesses should be a person to whom information will be released.

Instructions for Blank Consent to Release Information and Records (FIG. 2-2)

Figure 2-2 is a blank consent to release information and records. The form has blank spaces with a number under each space. Before filling in any of the blanks, make several photocopies of the form. Use one copy as a work copy, one or more as originals, and the rest as future work copies or originals. Fill out the work copy first and be sure it is correct, then type or print in the blanks on your original or originals.

The following numbered instructions match the numbers under the blanks in the form:

(1) Enter the full name(s) of the person(s) signing the consent. If the signer is consenting to the release of information and records regarding another person, explain the relationship between the signer and the other person, and give the names of both persons. Put the name of the signer first.

(2) Enter the full address(es) of the signer(s) of the consent. If the signer is consenting to the release of information regarding another, describe the full address of that other person also. Put the address of the signer first.

(3) Enter the full name of the person who has the information or records. If an institution has the information or records, put "administrator and custodian of records of", and then the name of the institution.

(4) Enter the full address of the person or institution who has the information or records.

(5) Enter the information or records that the signer is consenting to have released. Explain if any and all information and records can be released, or if there are any restrictions on what can be released. If the records or information relate to a specific injury or to specific dates, list those specifics. The sample consent and the explanation of the sample consent earlier in this chapter contain wording for the release of all information and for the release of specific information.

(6) Enter the full name(s) of the person(s) or institution(s) to whom the information may be released. If the signer consents to the release of information to employees of a person or institution, explain that also.

(7) Enter the full address(es) of the person(s) or institution(s) to whom the information may be released.

(8,9,10) Enter the day, month, and year that the consent is signed.

(11) Enter the city, county, and state where the consent is signed.

(12) The signer(s) of the consent should sign his, her, on their full names on this line. If the signer is signing for information regarding another person, the signer should indicate his or her relationship to that other person and the name of that other person on this line.

(13) Enter the full names of two witnesses to the consent.

(14) Enter the full name(s) of the signer(s) of the consent.

(15) Enter the date that the consent is signed.

(16) Enter the full name(s) of the signer(s) of the consent.

(17,18,19) Enter the day, month, and year that the witnesses sign their names.

(20) The witnesses should sign their full names above these lines.

The following items should be completed by a notary public.

(21) Enter the state where the consent is signed and notarized.

(22) Enter the county where the consent is signed and notarized.

(23) Enter the name of the notary public.

(24) Enter the state where the notary public resides and is authorized to notarize documents.

(25) Enter the date that the consent is signed and notarized.

(26) Enter the full name(s) of the person(s) who signed the consent.

(27,28,29) Enter the day, month, and year that the consent is signed and notarized.

(30) The notary public should sign his or her name on this line.

(31) Enter the date the notary public's commission expires.

(32) The notary public should affix his or her seal to the document.

After the consent is signed, witnessed, and notarized, the signer should make several copies of the consent. The signer may want to sign more than one original consent. The reason for this is that the person or institution who has the information or records will probably want to keep an original consent. If the institution loses the consent, the signer can present a second original consent without having to have another consent witnessed and notarized.

Consent to Release Information and Records

I, Jane M. Jones, whose address is 333 West Third Street, Waynecastle, Pennsylvania, 17294, hereby give my consent to and authorize the administrator and custodian of the records of St. James Hospital, whose address is 62 East 14th Street, Waynecastle, Pennsylvania, to release any and all information and records regarding me, including but not limited to X-rays, charts, reports, and information and records concerning the injuries I sustained in an automobile accident on June 4, 1989, for which I was hospitalized in St. James Hospital from June 4, 1989 to June 6, 1989, to Max M. Mumfee, my attorney, whose address is 111 West Fourth Street, Waynecastle, Pennsylvania, 17294, or to anyone employed by Max M. Mumfee. I also hereby give my consent to any officer or employee of St. James Hospital to talk to Max M. Mumfee or employees of Max M. Mumfee concerning my medical history, or any other subject concerning me.

I release St. James Hospital from any liability for releasing information or records in reliance on this consent.

Signed this 18th day of June, 1989, at 333 West Third Street, Waynecastle, Pennsylvania, 17294.

_____

Jane M. Jones

We, Allen M. Johnson and Frederick L. Roth, hereby acknowledge that we witnessed Jane M. Jones, who is known to us personally, sign the above consent to release information and records on June 18, 1989, in our presence, and that Jane M. Jones acknowledged to us and it appeared to us that she signed said consent freely and voluntarily.

Dated this 18th day of June, 1989.

_____

Allen M. Johnson

_____

Frederick L. Roth

COMMONWEALTH OF
PENNSYLVANIA   )
) ss.
COUNTY OF BURR   )

Fig. 2-1. (Cont'd). *Page 2 of 2* **13**

I, Wanda C. Twobucks, a resident of and notary public in and for the Commonwealth of Pennsylvania, who am duly commissioned and sworn and legally authorized to administer oaths and affirmations, hereby certify that on June 18, 1989, Jane M. Jones, who is known to me personally to be the signer of the above consent to release information and records, appeared before me and, after being first duly sworn by me under penalty of perjury, swore on her oath to the truth of the facts in the above consent, and signed and acknowledged said consent in my presence, of her own free will, and for the purposes explained in said consent.

Subscribed and sworn to before me this 18th day of June, 1989.

_____

Notary Public

(SEAL)   My Commission Expires: 2/09/90

Consent to Release
Information and/or Records

I, _____
(1)

_____, whose address(es)

is/are _____
(2)

_____,

respectively, hereby give my consent to and authorize _____
(3)

_____,

whose address is _____
(4)

_____,

to release _____
(5)

_____

_____

_____

_____

to _____
(6)

_____

_____,

whose address is _____
(7)

_____

_____.

I release the above-named person or institution from any liability for release of information or records in reliance on this consent.

Signed this _____ day of _____, _____,
(8)   (9)   (10)

at _____.
(11)

_____
(12)

_____
(12)

We, _____
(13)

_____, hereby acknowledge

that we witnessed _____,
(14)

_____, who is known to us personally,

sign the above consent on _____,
(15)

in our presence, and that _____
(16)

_____

acknowledged to us and it appeared to us that he/she signed said consent freely
and voluntarily.

Dated this _____ day of _____, _____.
(17)   (18)   (19)

_____
(20)
First Witness

_____
(20)
Second Witness

STATE OF _____)
(21)
) ss.
COUNTY OF _____)
(22)

I, _____,
(23)

a resident of and notary public in and for the State of _____,
(24)

who am duly commissioned and sworn and legally authorized to administer oaths

and affirmations, hereby certify that on _____,
(25)

_____,
(26)

who is known to me personally to be the signer of the above consent to release
information and records, appeared before me and, after being first duly sworn by

Fig. 2-2. (Cont'd). *PAGE 3 of 3* **17**

me under penalty of perjury, swore on his/her oath(s) to the truth of the facts in the above consent, and signed and acknowledged said consent in my presence, of his/her own free will, and for the purposes explained in said consent.

Subscribed and sworn to before me this _____ day of _____,
                                          (27)   (28)

_____.
    (29)

_____
                                       (30)
Notary Public

(SEAL)   My Commission Expires: _____
(32)   (31)

Chapter 3

Request for Credit Information and Request for Explanation of Denial of a Credit Application

A request for credit information is a written document signed by a consumer asking a credit reporting agency or creditor for information that the agency or creditor has in its file on the consumer.

A credit reporting agency is a company that collects financial information about people or companies. It provides that information to lending institutions, such as banks, which use the information to decide whether or not to lend money to a person or company. A credit reporting agency does not have to charge for its services. It can be a group of merchants who collect financial information and share that information with each other at no cost.

A request for explanation of denial of a credit application is a written document signed by a consumer asking a lending institution, such as a bank, to explain why the lending institution denied a credit application, or granted the application but required a higher interest rate.

When a lender denies a credit application or grants it but requires a higher interest rate, the lender will tell the consumer whether or not the denial was based on information obtained from a credit agency or from someone other than a credit agency. If the denial is based on information from a credit agency, the lender will tell the consumer the name and address of the agency. If the denial is based on information from someone other than a credit agency, the lender will explain that, but will not necessarily give the name and address of the source of the information.

If a lender uses information from a credit agency in denying a consumer's credit application, the consumer should send a request for credit information to the credit agency. If a lender uses information from someone other than a credit agency in denying a consumer's credit application, the consumer should send a request for explanation of denial of a credit application to the lender to discover the source of the information that led to the denial of credit. The consumer can then contact that source to discover and possibly correct the information that led to the denial of credit.

THE FAIR CREDIT REPORTING ACT (FCRA)

The Fair Credit Reporting Act (FCRA) is a federal law. It is Title VI of the Federal Truth In Lending Act, and is contained in Volume 15 of the United States Code, beginning at Section 1681. The U.S. Code contains all the laws passed by the U.S. Congress. Most county courthouses have a library containing the U.S. Code.

The purpose of the FCRA is to require consumer credit reporting agencies to be fair to consumers in investigating and reporting on consumers' credit. The FCRA does this in many ways, including requiring credit reporting agencies, upon request by a consumer, to disclose to a consumer the nature and substance of all information in their files on the consumer. Also, the FCRA requires a lending institution, upon request by a consumer, to disclose to the consumer the reasons for denying a consumer's credit application and the nature and scope of any investigation of the consumer requested by the lending institution.

The FCRA applies to *consumer* credit reporting agencies and *consumer* credit reports. A "consumer" is someone who seeks credit for personal, family, or household purposes.

You can use the two forms in this chapter to find out why a lender denied your credit application. You can also use these forms to discover any information in your credit file that is hurting your credit. The forms also help you ensure that a lender treats you fairly when you apply for credit.

Sample Request for Credit Information (FIG. 3-1)

Figure 3-1 is a sample request for credit information. This sample includes the following information that all requests for credit information should include:

- Date the consumer sent the request
- Full name and address of the credit agency to which the consumer sent the request
- Request for all the information the agency has about the consumer
- Request for the sources of the information
- Request for the names and addresses of anyone to whom the credit agency has given information about the consumer
- Information about the consumer that will help the agency correctly identify the consumer
- Address where the consumer wants the requested information sent
- Signature of the consumer
- Notarization

A request for credit information should ask for all the information that the agency has about the consumer. The agency is not required to disclose medical information. For that reason, the sample does not request medical information.

If a consumer discovers that some of the information in an agency's file is inaccurate, the consumer should send the agency whatever evidence proves that the information in its file is incorrect. The consumer should request that the agency correct its file, and that the agency tell any lenders or other people who received the incorrect information that the file has been corrected. As an added precaution, the consumer should contact those people to inform them that the credit agency gave them incorrect information.

By discovering the names and addresses of the sources of information about the consumer, the consumer can directly contact the sources and correct any mistakes made by the sources.

A request for credit information does not always have to be notarized. Because some agencies require notarized requests to be sure that the person signing the request is the person that the requested information relates to, the consumer's signature should be notarized.

Fig. 3-1. Request for Credit Information (Sample). *Page 1 of 2* **21**

DATE: 1/06/89

TO: Smith Credit Agency
     222 Third Street
     Waynecastle, Pennsylvania 17294

Dear Sirs:

   I hereby exercise my rights under federal law to request that you provide me with all the information that you have about me, except for medical information.

   I hereby request that you tell me the names and addresses of the sources of the information that you have about me, and that you tell me the names and addresses of any person, company, or institutions to whom you have given any information about me.

   My full name is John James Jones. My wife's name is Mary Ellen Jones. For the last five years I have lived at 333 4th Street, Waynecastle, Pennsylvania, 17294. My social security number is 012-34-5678. My wife's social security number is 876-54-3210. My date of birth is 01/09/47. My present employer is Acme Produce, 111 6th Street, Waynecastle, Pennsylvania, 17294. My home telephone number is (717) 555-4444. My business telephone number is (717) 555-3333.

   Please send the above information to 333 4th Street, Waynecastle, Pennsylvania, 17294.

                    Sincerely,

                    _____

                    John James Jones

COMMONWEALTH OF
PENNSYLVANIA   )
) ss.
COUNTY OF BURR   )

    I, Wanda C. Twobucks, a resident of and notary public in and for the Commonwealth and county named above, who am duly commissioned and sworn and legally authorized to administer oaths and affirmations, hereby certify that on January 6, 1989, John James Jones, who is known to me personally to be the signer of the above request for explanation of denial of a credit application, appeared before me and, after being first duly sworn by me under penalty of perjury, swore on his oath to the truth of the facts contained in the above request, and signed and acknowledged said document in my presence, of his own free will, and for the purposes explained in the request.

    Subscribed and sworn to before me this 6th day of January, 1989.

_____

Notary Public
(SEAL)   My Commission Expires: 2/09/90

Sample Request for Explanation of Denial of a Credit Application (FIG. 3-2)

Figure 3-2 is a sample request for explanation of denial of a credit application. The sample includes the following information that all such requests should include:

- Date the consumer sent the request
- Full name and address of the lender to which the request is sent
- Request for a complete explanation of the reasons for denying credit
- Request for the nature and sources of information received from anyone other than a credit reporting agency
- Information about the consumer that will help the lender correctly identify the consumer
- Address where the consumer wants the explanation sent
- Signature of the consumer
- Notarization

When a lender denies a credit application, the lender will tell the consumer whether or not its action is based on information from a credit reporting agency or from someone other than a credit reporting agency. If the lender's action is based on information obtained from a credit reporting agency, the lender will tell the consumer the name of that agency. For that reason, it is only necessary, in this sample, to ask for the nature and sources of information obtained from anyone other than a credit reporting agency.

By discovering the nature and sources of the information that led to the denial of credit, the consumer can contact the sources and correct any mistakes made by the sources. If some of the information given by a source is inaccurate, the consumer should send the source whatever evidence proves that the information in its file is incorrect. The consumer should request that the source correct its file, and that the source tell any lenders or other people who received the incorrect information that the source has corrected its file. To be safe, the consumer should write directly to any lenders or other people who received the incorrect information and send them whatever proof is necessary to correct their files.

By requesting the nature and scope of any investigation of the consumer requested by the lender, the consumer will find out if any credit agency prepared a consumer report about the consumer. The consumer can obtain a copy of that report by sending a request for credit information to the credit agency that prepared the report.

A request for explanation of denial of a credit application does not always have to be notarized. Some agencies require notarized requests to be sure that the person signing the request is the person that the requested information relates to. For that reason, the consumer's signature should be notarized.

DATE: 1/06/89

TO: First State Bank
       222 Third Street
       Waynecastle, Pennsylvania 17294

Dear Sirs:

On December 29, 1988, you denied my application for credit at your bank. I hereby exercise my rights under federal law to request that you provide me with the complete and accurate reasons for this action.

I request that you tell me the nature and sources of any information about me that you received from anyone other than a credit reporting agency. I also request that you tell me the nature and scope of any investigation of me that you requested.

My full name is John James Jones. My wife's name is Mary Ellen Jones. For the last five years I have lived at 333 4th Street, Waynecastle, Pennsylvania, 17294. My social security number is 012-34-5678. My wife's social security number is 876-54-3210. My date of birth is 01/09/47. My present employer is Acme Produce, 111 6th Street, Waynecastle, Pennsylvania, 17294. My home telephone number is (717) 555-4444. My business telephone number is (717) 555-3333.

Please send the above information to 333 4th Street, Waynecastle, Pennsylvania, 17294.

                          Sincerely,

                          _____
                                    John James Jones

Fig. 3-2. (Cont'd). *Page 2 of 2* **25**

COMMONWEALTH OF
PENNSYLVANIA)

) ss.

COUNTY OF BURR)

I, Wanda C. Twobucks, a resident of and notary public in and for the Commonwealth and county named above, who am duly commissioned and sworn and legally authorized to administer oaths and affirmations, hereby certify that on January 6, 1989, John James Jones, who is known to me personally to be the signer of the above request for credit information, appeared before me and, after being first duly sworn by me under penalty of perjury, swore on his oath to the truth of the facts contained in the above request, and signed and acknowledged said request in my presence, of his own free will, and for the purposes explained in the request.

Subscribed and sworn to before me this 6th day of January, 1989.

_____

Notary Public

(SEAL)   My Commission Expires: 2/09/90

Instructions for Blank Forms

This chapter includes two blank forms. Figure 3-3 is a blank request for credit information. Figure 3-4 is a blank request for explanation of denial of a credit application.

The forms have blank spaces with a number under each space. Before filling in any of the blanks, make several photocopies of the form you need. Use one copy as a work copy, one as an original, and the rest for future work copies or originals. Fill out the work copy first and be sure it is correct, then type or print in the blanks on your original form.

Request for Credit Information (FIG. 3-3)   The following numbered instructions match the numbers under the blanks in the form:

(1) Enter the date that you sign the request.

(2) Enter the name and address of the person or company to whom you are sending the request.

(3) Enter your full name. If you and your spouse are requesting information from a credit agency, each of you should prepare and sign a separate request.

(4) Enter the full name of your spouse. If you do not have a spouse, put "none" here.

(5) Enter the address or addresses where you have lived for the last five years. Include the dates when you lived at each of those addresses.

(6) Enter your social security number.

(7) Enter your spouse's social security number. If you have no spouse, put "none" here.

(8) Enter your date of birth.

(9) Enter the name of your employer. If you are self-employed, put "self" in this blank. If you are unemployed, put "none" in this blank.

(10) Enter the address of your employer. If you are self-employed, put the address of your business in this blank. If you are unemployed, put "not applicable" in this blank.

(11) Enter your home telephone number, including the area code.

(12) Enter your business telephone number, including the area code. If you have none, put "none" in this blank.

(13) Enter the address where you want the information sent.

(14) Sign your full name in front of a notary public.

The following items should be completed by a notary public:

(15) Enter the state where the request is notarized.

(16) Enter the county where the request is notarized.

(17) Enter the name of the notary public.

(18) Enter the date the request was signed.

(19) Enter the full name of the person signing the request.

(20,21,22) Enter the day, month, and year that the request was signed.

(23) The notary public should sign here.

(24) The notary public should enter the date that his or her commission expires.

(25) The notary public should affix his or her seal to this request.

After the request is signed and notarized, you should make at least one copy of the request for your files. You should send the original request for credit information to the credit agency or other person or organization that has the information you are requesting.

Request For Explanation of Denial of a Credit Application (FIG. 3-4)   The following numbered instructions match the numbers under the blanks in the form:

(1) Enter the date that you sign the request.

(2) Enter the name and address of the lending institution to whom you are sending the request.

(3) Enter the date the lender denied your application for credit, or granted the application for credit but raised the cost of the credit that you were trying to obtain.

(4) Enter the type of application that you made. For instance, if you applied for a car loan, say, "application for an automobile loan".

(5) Enter an explanation of exactly how the lender responded to your application. If the lender denied your application, say that. If the lender granted your application but increased the cost of the loan, say that.

(6) Enter your full name. If you and your spouse are requesting an explanation of a denial of a joint credit application, each of you should prepare and sign a separate request.

(7) Enter the full name of your spouse. If you do not have a spouse, put "none" here.

(8) Enter the address or addresses where you have lived for the last five years. Include the dates when you lived at each of those addresses.

(9) Enter your social security number.

(10) Enter your spouse's social security number. If you have no spouse, put "none" here.

(11) Enter your date of birth.

(12) Enter the name of your employer. If you are self-employed, put "self" in this blank. If you are unemployed, put "none" in this blank.

(13) Enter the address of your employer. If you are self-employed, put the address of your business in this blank. If you are unemployed, put "not applicable" in this blank.

(14) Enter your home telephone number, including the area code.

(15) Enter your business telephone number, including the area code. If you have none, put "none" in this blank.

(16) Enter the address where you want the information sent.

(17) Sign your full name in front of a notary public. The following items should be completed by a notary public.

The following items should be completed by a notary public:

(18) Enter the state where the request is notarized.

(19) Enter the county where the request is notarized.

(20) Enter the name of the notary public.

(21) Enter the date the request is signed.

(22) Enter the signer's full name.

(23,24,25) Enter the day, month, and year that the request is notarized.

(26) The notary public should sign here.

(27) The notary public should enter the date that his or her commission expires.

(28) The notary public should affix his or her seal to this request.

After the request is signed and notarized, you should make at least one copy of the request for your files. You should send the original request for explanation of denial of a credit application to the lending institution that denied your credit application.

Fig. 3-3. Request for Credit Information (Blank). *Page 1 of 2* **29**

Request for Credit Information

DATE: _____
                (1)

TO: _____
                    (2)

_____

_____

_____

Dear Sirs:

   I hereby exercise my rights under federal law to request that you provide me with all the information that you have about me, except for medical information.

   I hereby request that you tell me the names and addresses of the sources of the information that you have about me, and that you tell me the names and addresses of any person, company, or institution to whom you have given any information about me.

   My full name is _____.
                                        (3)

My spouse's name is _____.
                                    (4)

My addresses for the last five years and the dates when I lived at each are:

_____
                (5)

_____

_____

_____

_____

_____

My social security number is _____-_____-_____. My spouse's social
                                         (6)

security number is _____-_____-_____. My date of birth is _____
                                (7)   (8)

_____. My present employer is _____
                                                               (9)

_____ ,

_____

_____ .
                (10)

My home telephone number is (   )_____. My business
                                              (11)

telephone number is (   )_____.
                                 (12)

    Please send the above information to _____

_____

_____.
                              (13)

             Sincerely,

_____
                                                  (14)

STATE OF _____)
                  (15)

) ss.

COUNTY OF _____)
                    (16)

    I, _____, a resident
                            (17)

of and notary public in and for the state and county named above, who
am duly commissioned and sworn and legally authorized to administer
oaths and affirmations, hereby certify that on _____,
                                                              (18)

_____,
                        (19)

who is known to me personally to be the person who signed the above
request for credit information, appeared before me and, after being first duly
sworn by me under penalty of perjury, swore on his/her oath to the truth of
the facts contained in the above document, and signed and acknowledged
said document in my presence, of his/her own free will, and for the purposes
explained in said document.

    Subscribed and sworn to before me this _____ day of
                                                        (20)

_____, _____.
          (21)   (22)

_____
                                                  (23)

Notary Public

(SEAL)   My Commission Expires: _____
  (25)   (24)

Request for Explanation of Denial
of a Credit Application

DATE: _____
        (1)

TO: _____
                    (2)

_____

_____

_____

Dear Sirs:

On _____, you responded to my
                    (3)

_____
                    (4)

_____,

as follows: _____
                    (5)

_____

_____

_____.

I hereby exercise my rights under federal law to request that you provide me with the complete and accurate reasons for this action.

I request that you tell me the nature and sources of any information about me that you received from anyone other than a credit reporting agency. I also request that you tell me the nature and scope of any investigation of me that you requested.

My full name is _____.
                                (6)

My spouse's name is _____.
                                (7)

My addresses for the last five years and the dates when I lived at each are:

_____
                    (8)

_____

_____

_____

_____

_____

My social security number is _____–_____–_____. My spouse's social
                                         (9)

security number is _____–_____–_____. My date of birth is (12)
                                  (10)

_____. My present employer is _____
          (11)

_____,

_____
                                  (13)

_____.

My home telephone number is (   )_____. My business
                                           (14)

telephone number is (   )_____.
                                 (15)

Please send the above information to _____
                                                        (16)

_____

_____.

Sincerely,

_____
                                                             (17)

STATE OF _____)
                      (18)
) ss.

COUNTY OF _____)
                        (19)

I, _____,
                                           (20)

a resident of and notary public in and for the state and county named above,
who am duly commissioned and sworn and legally authorized to administer oaths

and affirmations, hereby certify that on _____,
                                                              (21)

_____,
                        (22)

who is known to me personally to be the person who signed the above request for
explanation of denial of a credit application, appeared before me and, after being
first duly sworn by me under penalty of perjury, swore on his/her oath to the truth
of the facts contained in the above document, and signed and acknowledged said
document in my presence, of his/her own free will, and for the purposes explained
in said document.

Fig. 3-4. (Cont'd). *Page 3 of 3*   **33**

Subscribed and sworn to before me this _____ day of _____,
(23) (24)

_____.
(25)

_____
(26)

Notary Public

(SEAL)   My Commission Expires: _____
(28)   (27)

Chapter 4
Affidavit

An affidavit is a written document in which a person, known as an *affiant*, makes a statement and swears under oath to the truth of that statement in front of a person authorized to give oaths, usually a notary public.

Since an affidavit is a sworn statement made upon oath, it is similar to a statement made by a witness in a trial. A person who makes an affidavit could be guilty of perjury if he or she knowingly makes a false statement in the affidavit. Because there is a greater penalty for lying under oath than for lying without an oath, there is more motivation to tell the truth.

An affidavit also ensures that the person named as affiant in the affidavit is the same person as the one who signed the affidavit. The notary public states in the affidavit that he or she knows that the person named in the affidavit is the same person as the one who signed it.

Affidavits have a variety of uses. Applications for jobs, for driver's licenses, and for other licenses often require an affidavit. Banks sometimes require affidavits from a deceased person's heirs before the bank will release funds to the heirs. Banks or hospitals sometimes require affidavits from the person holding a power of attorney before they will honor that power of attorney. (See Chapter 15 for an explanation of this.)

TYPES OF AFFIDAVITS

The most common type of affidavit is one in which an individual swears to facts that he or she knows are true. Someone acting in an official capacity, such as a state commissioner or someone acting on behalf of a corporation, can make an affidavit on behalf of a governmental body or corporation. A blind person or a person who cannot read or write the language used in an affidavit can make an affidavit. In each of these cases, the form of the affidavit will be different.

State laws are different as to the forms of affidavits in special situations. This chapter provides a form for the most common type of affidavit, not for every possible type of affidavit. If you need an affidavit for a special situation, such as a corporate affidavit or an affidavit by a blind person, consult a local attorney.

Affidavit

COMMONWEALTH OF
PENNSYLVANIA   )
) ss.
COUNTY OF BURR   )

I, Jane M. Jones, being first duly sworn, upon my oath do solemnly swear under penalty of perjury that:

1. I am a resident of 222 Third Street, Waynecastle, Pennsylvania, 17294, County of Burr.

2. I am making this affidavit for the purpose of obtaining a new title to my 1985 Honda Accord automobile, Serial No. 1234, Model No. 5678, Vehicle ID No. 9101112, License No. 131415, licensed in Pennsylvania.

3. On February 2, 1989, I discovered that I had lost the title that was sent to me for the above vehicle.

4. I have diligently searched for the title, but cannot find it.

5. The only reason for my application for a new title is my loss of the original title.

6. I am the sole and lawful owner of the above vehicle.

7. I hereby request that a duplicate title be sent to me for the above vehicle.

Signed at 222 Third Street, Waynecastle, Pennsylvania, 17294, on February 4, 1989.

_____

Jane M. Jones

I, Wanda C. Twobucks, a resident of and notary public in and for the Commonwealth of Pennsylvania, who am duly commissioned and sworn and legally authorized to administer oaths and affirmations, hereby certify that on February 4, 1989, Jane M. Jones, who is known to me personally to be the affiant in the above affidavit, appeared before me and, after being first duly sworn by me under penalty of perjury, swore on her oath to the truth of the facts in the above affidavit, and signed and acknowledged said affidavit in my presence, of her own free will, and for the purposes explained in said affidavit.

Subscribed and sworn to before me this 4th day of February, 1989.

_____

Notary Public
My Commission Expires: 02/09/90

(SEAL)

Sample Affidavit (FIG. 4-1)

Figure 4-1 is a sample affidavit. The sample contains the following information that all affidavits should contain:

- Full name and address of the person (affiant) making the affidavit.
- A statement that, under the penalty of perjury and under oath, the affiant swears to the truth of the facts in the affidavit. This statement is what makes knowingly false statements in the affidavit perjury.
- An explanation of why the affiant is making the affidavit.
- A statement of the facts that the affiant swears are true. These facts should be listed in numbered paragraphs. At least one state, New Jersey, requires numbered paragraphs in affidavits. In the sample, the affiant swears as to her identity and address, as to her losing and searching for the title to her car, as to her being the sole owner of the car described, as to the reason for making the affidavit, and as to where and when she signed the affidavit. If an affiant *believes* a fact is true but is not *sure* whether or not it is true, he or she can state that the fact is true "to the best of my knowledge and belief".
- Description of where and when the affiant signed the affidavit.
- Signature of the affiant in front of a notary public. An affiant should sign an affidavit in front of a notary public for the state where the affiant signs the affidavit. The notary public must know the affiant personally so the notary public can certify that the person who signed the affidavit is the same person as the person referred to in the affidavit. The notary public should ask the affiant to raise his or her right hand and ask the affiant whether he or she swears upon his or her oath under penalty of perjury that the statements contained in the affidavit are true and that he or she is the person referred to in the affidavit. After so swearing, the affiant should sign the affidavit. The notary public should then sign the affidavit, indicate the date that his or her commission expires, and affix his or her seal to the affidavit.

Instructions for Blank Affidavit (FIG. 4-2)   Figure 4-2 is a blank affidavit. The form has blank spaces with a number under each space. Before filling in any of the blanks, make several photocopies of the form. Use one copy as a work copy, one or more as originals, and the rest for future work copies or originals. Fill out the work copy first and be sure it is correct, then type or print in the blanks on your original(s).

The following numbered instructions match the numbers under the blanks in the form:

(1) Enter the name of the state where you sign the affidavit, which should be the same state where the notary public is authorized to administer oaths.
(2) Enter the name of the county where you sign the affidavit.
(3) Enter your full name.
(4) Enter your residence address.
(5) Enter in numbered paragraphs the facts that you swear are true. Include an explanation of why you are making the affidavit.
(6) Enter the address where you sign the affidavit, including the state and county.
(7) Enter the date you sign the affidavit.
(8) Before you sign the affidavit, the notary public should ask you to raise your right hand. The notary public should ask you whether you solemnly swear upon your oath under penalty of perjury that you are the affiant referred to in the affidavit, that the facts in the affidavit are true and made of your own free will, and that you are making the affidavit for the purposes explained in the affidavit. After answering these questions, you should sign your full name on this line.

The following items should be completed by a notary public:

(9) Enter the name of the notary public.

(10) Enter the date the affiant signs the affidavit.

(11) Enter the affiant's name.

(12,13,14) Enter the day, month, and year the affidavit is signed.

(15) The notary public should sign his or her full name here.

(16) Enter the date the notary public's commission expires.

(17) The notary public should affix his or her seal to the affidavit.

After you and the notary sign the affidavit, you should keep the original affidavit. You may want to sign more than one original affidavit. The reason for this is that you may need to give an original affidavit to a certain institution or person. Having more than one original allows you to do this and still have original affidavits to provide to other people or institutions.

Fig. 4-2. Affidavit (Blank). *Page 1 of 2* **39**

Affidavit

STATE OF _____)
         (1)

) ss.

COUNTY OF _____)
         (2)

I, _____,
         (3)

whose residence address is _____
         (4)

_____,

being first duly sworn, upon my oath do solemnly swear under penalty of perjury

that (5)

Signed at _____
         (6)

_____,

on _____.
         (7)

_____
         (8)

         Affiant

I, _____,
(9)

a resident of and notary public in and for the state and county named above, who am duly commissioned and sworn and legally authorized to administer oaths and

affirmations, hereby certify that on _____,
(10)

_____,
(11)

who is known to me personally to be the affiant in the above affidavit, appeared before me and, after being first duly sworn by me under penalty of perjury, swore on his or her oath to the truth of the facts in the above affidavit, and signed and acknowledged said affidavit in my presence, of his or her own free will, and for the purposes explained in said affidavit.

Subscribed and sworn to before me this _____ day of _____,
(12)   (13)

_____.
(14)

_____
(15)

Notary Public

(SEAL)   My Commission Expires: _____
(17)   (16)

Chapter 5
Simple Will

A will is a legal document which contains a person's instructions for his or her property and other affairs after death. The person signing the will is known as the *testator* if he is a man, and the *testatrix* if she is a woman. A will may include a *codicil*, which is an addition to a will signed by a testator or testatrix after signing the original will.

This chapter discusses writing your own *simple* will. Simple wills give simple funeral and burial instructions, may have a few specific gifts, divide the rest of the property in an uncomplicated way, name an *executor* or *executrix* to manage the estate, and name a *guardian* for minor children if one is necessary.

Wills that try to disinherit a spouse are not simple wills. Most states have laws restricting someone's right to disinherit a spouse. Wills that create trusts are not simple wills. (Trusts will be explained later in this chapter.) Wills that restrict the use of property after death are not simple wills, nor are wills that involve complex methods of dividing or managing property. Couples with stepchildren often need more than simple wills to protect the rights of the stepchildren.

WHO CAN WRITE A WILL

Any person who is 18 years of age or older (16 in Louisiana, 14 in Georgia, and 19 in Wyoming) and who is of sound mind may make a will.

What does "of sound mind" mean? It means that you know who the natural objects of your love are, such as your family. It means that you know the nature and extent of your property and the consequences of your will. It means that you are acting voluntarily when you make your will.

WHAT HAPPENS IF YOU DIE WITHOUT A WILL

What happens to your property if you die without a will depends on whether or not you owned property jointly with right of survivorship, jointly without right of survivorship, or were the sole owner of property.

What happens to joint property with right of survivorship? Property owned jointly with right of survivorship automatically belongs to the other joint owner at your death, regardless of what your will says.

Whether joint ownership is with or without right of survivorship depends upon the wording of the title to the property. The following language creates joint ownership with right of survivorship: "John Smith and William Jones, each as to an undivided one-half interest, to be held jointly with right of survivorship, not as tenants in common", or in states that recognize joint tenancies, "John and Mary Smith, as joint tenants". Other language is sometimes used to create joint ownership with right of survivorship, but this author believes the preceding wording is the clearest. A *tenancy in common* is joint ownership without right of survivorship.

What happens to joint property without right of survivorship? Joint property owned without right of survivorship does not automatically belong to the other joint owner at your death. It is controlled by your will. If you do not have a will, it is controlled by the will written for you by your state. These state wills are called the *laws of interstate succession*.

The following wording will create joint ownership without right of survivorship in all states: "John Smith and Mary Smith, as tenants in common".

What happens to property owned alone? Your will controls property you own alone. If you do not have a will, the will written for you by your state controls the property.

Probate. Technically, *probate* means to prove that a will is genuine and was properly signed, however, probate has come to mean the court process of managing a person's affairs after his or her death.

Writing a will does not avoid probate. A will tells a probate court what to do with property you own alone and property you own jointly without right of survivorship.

Joint ownership with right of survivorship avoids probate. Ownership belongs to the surviving joint owner automatically, without probate, and without looking at the will of the deceased.

Life insurance, pension funds, and individual retirement accounts (IRAs) avoid probate if they name a beneficiary other than your estate, and if that beneficiary is still alive at the time of your death. The beneficiary receives the proceeds of these accounts and policies directly, without probate.

A revocable trust can also avoid probate. The next chapter of this book discusses the details of avoiding probate.

The will written for you by your state. If you die without a will, your state has written a will for you. These wills vary from state to state. In most states, your spouse will get one-third to one-half of your property, and your children will get the rest. If you die without children, your spouse usually gets one-half of your estate, but gets all of your estate in some states. In states where your spouse gets one-half of your estate, the other one-half is divided among parents, brothers, sisters, and children of deceased brothers and sisters.

The laws of interstate succession are so varied that it is not possible to summarize them here. If you want to find out what the laws of interstate succession are in your state, go to the library at your county courthouse or a law school library in your state. Ask the librarian to show you where to find the state laws regarding descent of property upon death, or the laws of interstate succession.

People often do not want their property distributed according to the will written for them by their state. The solution is simple. Make sure you have a valid will of your own.

REASONS FOR WRITING A WILL

The following are some important reasons why you should have a will:

You are dissatisfied with the will your state has written for you. If you do not like the will your state has written for you, you should write your own will. Under the wills written by all 50 states, stepchildren and friends get nothing. If you want stepchildren or friends to receive property upon your death, you should make a will.

Some people do not like the will their state has written for them because it gives property to an estranged child or someone else that they do not want to get their property. A will can make sure that your estate is distributed as you wish.

Giving specific gifts. If you want certain people, charities, or organizations to get property from your estate, you should have a will. In your will, you can leave certain items or money to whomever you want.

Creating trusts. Trusts have many uses. A trust names a person, called a *trustee*, to manage property for the benefit of another, called a *beneficiary*. You can create a trust in your will.

A trust can ensure that a competent trustee will manage the property of a minor, handicapped, or elderly beneficiary. A trust can also protect someone who has trouble managing money.

Trusts are useful in reducing income or inheritance taxes. If you need to consider creating trusts in your will to reduce taxes, your estate is probably so large that a simple will may not be adequate for you. Chapter 6 explains trusts in greater detail.

Naming an executor or trustee. In your will, you name an executor or executrix. The executor or executrix handles your affairs after your death. You also name a trustee, if you create a trust in your will. If you do not have a will, the probate court will choose your executor or trustee, if one is necessary. The court's choice may not be the person you would have chosen.

Naming a guardian for minors. In your will, you can name a person to be the guardian of your minor children and their property. If you do not have a will, the court will choose a guardian for your minor children and their property. The court's choice may not be the person you would have chosen.

Saving the cost of a bond for your executor, trustee, or guardian. If you do not have a will and it is necessary to appoint an executor, trustee, or guardian in your estate, the court will require that person to buy a bond to protect your property against misuse. The larger the estate, the larger the bond and the greater the cost of the bond. You can save this cost by providing in your will that your executor, trustee, or guardian should serve without bond. In most cases, the court will honor your instructions.

Avoiding disputes about division of property. If you do not have a will, different heirs may have different ideas about how to divide your property. There may be disputes about the value of jewelry or land. Some heirs may want to live in the family home, while others may want to sell it. You can avoid these disputes by making these decisions in your will.

Burial instructions. In your will, you can explain the type of funeral and burial that you want.

Sample Wills (FIGS. 5-1 and 5-2) and Affidavit of Witnesses (FIG. 5-1A)

Although some states allow oral wills in certain circumstances, a will should be in writing. It can be handwritten or typed. If it is handwritten, it should be written in nonerasable ink. A person can write his or her own will in all states.

Once you have written your will, do not make any changes in it. If you want to change the will, rewrite the entire will. The will should not have any mistakes in it. If the will is not perfect, rewrite the entire will before you sign it.

Figures 5-1 and 5-2 are two sample wills. The paragraph numbers of the explanation which follows correspond with the paragraph numbers of the samples. Figure 5-1A is a sample affidavit to accompany FIG. 5-1.

Paragraph 1   The first paragraph of your will should contain your full legal name and the state where you live. It should explain that you intend to make a will and that you revoke all previous wills and codicils, so there is no confusion that you intend this will to control your affairs after your death. A codicil is an addition or amendment to a will. You should destroy any previous wills and codicils when you sign the new will.

Some states require that you *publish* your will. Publishing a will means that you declare to the witnesses that you intend the document they are witnessing to take effect as your will.

Paragraph 2   The second paragraph should describe your family situation. You should state whether you are single or married. You should give the full names of your spouse and children, whether or not you leave them anything in your will.

To have the capacity to make a will, you must know who the natural objects of your love are. Because the members of your family are the natural objects of your love, naming the members of your family in your will shows that you know who the natural objects of your love are. If you do not have a spouse or children, name your closest relatives, such as parents or brothers and sisters, for the same reason.

If you are not leaving anything to your spouse or one or more of your children, or some other person who would receive property from your estate if you did not write a will, you should add a sentence to your will saying that you are intentionally omitting that person from your will. Such a clause makes it clear that you did not omit that person unintentionally. If a court decides that you omitted the person unintentionally, that person might be able to obtain a portion of your estate.

Paragraph 3   The third paragraph should explain your funeral and burial instructions, but often no one reads the will until after the funeral. You do not have to say anything in your will about this. The best practice is to make funeral and burial arrangements outside the will and refer to these arrangements in the will. Let your family know the arrangements you have made and any preferences you have regarding your funeral or burial.

Paragraph 4   The fourth paragraph should explain how you want your debts to be paid. Most people prefer to have all their debts paid before any property is distributed to anyone. Some people want the person receiving land or other property to pay the debt on that property. This does not mean that a mortgage on land has to be paid in full. It means that the person receiving the land must honor the obligations of the mortgage, which usually means making monthly payments.

Be specific as to whether debts are to be paid before property is given to someone under the will, or whether the person receiving the property is the only one responsible for the debt. Figure 5-2 makes it clear who is to pay the mortgage on the property left to the testatrix's daughter.

Paragraph 5   The fifth paragraph should explain what you want done with your property after your debts are paid.

You should list specific gifts first, describing each gift clearly, so there is no confusion as to what the gift is. You should explain what happens to the gift if the person you leave it to dies before you. People usually want the gift to go to the child of the person who was originally supposed to receive the gift, or to go to the *residuary estate*. The residuary estate is the property that is left in your estate after debts are paid and after you make specific gifts.

Last Will and Testament
of
John James Smith

1. I, John James Smith, a resident of the Commonwealth of Pennsylvania, declare and publish this as my Will and revoke all previous Wills and Codicils.

2. I am married to Mary Jane Smith. I have two daughters, Patricia Ann Smith and Alice Kathryn Smith.

3. I want a simple, inexpensive burial, with no funeral or graveside service.

4. I want my legally enforceable debts, taxes, and expenses of my estate paid immediately out of my estate, before any property is distributed to anyone under this Will.

5. I give everything to my wife, Mary Jane Smith. If my wife, Mary Jane Smith, dies before me, I give everything equally to my children, including any children born or adopted after I write this Will. If one of my children dies before me, that child's share is to be divided equally among his or her children who are surviving at the time of my death. If one of my children dies before me and said child does not have any children surviving at the time of my death, said deceased child's share of my estate shall be divided equally among my other children who are surviving at the time of my death. "Children" does not include stepchildren, but does include adopted and illegitimate children.

6. I appoint my wife, Mary Jane Smith, as executrix of my estate. If she does not or cannot serve as executrix, I appoint my brother, Joseph William Smith, as executor. I do not want either of them to have to file a bond. I give them the power to sell or not sell, or deal with my property in any way they feel is in the best interest of my estate.

7. If my wife, Mary Jane Smith, dies before me, I appoint my brother, Joseph William Smith, and his wife, Ann Marie Smith, as guardians of my minor children and their property. I want them to serve without bond.

8. Dated this 5th day of January, 1989.

_____

Testator

The above Will was signed, declared, and published as his Will by John James Smith in our presence, and at his request we have signed our names to this Will as witnesses, this 5th day of January, 1989.

Witness _____

Residing _____

_____

Witness _____

Residing _____

_____

Fig. 5-1A. Affidavit to use with will (Sample). *Page 1 of 1* **47**

Affidavit

COMMONWEALTH OF
PENNSYLVANIA   )
) ss.
COUNTY OF BURR   )

I, John James Smith, the testator, signed my name to the above will this 5th day of January, 1989, and being first duly sworn, do solemnly swear upon my oath to the undersigned authority that I sign and execute this instrument as my will, that I sign it voluntarily, that I execute it as my free and voluntary act for the purposes therein expressed, that I am 18 years of age or older, that I am of sound mind, and that I am under no constraint or undue influence.

We, Robert Allen Jones and Mary Jane Jones, being first duly sworn, do solemnly swear upon our oaths to the undersigned authority that in our presence and in the presence of each other, John James Smith signed the above instrument on the 5th day of January, 1989, asked each of us to witness the will, and declared to us that the above will was his last will and that he signed it voluntarily. We signed said will as witnesses in the presence of John James Smith and in the presence of each other. At the time of signing said will, John James Smith appeared to us to be of sound mind and to be signing said will voluntarily. Each of us has attained the age of 18 and is otherwise competent to witness a will.

John James Smith

Robert Allen Jones

Mary Jane Jones

SUBSCRIBED, SWORN TO, AND ACKNOWLEDGED before me by John James Smith, Robert Allen Jones, and Mary Jane Jones, each of whom is known to me personally, this 5th day of January, 1989.

Notary Public
My Commission Expires: 01/10/90

(SEAL)

If you leave a gift to someone in your will, you can still sell or give that gift to someone else while you are alive. If you do, the person who was to receive the gift in your will does not get the gift at your death.

After making specific gifts, if any, you should explain who is to receive your residuary estate. You should explain what you want done with your residuary estate if the person or persons you leave it to die before you. By doing this, you avoid having to rewrite your will if your first choice dies before you do.

You should explain whether you want children born or adopted after you make the will to share in your property. Even though you do this, you should prepare a new will after a new child is born or after you adopt a child. Almost all states have laws that provide that a child born or adopted after you make a will has the right to claim a portion of your estate. You should explain what you mean by "children". If you want to include illegitimate or adopted children in your will, you should say so.

You should make a new will after a marriage or a divorce. In a few states, a marriage after making a will revokes the will. In almost all states, a divorce revokes the portions of the will leaving property to the divorced spouse.

Paragraph 6   The sixth paragraph appoints a person to serve as executor (or executrix) of your estate. It also names an alternate so you do not have to rewrite your will if your first choice dies before you.

A probate court will appoint as executor the person whom you name in your will, unless there is a good reason not to appoint that person, such as the complete incapacity of that person at the time of your death.

An executor appointed by a court gathers a deceased person's property and pays all valid debts. Creditors of the deceased are usually given several months to file claims against the estate. After the time for filing claims has passed, an executor distributes the deceased person's property to the people named in the will, or to the deceased person's heirs if there is no will. *Heirs* are people who are entitled to a deceased person's property according to the will written for the deceased person by the deceased person's state.

A probate court requires an executor to file a bond to protect the estate from his or her misuse of estate property. If you trust your executor, you can save the cost of this bond by directing in your will that your executor should serve without bond.

You should appoint as executor a capable person whom you trust. You can name more than one person. Many people name their spouse as first choice, and a child or close relative as alternate.

You should explain in your will what powers you want your executor to have. If you want to leave all decisions about selling and managing property to your executor, say so in your will. Figure 5-1 does not detail the powers of the executrix as much as FIG. 5-2 does. It is not always necessary to detail the powers, but it is wise to do so. Detailing the powers may help an executor convince some person or a probate court that the testator intended the executor to have the power to perform a particular act.

Paragraph 7 (FIG. 5-1 only)   The seventh paragraph in FIG. 5-1 names guardians to protect minor children and their property. Choosing a guardian for minors can be a difficult decision. The age of the guardian and his or her financial situation are important. Before you write your will, discuss this choice with the person you are thinking of naming as guardian.

A court may require a guardian to file a bond to protect a child's property from misuse by the guardian. You can save the cost of this bond if you direct in your will that the guardian should serve without bond.

A guardianship ends when a child becomes an adult, which is age 18 in almost all states. The child's property is then given to the child.

Last Will and Testament
of
Mary Ellen Jones

1. I, Mary Ellen Jones, a resident of the State of California, declare and publish this as my Will and revoke all previous Wills and Codicils.

2. I am not presently married. I have two children, Jennifer Marie Jones and Edward Allen Jones.

3. I direct that my body be cremated, and my remains buried in Adams Cemetery, in Redwood, California, where I have already purchased a burial plot.

4. I direct that my legally enforceable debts, taxes, and expenses of my estate be paid out of my estate, before any property is distributed to anyone under this Will, except that if the land that I describe below to be given to my daughter still has a mortgage on it at the time of my death, my daughter, Jennifer Marie Jones, should be solely responsible for that mortgage if she receives that property.

5. I give my interest in my house and farm of approximately five acres, located at 11223 South Middle Fork Lane, Redwood, California, 98765, without any of the personal property in the home or on the farm, to my daughter, Jennifer Marie Jones. If she dies before me, this property falls into my residuary estate.

I give $10,000.00 to my son, Edward Allen Jones. If he dies before me, this money falls into my residuary estate.

I give all the rest of my property, which is my residuary estate, equally to my children who are surviving at the time of my death, including any children born or adopted after I write this Will. If one of my children dies before me, his or her share should be equally divided among my other children who are surviving at the time of my death. "Children" does not include stepchildren, but does include adopted and illegitimate children.

6. I appoint my two present children as co-executors of my estate, to serve without bond. I give them the power to sell or not sell, or deal with my property in any way they feel is in the best interest of my estate, including, but not limited to, the power to make all decisions regarding claims against my estate, to employ attorneys, advisers, or other agents on behalf of my estate, to begin or continue any litigation regarding my estate, to keep or dispose of any property of my estate, to continue to operate, sell, or otherwise deal with any interest I have in any business at the time of my death, and to mortgage, pledge, lease, rent, insure, repair, or otherwise manage any other property belonging to my estate.

7. If any part of this Will is held to be inoperative, I want the remainder of my Will to be fully operative.

8. If at the time of my death I own any community property, this Will refers only to my community property interest in that property.

9. Dated this 6th day of February, 1989.

_____

Testatrix

The above Will was signed, declared, and published as her Will by Mary Ellen Jones in our presence, and at her request we have signed our names to this Will as witnesses, this 6th day of February, 1989.

Witness _____

Residing _____

_____

Witness _____

_____

Paragraph 7 (FIG. 5-2 only)   The seventh paragraph in FIG. 5-2 is known as a *savings clause*. This clause provides that if any portion of the will is invalid for some reason, the rest of the will remains valid.

Paragraph 8 (FIG. 5-2 only)   The eighth paragraph in FIG. 5-2 explains that if the maker of the will owns any community property, the will only attempts to control the maker's interest in the community property, not all of the community property. There are nine community property states: Arizona, California, Idaho, Louisiana, Nevada, New Mexico, Texas, Washington, and Wisconsin. Under community property laws, only a deceased person's one-half share of community property may be distributed by the deceased person's will.

Paragraph 8 (FIG. 5-1), Paragraph 9 (FIG. 5-2)   The last paragraph of your will should indicate the date you sign your will. Directly underneath the date, you should sign your will with your full legal name in front of at least two witnesses and a notary public.

Washington, D.C. and all states except Vermont require only two witnesses to a will. Vermont requires three witnesses. Figure 5-3 lists how many witnesses are required by each state and the minimum age for making a will in each state. Only Louisiana requires that the testator sign every page of the will.

Figure 5-1A is an affidavit attached to FIG. 5-1. A will is valid even if it has no affidavit attached. But if the witnesses do not sign an affidavit and it becomes necessary to probate the will, the witnesses may have to be located. Finding the witnesses could delay completion of the probate. If the witnesses and the testator sign an affidavit in front of a notary, usually it is not necessary to find the witnesses in order to probate the estate.

None of the witnesses to your will should have an interest in the will. A witness has an interest in the will if he or she is named in the will to receive property, or if he or she would receive property from the testator's estate if the testator died without a will. Having an interested witness could invalidate the entire will. Some states allow interested witnesses to witness a will, but many states do not.

You should go through the following ritual when signing your will and the affidavit that accompanies it:

1. The testator (or testatrix), the witnesses, and the notary should assemble.
2. The testator should sign the will with his or her full name.
3. The testator should tell the witnesses and the notary that the document he or she signed is his or her will, and that he or she signed it voluntarily. The testator should then ask the witnesses to witness the will and to sign the affidavit after the will.
4. The witnesses should each sign the will.
5. The notary public should administer an oath to the testator and the witnesses asking whether they solemnly swear upon their oaths and under penalty of perjury to the truth of the statements that they are about to make regarding the will. The testator should raise his or her right hand and declare under oath to the notary public that the document he or she signed is his or her Last Will and Testament, and that he or she signed it in the presence of the witnesses, voluntarily, and without constraint or undue influence. The testator should also swear that he or she signed the will while of sound mind, while being at least 18 years of age (14 in Georgia, 16 in Louisiana, and 19 in Wyoming) and for the purposes stated in the will. The testator should then sign the affidavit to the will. The witnesses should raise their right hands and declare under oath to the notary that in their presence and in the presence of each other the testator told them the document they witnessed was his or her will. The witnesses should also swear that in their presence and in the presence of each other, the testator: (1) signed the will of his or her own free will, (2) appeared at the time of signing to be of sound mind and of legal age, and (3) requested that the witnesses sign the will as witnesses and sign the affidavit after the will and the witnesses did so. The witnesses should also swear that they are each at least 18 years of age (19 in Wyoming). The witnesses should then sign the affidavit to the will.

6. The notary should complete the remainder of the affidavit, filling in all blanks, and notarize the affidavit. You should then staple the original affidavit to the original will.

State Laws on Wills (FIG. 5-3)

Figure 5-3 describes the minimum age requirement for making a will and the number of witnesses needed to witness a will in each state and the District of Columbia. It refers to the sections of each state's laws that govern these requirements. You can find these laws by going to a law library in your state. A law library is located at your county courthouse. Ask the librarian to help you find the laws.

Figure 5-3 is based on 1987 and 1988 laws. The state legislatures of the 50 states meet at different times. Some legislatures only meet once every two years. When a state legislature passes a law, the legislature or a publishing company publishes that law at a later time. Several months can pass before the legislature or publisher sends that law to the libraries around the country. As you read these words, months or years will have also passed from the time this book was edited, printed, and distributed. For these reasons, this book, like all legal books, cannot be absolutely current.

Figure 5-3 indicates whether the information for a particular state is based on the 1987 or 1988 laws of that state. If you want to confirm whether or not your state has changed its laws, go to a law library in your state and read the most current version of the law referred to in FIG. 5-3. If the law in your state has changed, the new law will usually have the same number as the old law. Check what are known as the "pocket parts" of your state's laws. Pocket parts are supplements which contain the latest revisions of a state's laws.

Laws regarding the minimum age for making a will and the number of witnesses needed to witness a will are not expected to change, except that eventually Vermont may reduce the number of witnesses required for a will to two witnesses and Wyoming may lower the age for signing and witnessing a will to 18 years.

ESTATE TAXES

Your estate may be subject to state and federal estate taxes. For purposes of federal taxes, your estate includes your individual property, your share of joint property, insurance on your life, pension and death benefits, property you transferred during life but retained control of, and any other property you owned at the time of your death.

For deaths in 1987 and thereafter, federal law imposes no estate taxes on any amount transferred to a surviving spouse, nor on the first $600,000 transferred to non-spouses.

State estate taxes vary widely. Some states do not have an estate tax. You should consult your accountant to find out the details of the estate tax laws for your state. You can also contact your state department of revenue for estate tax returns and instructions.

Fig. 5-3. State Laws on Wills   **53**

State	Minimum Age for Making a Will	Number of Witnesses Required	Sections/Year of Update
Alabama	18	2	43-8-130, -131/1987
Alaska	18	2	13.11.150, .155/1987
Arizona	18	2	14-2501, -2502/1987
Arkansas	18	2	60.401, .403/1987
California	18	2	Probate Code 6100, 6110/1988
Colorado	18	2	15-11-501, -502/1987
Connecticut	18	2	45-160, -161/1987
Delaware	18	2	12-201, -202/1987
District of Columbia	18	2	18-102, -103/1988
Florida	18	2	732. 501, .502(4)/1988
Georgia	14	2	53-2-20, -22, -40/1988
Hawaii	18	2	560:2-501, -502/1987
Idaho	18	2	15-2-501, -502/1988
Illinois	18	2	110 ½-4-1, -3/1988
Indiana	18	2	29-1-5-1, -3/1988
Iowa	18	2	633.264, .279/1988
Kansas	18	2	59-601, -606/1987
Kentucky	18	2	394.020, .040/1987
Louisiana	*	*	*/*
Maine	18	2	18A-2-501, -502/1987
Maryland	18	2	Estates and Trusts 4-101,-102/1987
Massachusetts	18	2	191-1/1987
Michigan	18	2	27.5121, .5122/1988
Minnesota	18	2	524.2-501, -502/1988
Mississippi	18	2	91-5-1/1987
Missouri	18	2	474.310, .320/1988
Montana	18	2	72-2-301, -302/1987
Ncbraska	18	2	30-2326, -2327/1987
Nevada	18	2	133.020, .040/1987
New Hampshire	18	2	551-1, -2/1988
New Jersey	18	2	3B-3-1, -2/1988
New Mexico	18	2	45-2-501, -502/1987
New York	18	2	Estates, Powers, and Trusts Law 3-1.1, -2.1/1988
North Carolina	18	2	31-1, -3.3/1987
North Dakota	18	2	30.1-08-01, -02/1987
Ohio	18	2	2107.02, .03, .04/1988
Oklahoma	18	2	84-41, -55/1988
Oregon	18	2	112.225, .235/1987
Pennsylvania	18	2	20-2501, -2502/1988
Rhode Island	18	2	33-5-2, -5/1987
South Carolina	18	2	62-2-501, -502/1987
South Dakota	18	2	29-2-3, -6/1988
Tennessee	18	2	32-1-102, -104/1987
Texas	18	2	Probate Code 57, 59/1988
Utah	18	2	75-2-501, -502/1988
Vermont	18	3	14-1, -5/1988
Virginia	18	2	64.1-46, -47, -49/1988
Washington	18	2	11.12.010, .020/1988
West Virginia	18	2	41-1-1, -2, -3/1988
Wisconsin	18	2	853.01, .03/1988
Wyoming	19	2	2-1-301(xxvi); 2-6-101, -112; 8-1-102(a)(iii)/1987

* In Louisiana, a minor over the age of 16 can prepare a will, except leaving property to a tutor, a preceptor or an instructor (Civil Code 1477, 1478). Two witnesses are required. The will should be notarized. The testator or testatrix should sign every page of the will. The attestation clause, which is the clause between the testator's signature and the witnesses' signatures, should indicate that the testator or testatrix not only signed the will at the end, but signed the will on each separate page. (Title 9, Section 2442) (1988 Update). **The blank forms in this chapter cannot be used in Louisiana.**

Instructions for Blank Will and Affidavit of Witnesses

Figure 5-4 is a blank will. Figure 5-5 is a blank affidavit to use with a will. You can use these forms in all states except Louisiana. (Louisiana requires formalities other states do not require.) Each form includes blank spaces with a number under each blank. Before filling in any of the blanks, make several photocopies of the form. Use one or more copies as work copies, one as an original, and the rest for future work copies or originals. Fill out a work copy first and be sure it is correct, then fill in the blanks on your final copy. Use ink or nonerasable ballpoint pen, or a typewriter.

Blank Will (FIG. 5-4)   The following numbered instructions match the numbers under the blanks in FIG. 5-4. For simplicity, in these instructions and the ones that follow, the term *testator* means "testator or testatrix" and the term *executor* means "executor or executrix."

(1) Enter the full name of the testator.

(2) Enter the full name of the testator.

(3) Enter the state of residence of the testator.

(4) Enter whether the testator is married or not married.

(5) If the testator is married, enter the full name of the spouse. If there is no spouse, put "not applicable" in this blank.

(6) Enter, in words, the number of children that the testator has. If there are none, put "no" in this blank.

(7) Enter the full names of all the testator's children. If there are none, put "not applicable" in each of these blanks.

(8) Enter any funeral or burial instructions that the testator wishes to give. If there are none, put "none" in this blank.

(9) Enter instructions for the payment of debts. See the sample wills and the explanation of the samples for different wordings that you can use here.

(10) Enter the instructions for division of property upon the testator's death. Be sure to include a clause explaining that the omission of a spouse, child, or other heir is intentional, if such a clause is appropriate. List specific gifts first. Explain whether the person receiving a specific gift is responsible for paying any debt owed on that gift, or whether the estate should pay that debt before the specific gift is given to the beneficiary. Be sure to name alternates for both specific gifts and for the residuary estate.

(11) Enter the full name(s) of the executor(s).

(12) Enter the full name(s) of the alternate executor(s).

(13) If there are no minor children, put "not applicable" in this blank. If there are minor children, enter the full name(s) of the guardian(s) appointed to care for minor children and their property.

(14) If there are no minor children, put "not applicable" in this blank. If there are minor children, enter the full name(s) of any alternate guardian(s) for minor children and their property.

(15,16,17) Enter the day, month, and year that the will is signed.

(18) The testator, at least two witnesses, and a notary public should assemble. The testator should sign his or her full name on this line in the presence of the witnesses and the notary public, and then follow the signing ritual explained earlier in this chapter.

(19) Enter the full name of the testator.

(20,21,22) Enter the day, month, and year that the will is signed.

(23) The first witness should sign his or her full name on this line in front of the testator, the other witnesses, and the notary.

(24) Enter the address of the first witness on these lines.

(25) The second witness should sign his or her full name on this line in front of the testator, the other witnesses, and the notary.

(26) Enter the address of the second witness on these lines.

(27) In Vermont, the third witness should sign his or her full name on this line in front of the testator, the other witnesses, and the notary. In all other states, put "not applicable" on this line.

(28) In Vermont, enter the address of the third witness on these lines. In all other states, put "not applicable" on these lines.

Blank Affidavit (FIG. 5-4A) The following numbered instructions match the numbers under the blanks in FIG. 5-4A:

(1) Enter the name of the state where the affidavit is signed.

(2) Enter the county where the affidavit is signed.

(3) Enter the name of the testator.

(4,5,6) Enter the day, month, and year that the testator signed the will.

(7) Enter 18 in all states except Wyoming (19) and Georgia (14).

(8) Enter the full names of the witnesses on this line.

(9) Enter the full names of the testator on this line.

(10,11,12) Enter the day, month, and year that the will is signed.

(13) Enter the full name of the testator on this line.

(14) Enter the full name of the testator on this line.

(15) Enter 18 in all states, except 19 in Wyoming.

(16) The testator, the witnesses, and the notary public should assemble and follow the signing ritual described earlier in this chapter. The testator should sign his or her full name on this line in front of the notary.

(17) The first witness should sign his or her full name on this line in front of the notary.

(18) The second witness should sign his or her full name on this line in front of the notary.

(19) In Vermont, the third witness should sign his or her full name on this line in front of the notary. In all other states, put "not applicable" on this line.
The following items should be completed by a notary public:

(20) Enter the full names of the testator and witnesses on this line.

(21,22,23) Enter the day, month, and year that the affidavit is signed.

(24) The notary public should sign his or her name on this line.

(25) Enter the date the notary public's commission expires.

(26) The notary public should affix his or her seal to the left of his or her signature.

WHERE TO KEEP YOUR WILL

After you staple the original affidavit to the original will, you should put your signed will and affidavit in an envelope and store them in a secure place, along with your other important papers. Safe deposit boxes can be a problem. Some banks will not allow anyone access to the safe deposit box unless a probate court authorizes an executor or executrix to open the box. If you put your will in a safe deposit box, ask the bank to write you a letter indicating that the bank will allow any person who is a joint signer on the box or the person named as executor or executrix in your will to have access to the box upon your death, even if there is no probate of your estate.

You may wish to make copies of your will and affidavit for the executor or executrix named in the will, any guardian named in the will, your spouse, or your children.

Fig. 5-4. Will (Blank). *Page 1 of 3* **57**

Last Will and Testament
of

_____
(1)

1. I, _____,
(2)

a resident of the State of _____,
(3)

declare and publish this as my Will and revoke all previous Wills and Codicils.

2. I am _____. My
(4)

spouse's full name is _____.
(5)

I have _____ children, whose names are:
(6)

_____ (7)	_____ (7)
_____ (7)	_____ (7)
_____ (7)	_____ (7)

All references to children in this Will include adopted children, children born or adopted after I write this will, and illegitimate children, but do not include stepchildren.

3. I give the following funeral and burial instructions:

_____
(8)

_____

_____

_____

_____

_____

4. Upon my death, I want my debts paid as follows:

_____
(9)

_____

_____

_____

_____

_____

5. Upon my death, I want my property distributed as follows:

_____
(10)
_____
_____
_____
_____
_____
_____
_____
_____
_____
_____
_____.

6. I appoint _____
(11)
as executor or executrix of my estate. I appoint _____
(12)
_____ as alternate.
Any executor or executrix shall serve without bond. I give my executor or executrix the power to sell or not sell, or deal with my property in any way he or she feels is in the best interest of my estate, including, but not limited to, the power to make all decisions regarding claims against my estate, to begin or continue any litigation regarding my estate, to employ attorneys, advisers, or other agents on behalf of my estate, to keep or dispose of any property of my estate, to continue to operate, sell, or otherwise deal with any interest I have in any business at the time of my death, and to mortgage, pledge, lease, rent, insure, repair, or otherwise manage any property belonging to my estate.

7. If at the time of my death I have minor children who survive me, and if the other

parent(s) of said children die(s) before me, I appoint _____
(13)

to act as guardian(s) for my minor children and their property. I appoint

_____
(14)

_____
as alternate(s). Any guardian shall serve without bond.

8. If any part of my Will is held to be inoperative in any way, I want the rest of my Will to remain operative.

9. If any of my property at the time of my death is community property, this Will refers only to my community property interest in such property.

Dated this _____ day of _____, _____.
(15)   (16)   (17)

_____
(18)
Testator/Testatrix

Fig. 5-4. (Cont'd). *Page 3 of 3* **59**

The above Will was signed, declared, and published as his/her Will by

_____ in our presence, at his/her
(19)

request we have signed our names to this Will as witnesses this _____
(20)

day of _____, _____ .
(21)   (22)

Witness _____
(23)

Residing _____
(24)

_____

Witness _____
(25)

Residing _____
(26)

_____

Witness _____
(27)

Residing _____
(28)

_____

STATE OF _____)
                    (1)
) ss.
COUNTY OF _____)
                    (2)

I, _____,
                                                    (3)

the testator or testatrix, sign my name to the above Will on this _____ day of
                                                                                        (4)

_____, _____, and being first duly sworn, do solemnly swear
            (5)   (6)

upon my oath to the undersigned authority that I sign and execute this instrument as

my Will and that I sign it voluntarily, that I execute it as my free and voluntary act

for the purposes therein expressed, and that I am ____ years of age, or older, of

sound mind, and under no constraint or undue influence.

We, _____
                                                    (8)

_____,

being first duly sworn, do solemnly swear upon our oaths to the undersigned authority

that, in our presence and in the presence of each other, _____
                                                                                        (9)

_____ signed the above instrument on the _____

day of _____.
            (10)   (11)   (12)

asked each of us to witness the Will, and declared to us that the above Will was his/her

Last Will, and that he/she was signing it voluntarily. We signed said Will as witnesses

in the presence of _____
                                                    (13)

and in the presence of each other, and at the time of signing said Will,

_____ appeared to us to be of sound mind and to be
                (14)

signing said Will voluntarily. Each of us has attained the age of _____ and is
                                                                                        (15)

otherwise competent to witness a Will.

_____
                                                                                (16)

Testator/Testatrix

_____
                                                                                (17)

First Witness

Fig. 5-4A. (Cont'd). *Page 2 of 2*   **61**

_____ (18)

Second Witness

_____ (19)

Third Witness

SUBSCRIBED, SWORN TO, AND ACKNOWLEDGED before me by

_____
(20)

_____

_____, each of whom is known to me personally, this _____ day of
(21)

_____, _____.
(22)   (23)

_____ (24)

Notary Public

(SEAL)   My Commission Expires: _____
(26)   (25)

Chapter 6
Joint Ownership Agreements That Avoid Probate

This chapter explains what probate is, when to use probate, and how and when to avoid probate. Following these explanations, this chapter provides and explains sample and blank affidavits of joint ownership and assignments creating joint ownership with right of survivorship, which you can use to avoid probate. By using these forms, you can save hundreds, or even thousands, of dollars in probate costs. You can also avoid the delay and frustration probate causes.

PROBATE

Technically, *probate* means to prove that a will is genuine and was signed properly, but probate has come to mean the court process of managing a deceased person's affairs.

Probate protects the wishes of the deceased person and the rights of heirs, people named in the will, and creditors of the deceased person. Probate also passes clear title to property from a deceased person to the people entitled to that property.

Probate begins when someone petition a probate court to admit a deceased person's will to probate, or to open a probate for someone who died without a will.

If a deceased person had a will, a probate court will decide whether or not it is valid. The probate court will appoint an *executor* (or *executrix*) to manage the affairs of the deceased person during the probate. The appointed person is an executor (or executrix) if he or she is named in a will. The appointed person is an *administrator* if there is no will.

The executor or administrator publishes a notice to creditors of the deceased. He or she sends notices to heirs of the deceased, to people named in the will, to the Internal Revenue Service, and to the state Department of Revenue. *Heirs* are people who receive a deceased person's property according to the will written for the deceased person by his or her state. The executor or administrator gives creditors a certain amount of time to file claims against the estate.

The executor or administrator discovers and protects the property of the deceased. He or she also discovers and pays legitimate debts. When the executor or administrator is ready to close the estate, he or she files an accounting with the court. The accounting explains what property the deceased person had at the time of his or her death, what receipts came into the estate, and what disbursements were made from the estate. The accounting also explains how the executor proposes to distribute any property left in the estate, and asks the court to transfer title to property to the people who are entitled to that property.

THE COSTS OF PROBATE

The costs of probate include filing fees, bond fees, publication fees, attorney's fees, accountant fees, appraiser fees, and executor or administrator fees.

Filing Fees. A probate court requires a filing fee to open a probate. The size of the estate determines the amount of the filing fee. Fees differ among states and among counties within states. As an example, one court presently charges a filing fee of $34 for an estate of less than $10,000; $83 for an estate between $10,000 and $25,000; $153 for an estate between $25,000 and $50,000; $223 for an estate between $50,000 and $100,000; and $293 for an estate larger than $100,000.

Bond Fees. If a will directs that an executor shall serve without bond, a probate court usually will not require a bond. If there is no will, or if the will does not direct that the executor shall serve without bond, a court will require the executor or administrator to buy a bond to protect the estate from misuse of property by the executor or administrator.

The amount of the bond the court requires is related to the size of the estate. Different bonding companies charge different rates for these bonds. As an example, one company charges an annual premium of $20 for a bond of $4,000 or less, and gradually increases the premium for each additional $1,000 of the bond. A $25,000 bond costs $110 per year. A $75,000 bond costs $273 per year. The cost of the bond continues to increase as the amount of the bond increases.

Publication Fees. Probate requires publishing a notice in a local newspaper that tells the public where to file a claim against an estate. The executor publishes these notices for three or four consecutive weeks. The cost of the notice depends on the rates of the newspaper used. These notices usually cost between $50 and $100.

Attorney's Fees. Different attorneys use different methods to determine their fees in probate cases. Some attorneys charge an hourly rate, and base their fee on the time they spend on the case. Some charge a percentage of the value of the estate and often ask for extraordinary fees in excess of the percentage they normally charge. Courts rarely disallow a request for extraordinary fees. Especially where an attorney uses the percentage method, attorney's fees for an estate can be costly, as much as five percent of the total estate, or more.

Attorneys do most of the work that executors or administrators are supposed to do. Attorneys are more experienced than executors or administrators in performing the tasks required of executors or administrators. Those tasks include:

- gathering information regarding the estate
- filing the petition to open a probate
- collecting the assets of the estate
- inventorying and valuing the property of the estate
- contacting the heirs and beneficiaries of the estate
- preparing necessary tax returns
- obtaining tax releases from the IRS and the state Department of Revenue
- preparing the final accounting
- preparing the petition for distribution
- preparing the petition to close the estate
- preparing the legal documents to transfer assets from the estate to the people entitled to the property at the close of the estate

Accountant Fees. Some estates are so large or receive so much income during the probate that tax returns have to be prepared for the estate. Some attorneys do all of these returns, but accountants often prepare these returns. The cost of preparing these returns depends on the number and complexity of the returns. Some returns are relatively simple and cost $100 or less to prepare. Other returns are more complex. The cost of preparing complex returns can be several hundred or even several thousand dollars.

Appraiser Fees. The probate process often requires that an appraiser value the property in an estate for tax purposes or for the probate court. Appraiser fees vary among states and depend upon the extent of the property that is appraised. These fees can be several hundred dollars.

Executor or Administrator Fees. An executor or administrator of an estate is entitled to a fee for his or her work on the estate. These fees can be based on a percentage of the value of an estate or on the time spent on an estate. Executor fees can be several thousand dollars in larger estates.

WHEN TO USE PROBATE, WHEN TO AVOID IT

Critics of the probate system have said many bad things about probate. But probate is a tool. Sometimes, you should avoid probate. Sometimes, however, you should use probate. You can use probate to:

- pass clear title to property.
- cut off the claims of creditors.
- resolve disputes among heirs, people named in the will, or creditors.
- help reduce income or inheritance taxes.

Probate is unnecessary if all interested people agree on what to do with a deceased person's property, if no one is worried about creditors, if title to property can be passed without probate, and if there is no need to reduce income or estate taxes.

Using probate to pass title to property. When someone dies, title to his or her property must pass to whomever is entitled to the property. For example, if a father dies and has a will leaving land to one of his daughters, the daughter may not be able to sell the land without an order from a probate court transferring the title to the land from the father's name to the daughter's name. A will alone may not pass title to the daughter. Until a will has gone through probate, a court has never proven it to be authentic or properly executed.

In the above example, some title insurance companies will insure clear title in the daughter's name without probate if the daughter pays a larger premium for a title insurance policy and if all the heirs of the deceased person sign affidavits protecting the title company against claims by any heirs. Also, in some states title to land automatically passes to a deceased person's heirs or the people named in a deceased person's will. Unfortunately, this is not true in all states.

Using probate to cut off claims of creditors. State probate rules determine how much time an estate has to give creditors to file claims against the estate. Creditors must file their claims within four months or so after the date of first publication of the notice to creditors in the newspaper and are sometimes given one year from the date of death within which to file claims. Once that time has passed and the executor closes the estate, no creditor can make any claim against the estate, the executor, the heirs, or other people who received property from the estate. If a deceased person's family is worried about possible claims against his or her estate, they can use probate to set a time period within which creditors must file claims.

Using probate to resolve disputes. Sometimes heirs, or people named in a will, disagree about the validity or meaning of the will or about how to divide property. A probate court will decide these issues if the people involved cannot.

Using probate to reduce taxes. Most people do not have to worry about paying estate taxes on the federal level because their estates are too small. Presently, you can pass any amount of money to your spouse without any federal estate taxes, and up to $600,000 to a non-spouse without federal estate tax.

If you have a net worth greater than $600,000, your estate may be subject to some federal estate tax when you and your spouse die and leave property to other people. One way to reduce these taxes is to create trusts that double the $600,000 exemption. These trusts divide ownership of property between a husband and wife. By removing property from joint ownership with right of survivorship, which passes title without probate, these trusts require a probate of each spouse's estate in order to pass title to property to the surviving spouse and children. Probate is necessary to carry out this method of reducing taxes.

HOW TO AVOID PROBATE

Joint ownership with right of survivorship, revocable trusts, and properly naming beneficiaries in life insurance policies, pension funds, and retirement accounts can avoid probate.

Joint ownership with right of survivorship. Owning all of your property jointly with right of survivorship with one or more other people avoids probate. When one owner dies, ownership of the property automatically belongs to the surviving joint owner(s). Probate is not necessary to pass title to the property.

Joint ownership with right of survivorship has advantages and disadvantages.

ADVANTAGES

- The property belongs to the survivor without the costs and delays of probate.
- The property belongs to the survivor free of the claims of creditors of the deceased person, except for mortgages or other liens attached to property before death.
- The property belongs to the survivor without public notices.

DISADVANTAGES

- If joint ownership is between a husband and wife, it only avoids probate when the first spouse dies. If both die in a common accident, probate may be necessary to pass title to children or other people.
- Joint ownership gives all joint owners a present interest in the property. All owners have to agree to sell the property.
- If one joint owner becomes incompetent, the other joint owner may have to go to court to create a guardianship to sell or deal with the incompetent person's interest in the property. You can avoid this if, before becoming incompetent, one joint owner gives the other joint owner a valid durable power of attorney. Chapter 15 of this book explains powers of attorney.
- While both joint owners are alive, the creditors of either may be able to reach a joint owner's interest in joint property.
- When a parent owns property jointly with right of survivorship with one child, the property belongs to that one child when the parent dies. Unless there is strong evidence that the parent intended other children to share in the property, other children will not get any of the property.
- Making someone a joint owner of your property is a gift to them of the portion of the property that you give them. You may have to file a gift tax return, and, if the gift is large enough, may have to pay a gift tax. Also, creating joint ownership

with right of survivorship may result in losing a tax advantage, known as a stepped-up basis. This tax advantage is too complex to explain in this book. For these two reasons, no one should change the ownership of their assets to create joint ownership with right of survivorship without first consulting an accountant to find out what the tax effects of the transfer will be.

Revocable trusts. You can create a revocable trust while you are alive to avoid probate. In a trust, one person, called a *trustee*, manages property for another person, called a *beneficiary*. A *revocable trust* is a trust that you can revoke or change after you create it.

A revocable trust takes all of your property and transfers it into the name of a trustee, who can be you. The trust agreement names as the beneficiaries the people whom you want to get your property at your death.

The trust agreement directs that while you are alive, you can sell or use the property in the trust in any way you want. When you die, the revocable trust agreement names a successor trustee to succeed you as trustee. The agreement directs that, at your death, the successor trustee should distribute the trust's property among the beneficiaries, without probate. This type of trust allows you to maintain control over your property while alive, and yet pass that property without probate upon death.

At the time you create a revocable trust, you have to change the titles to all of your property into your name as trustee.

Revocable trusts have advantages and disadvantages.

ADVANTAGES

- A revocable trust passes title to property without the costs, delays, and publicity of probate.

- If there are two creators, the trust can pass property without probate when both die, as well as when the first dies.

- The trust maintains control over the property while the creator(s) is/are alive.

- The trust is not a present gift to the beneficiaries, and therefore does not result in a taxable gift to them.

- The trust does not pass property to the beneficiaries until death, and therefore preserves the "stepped-up basis" tax advantage.

DISADVANTAGES

- The trust requires preparing and signing a trust agreement.

- It requires changing titles to all property to the name of the trustee and maintaining them in that name.

- Having an attorney prepare the trust will cost more than the costs of avoiding probate through joint ownership with right of survivorship.

- These trusts can be confusing to the creator, to the beneficiaries, and to some banks and other institutions that are not experienced with them. Joint ownership with right of survivorship is easier for people to understand and to work with.

Life Insurance. Life insurance, pension funds, and individual retirement accounts (IRAs) can avoid probate by naming a specific beneficiary other than the estate of the insured. If the beneficiary of these accounts or policies is your estate, the checks for the proceeds of the accounts or policies will be made out to "the estate of" the deceased person. An estate may have to be opened so that the "estate" can cash the check.

You can avoid probate of insurance policy proceeds, IRAs, and other accounts if the beneficiaries are specific persons who are living at the time of your death. The bank or insurance company will pay the proceeds directly to the beneficiary without probate. You should name an alternate, sometimes called a *contingent*, beneficiary. By doing so, you avoid probate even if the primary beneficiary dies before the insured.

The costs of avoiding probate. If you avoid probate by joint ownership with right of survivorship, your costs will be far less than the costs of probate. You will not pay probate filing fees, a bond fee, a publication fee, or an executor's or administrator's fee, and your attorney's fees will be greatly reduced. Your costs will be about $50 or less for recording new deeds and changing titles to vehicles, and about $300 or less in attorney's fees for preparation of deeds and other documents (if you have an attorney prepare the documents). Accountant and appraiser fees in avoiding probate will not vary much from probate fees because avoiding probate does not avoid having to file tax returns.

If you use a trust agreement to avoid probate, your costs should be far less than the costs of probate. You will not have to pay probate filing fees, bond fees, publication fees, or an executor's or administrator's fee. Your attorney's fees for preparing the trust agreement and changing the titles to your property should be less than the attorney's fees for probating your estate, but, again, your accountant and appraiser fees will not vary much from probate fees.

AVOIDING PROBATE THROUGH JOINT OWNERSHIP

If you have reviewed the advantages and disadvantages earlier in this chapter, have consulted an accountant about the tax effects of creating joint ownership with right of survivorship, and have decided to avoid probate through joint ownership, this section will tell you how to avoid probate using joint ownership. The procedure differs with different types of property, so this section discusses each type of property separately.

Bank accounts, safe deposit boxes, and brokerage accounts. Having a joint signer on your bank accounts, safe deposit box, and brokerage accounts can avoid probate if only one signature is required to withdraw money or property. These accounts have "signature cards," which are cards signed by anyone who is authorized to withdraw money from the account. Those cards indicate whether one or more signatures are required to withdraw money from the accounts.

If the signature card for your account or safe deposit box does not allow only one joint owner to withdraw money or property, ask your bank or brokerage house to amend the signature card to do so. Explain that you want to own the account or box jointly with right of survivorship, so the surviving joint owner will automatically own the account or box when one of the joint owners dies. They will know how to amend the signature cards to do this.

Some banks and brokerage firms have blocked withdrawals from accounts and safe deposit boxes when one joint owner dies. Ask your bank or brokerage firm to confirm in writing that this will not happen to your account or box, and that upon the death of one joint owner the surviving joint owner will have immediate access to bank accounts, safe deposit boxes, and brokerage accounts.

Stocks, bonds, certificates of deposit, and vehicles. For stocks, bonds, certificates of deposit, and vehicles, the wording of the stock or bond certificate, of the certificate of deposit, or of the title to the vehicle determines whether or not ownership is joint with right of survivorship. The key words are "or the survivor" or "with right of survivorship" or "as joint tenants". The words to avoid are, "as tenants in common". *Without words of explanation a tenancy in common is often created.*

If the wording on your titles or certificates does not create joint ownership with right of survivorship, contact your Department of Motor Vehicles, the bank that issued the certificate of deposit, or the company that issued the stock or bond. Ask them to change the title or certificate to create joint ownership with right of survivorship. They should know the language to use to do that in your state. If they do not, tell them to use this language, "John R. Jones or Mary M. Jones, or the survivor, as joint tenants, not as tenants in common".

Life insurance, pension funds, and IRAs. Life insurance, pension funds, and IRAs avoid probate by having a specific beneficiary other than the estate of the insured, as explained earlier in this chapter. Check your documents to be sure the beneficiary designations are correct. If they are not, contact your insurance agent, bank, or brokerage firm to name primary and alternate beneficiaries.

Interests in business. If a business is a corporation, the stockholders will have stock certificates. Creating joint ownership with right of survivorship for stock certificates was discussed above.

If a business is a partnership, the written partnership agreement should explain what happens to a partner's interest upon his or her death. The following is an example of a provision which avoids probate when one partner dies:

> *The partners, John James Smith and Fredrick Allen Jones, agree that their interests in this partnership and in all partnership property are held jointly with right of survivorship, not as tenants in common. Upon the death of one of the partners, the partners intend that the deceased partner's interest in the partnership and all partnership property shall belong automatically to the other surviving partner, without probate.*

In addition to the above clause, all titles to partnership property should be held in the name of the partnership or by all the partners jointly with right of survivorship. This chapter already explained how to contact the Department of Motor Vehicles to change titles for vehicles. If the partnership is registered with the federal, state, county, or city government or other organization, the registration should indicate that the partners own the business jointly with right of survivorship. Contact the organization or government department where the business is registered and explain that you want to be sure that when one partner dies, the other partners will automatically control the business without need for probate. Ask them if you need to amend the registration to accomplish this.

If the partners want a surviving partner to compensate a deceased partner's spouse for the deceased partner's interest in the partnership, the partnership agreement should set up a method to do so. For example, the partnership could maintain life insurance on the lives of the partners, with the partners' spouses as beneficiaries. In this way, the surviving spouse receives compensation for the deceased partner's interest in the partnership by receiving the proceeds of the insurance policy. The insurance company pays these proceeds to the surviving spouse without probate.

If you are the sole owner of a business, you have to change the business to a jointly owned corporation or partnership to avoid probate.

Literary works, musical compositions, patent rights, and royalties. An author, composer, or inventor may have a copyright or patent on his or her work. He or she may have a contract with a publisher or manufacturer for royalty payments. Authors, composers, and inventors can avoid probate of their rights under copyrights, patents, and royalty contracts by assigning one-half of their interest in those contracts to another person, to be held jointly with right of survivorship with that person. As discussed earlier, one of the disadvantages of this is that the joint owner becomes a present owner, with the right to one-half of any royalties.

A sample assignment, an explanation of the sample, and a blank assignment to avoid probate of copyrights, patents, and royalty contracts are provided later in this chapter.

Personal property without titles. For personal property without titles, you can create joint ownership by signing a joint property affidavit and/or signing an assignment.

When two or more people own untitled property together, they sign a joint property affidavit to create joint ownership with right of survivorship as to that property. A joint property affidavit is a document that all the joint owners sign, declaring that they own the untitled personal property jointly with right of survivorship.

When you own untitled personal property alone and want to add another person as a joint owner, you assign one-half of your interest in the property to the other person, to be held jointly with right of survivorship with that person.

Samples, explanations of the samples, and blank forms for a joint property affidavit and an assignment are provided later in this chapter.

Real property, mortgages, trust deeds, real estate contracts, rental agreements, and personal property sales contracts. If you own real property (land and buildings) free of all loans and liens, the wording of the deed to the property determines whether or not you own the property jointly with right of survivorship.

If you are buying or selling real property on a mortgage or trust deed, the wording of the mortgage or trust deed, of the promissory note that accompanies the mortgage or trust deed, and of the deed you received when you bought the property determines the type of ownership.

If you are buying or selling real property on a real estate contract, the wording of the contract of sale and of the seller's deed to the property determines the type of ownership.

If you are a landlord or renter in a rental agreement or a buyer or seller in a personal property sales contract, the wording of the rental agreement or contract determines the type of ownership.

The following wording creates joint ownership with right of survivorship in all states:

John and Mary Smith, each as to an undivided one-half interest, to be held jointly with right of survivorship, not as tenants in common.

Different states use different wording to create joint ownership. Some states recognize *joint tenancies* for real property. A joint tenancy is joint ownership with right of survivorship. If a deed reads, "John and Mary Smith, as joint tenants", or "John and Mary Smith, jointly with right of survivorship", or "John and Mary Smith, jointly with right of survivorship, not as tenants in common", John and Mary Smith already own the property jointly with right of survivorship. If a deed reads, "John and Mary Smith, as tenants in common", they do not own the property jointly with right of survivorship.

The wording you use to show joint ownership with right of survivorship must make it clear that, upon the death of one joint owner, the survivor gets the property. Such phrases as "or the survivor" or "with right of survivorship" accomplish that. The wording to avoid is "as tenants in common". A tenancy in common is joint ownership without right of survivorship. If you do not make it clear that you want joint ownership with right of survivorship, most states presume that you do not.

If the deed to your property is not joint with right of survivorship and you own property free of loans or liens, you have to sign a new deed to create joint ownership with right of survivorship. Chapter 10 of this book explains and provides samples and forms for deeds. Follow the instructions in that chapter to prepare a deed to create joint ownership with right of survivorship.

If you are buying property on a mortgage or trust deed, your trust deed or mortgage probably says that if you try to assign any interest in the trust deed or mortgage without the lender's written consent, the entire balance owing under the trust deed or mortgage becomes immediately due and payable. If the trust deed or mortgage does say that, you must contact your lender and obtain written permission before you assign any interest in the trust deed or mortgage.

If the lender in your trust deed or mortgage approves in writing the assignment of your interest in the trust deed or mortgage, follow the instructions in Chapter 10 to prepare the deed needed to create joint ownership with right of survivorship. Follow the instructions later in this chapter to prepare an assignment of the promissory note and of the trust deed or mortgage. With trust deeds and mortgages, the person you want to add as a joint owner may not want to be a joint owner. If your lender agrees to add a new joint owner to the promissory note and mortgage or trust deed, the new joint owner will be liable for the obligations under the promissory note and trust deed or mortgage. The compensation to the new joint owner is that the new joint owner will also own one-half of any equity that has been built up in the property. In addition, when you pay for the property in full, the new joint owner will own one-half of the property.

If you are buying or selling real property on a real estate contract, are a landlord or tenant in a rental contract, or are a buyer or seller in a personal property sales contract, and the wording of the contract does not create joint ownership with right of survivorship, you have to assign part of your interest in the contract to another person to avoid probate. For real estate contracts, you have to sign an assignment and a quitclaim deed. For rental agreements and personal property contracts, you only have to sign an assignment.

A real estate, personal property sales, or landlord/tenant contract may say that if one party tries to assign any interest in the contract without the other party's written consent, the entire balance owing under the contract becomes immediately due and payable. The contract may also say that such an assignment breaches the contract. If the contract does include clauses such as these, you must contact the other party and obtain written permission before you assign any interest in the contract. If the other party approves in writing the assignment of your interest in the contract, follow the instructions in Chapter 10 to prepare a quitclaim deed for an assignment of an interest in a real estate contract. Follow the instructions later in this chapter to prepare an assignment of an interest in a real estate contract, a personal property sales contract, or a rental contract.

Sample Affidavit of Joint Ownership (FIG. 6-1)

Chapter 4 explains affidavits in detail and provides sample and blank affidavits. Read that chapter before preparing the affidavit in this chapter.

Figure 6-1 is a sample joint ownership affidavit. It contains the following information that all affidavits of joint ownership should contain:

Full names and addresses of all the persons making the affidavit (the affiants).

Statement that the affiants swear to the affidavit upon their oaths and under the penalty of perjury. Swearing upon an oath and under penalty of perjury makes an affidavit different from any other statement that a person makes. It makes knowingly false statements in an affidavit perjury.

Explanation of why the affiants are making the affidavit. The sample explains that the purpose of signing the affidavit is to create joint ownership with right of survivorship of all untitled personal property, in order to avoid probate of that property when one of the joint owners dies. When a judge interprets a written document, he or she always tries to determine what the people who signed the document intended the document to do. Making that intent known helps ensure that the document accomplishes its purposes.

Statement of the facts that the affiants are swearing are true. In the sample, the affiants swear as to their identities, addresses, and reasons for making the affidavit. In addition, they swear that they own all of their untitled personal property jointly with right of survivorship.

Most people do not want to list all of their untitled personal property in a joint property affidavit. One reason not to do so is that the list will change as people buy and sell property in the future. So, if two people wish to declare that they own all of their present and future untitled personal property jointly with right of survivorship, they should not list specific property.

Affidavit of Joint Ownership

COMMONWEALTH OF PENNSYLVANIA   )
) ss.
        COUNTY OF BURR   )

We, the undersigned, John M. Jones, whose address is 222 Third Street, Waynecastle, Pennsylvania, County of Burr, 17294, and Mary L. Jones whose address is 222 Third Street, Waynecastle, Pennsylvania, County of Burr, 17294, being first duly sworn, upon our oaths do solemnly swear under penalty of perjury that:

1. We are making this affidavit for the purpose of creating joint ownership with right of survivorship of all untitled personal property owned by us, in order to avoid probate of that property upon the death of one of us.

2. We hereby declare that we own all of the untitled personal property in our possession, and will own all of the untitled personal property that comes into our possession in the future, as follows: Each as to an undivided one-half interest, jointly with right of survivorship, not as tenants in common. Upon the death of either of us, the survivor shall own the property automatically, without necessity of probate of said property.

Signed at 222 Third Street, Waynecastle, Pennsylvania, County of Burr, 17294, on February 2, 1989.

_____
                               John M. Jones

_____
Mary L. Jones

I, Wanda C. Twobucks, a resident of and notary public in and for the Commonwealth of Pennsylvania, who am duly commissioned and sworn and legally authorized to administer oaths and affirmations, hereby certify that on February 2, 1989, John M. Jones and Mary L. Jones, who are known to me personally to be the affiants in the above affidavit, appeared before me and, after being first duly sworn by me under penalty of perjury, swore on their oaths to the truth of the facts in the above affidavit, and signed and acknowledged said affidavit in my presence, of their own free will, and for the purposes explained in said affidavit.

Subscribed and sworn to before me this 2nd day of February, 1989.

_____
             Notary Public
(SEAL)   My Commission Expires: 2/09/90

If two people want to declare that they own certain personal property jointly with right of survivorship, the affidavit should list and accurately describe each item of untitled personal property that the parties are referring to.

The sample affidavit uses the following language to describe the type of ownership of untitled personal property: "each as to an undivided one-half interest, jointly with right of survivorship, not as tenants in common". As discussed earlier in this chapter, different states use different wording to create joint ownership with right of survivorship. The important factor in the wording is to make clear the intent of the parties. You can use the wording in the sample in any state because it makes the intent of the parties clear.

Description of when and where the owners signed the affidavit.

Signatures of the affiants in front of a notary public. The affiants should sign the affidavit in front of a notary public for the state where they sign the affidavit, which should be the same state where they reside. The notary public should ask the affiants to raise their right hands. The notary public should ask whether they solemnly swear upon their oaths and upon penalty of perjury that the statements contained in the affidavit are true. After so swearing, the affiants should sign the affidavit. The notary public should then fill out the acknowledgment portion of the affidavit, including the notary public's signature, the date his or her commission expires, and the seal of the notary public.

After the affiants sign an affidavit of joint ownership, they should keep the affidavit with their other important papers.

Sample Assignment Creating Joint Ownership with Right of Survivorship (FIG. 6-2)

Figure 6-2 is a sample assignment creating joint ownership with right of survivorship. You can use this type of assignment to create joint ownership with right of survivorship in promissory notes, trust deeds, mortgages, real estate contracts, rental contracts, personal property sales contracts, patents, literary works, and musical compositions.

The sample includes the following that all such assignments should include:

Name(s) and address where the recorder's office should send the assignment after recording it. The name(s) and address should be in the margin or at the top of the first page of the assignment.

Names, addresses, and marital status of the assignor and assignee. In Figure 6-2, the assignor was the sole owner of the property he is assigning to his wife. If two people own property together but not with right of survivorship and are signing the assignment to create right of survivorship, both people are assignors and both are assignees. If the assignor is married and the assignee is not his or her spouse, make the spouse an assignor, even if that spouse is not an owner of the property.

Description of the consideration involved in the assignment. Consideration is what the assignor gets in exchange for transferring the interest in the property to the assignee. In the sample, the consideration is $5.00 and love and affection.

In order for an assignment to be valid, there must be either *good* or *valuable* consideration. Good consideration is consideration that is personal. For instance, transferring property for love and affection is good consideration. Valuable consideration is consideration that has some value, for instance, money. Another form of valuable consideration is cancellation of a debt. In return for transferring real estate to the assignee, the assignee could forgive a debt owed by the assignor to the assignee.

When property, services, or cancellation of a debt are the consideration for transfer of property, some states require that an assignment state the value of the property, services, or the cancellation of the debt in terms of money.

Some states require that there be *nominal* consideration in assignments where the consideration is love and affection. Nominal consideration means a small amount of money, such as $5.00. Some states also require that in assignments where the consideration is love and affection, the assignment must state whether or not the assignor and assignee are blood relatives, and if so, their relationship.

Words of assignment. Every assignment must contain words of assignment that transfer the property from the assignor to the assignee. In the sample, those words are "grants, conveys, assigns, transfers, and sets over".

Description of what is assigned. In the sample, the assignor assigns to the assignee one-half of the assignor's interest in a real estate contract in which the assignor is the seller, in the future payments under the contract, and in the property involved in the contract. An assignment of a real estate contract should describe the date of the real estate contract, where it is recorded, the present unpaid balance of the contract, the interest rate under the contract, and the date that the interest is paid until. An assignment of an interest in a trust deed or mortgage should describe the same information.

If an assignor is assigning an interest in an unrecorded lease, promissory note, or personal property sales contract, the assignment should describe the date of the lease, note, or contract; the names of the parties in the lease, note, or contract; the property rented or sold in the lease or contract; whether the assignor is the seller, buyer, holder, signer, landlord, or renter in the lease, note, or contract; the unpaid balance owing under the lease, note, or contract; the interest rate if there is any; and the date that any interest owed is paid to. In addition, the assignor should attach a copy of the lease, note, or contract to the assignment, refer to and mark the copy as "Exhibit A", and say that Exhibit A is "attached here to and incorporated into this assignment by this reference".

If an assignor is assigning an interest in a patent, literary work, or musical composition, the assignment should describe the patent or copyright number, the year the patent or copyright was filed, and any royalty contract for the patent or copyright. In describing a royalty contract, an assignment should describe the date of any such contract, the parties to the contract, the property, patent, literary work, or musical compensation that is the subject of the contract, and when and where the contract was recorded if it was recorded. If the contract was not recorded, the assignor should attach a copy of the contract to the assignment, refer to and mark the copy as "Exhibit A", and say that Exhibit A is "attached here to and incorporated into this assignment by this reference".

The sample assigns to the assignee an undivided one-half interest in a real estate contract. An assignment must divide the ownership of whatever is being assigned into equal parts. In some states, joint ownership with right of survivorship has to be equal joint ownership. If, after the assignment, there will be two joint owners, each should own a one-half interest in the property. If, after the assignment, there will be three joint owners, each should own one-third, and so on.

If the assignor will not be one of the joint owners after the assignment, or if two people own property together but not with right of survivorship and are signing the assignment to create right of survivorship, what would be assigned would be "all our right, title, and interest in . . .", not a one-half interest.

How the property will be held after the assignment. The sample says that when the assignor transfers a one-half interest in the real estate contract to the assignee, the assignor and assignee will then own their one-half interests in an undivided manner, jointly with right of survivorship, not as tenants in common. The ownership is undivided because both owners own all of the property. One owner does not own a specific one-half of the property. Both own the whole. The ownership is joint with right of survivorship and not as tenants in common, because a tenancy in common is joint ownership *without* right of survivorship. A tenancy in common does not avoid probate.

If two people own property together but not with right of survivorship and are signing the assignment to create right of survivorship, the last two sentences of the second paragraph would read, "Assingees" interest shall be an undivided interest, jointly with right of survivorship, not as tenants in common. Upon the death of either assignee, the survivor shall automatically own the entire interest in said contract, payments, and property, without probate." You should use this same wording when the assignor will not be one of the joint owners of the property after the assignment.

Release of dower, curtesy, homestead, and community property rights. The sample does not mention dower, curtesy, homestead, or community property rights because the assignor and assignee in the sample are husband and wife. If the assignor and assignee are not husband and wife, the spouse of the assignor should be listed as an assignor and should sign a statement that the spouse gives up his or her dower, curtesy, homestead, and community property rights in the property assigned.

Some states give a husband or a wife certain rights in real property owned by his or her spouse, even if the real property is in the name of only one spouse. These rights are called *dower rights* on behalf of women, and *curtesy rights* on behalf of men. Many states have abolished dower and courtesy rights, but in the states that still have them, a final divorce of the parties that dissolves the marriage of the parties forever will eliminate dower and curtesy rights. An assignee only needs to have the present spouse of the assignor give up dower or curtesy rights.

In some states, a husband or wife has homestead or community property rights in his or her spouse's property. *Homestead rights* are the rights of a spouse to live in the family home until death. *Community property rights* exist in nine states: Arizona, California, Idaho, Louisiana, Nevada, New Mexico, Texas, Washington, and Wisconsin. Under community property laws, a spouse may have an interest in property owned by his or her spouse, even if title to the property is only in one spouse's name.

An assignee wants the spouse of an assignor to release homestead and community property rights so that the spouse of the assignor cannot make a claim against the property based on these rights.

Name(s) and address where the tax assessor should send real property tax statements in the future. The assessor should send future tax statements to the assignor and assignee if they are husband and wife. If the assignor and assignee are not husband and wife and do not live at the same address, use the name and address of the assignor.

Statement that the assignor does not guaranty what the assignee may use the property for. Some states require that an assignor make an assignee aware that there may be zoning laws which affect how the assignee may use the property.

Statement of the value of the property being transferred. Some states require that the assignor state the value of the property he or she transfers to the assignee before the assignee can record an assignment. This value should be the true market value of the property. In the sample, the value is $2,600.00 because that is one-half of the balance owed on the contract. As the seller in the contract, the assignor is transferring to the assignee one-half of the balance the buyer owes the assignor.

- If the assignor is the buyer in a real estate contract, the value of the property transferred would be one-half (one-third if there are two assignees) of the difference between the value of the property (what the assignor could sell the property for) and what the assignor still owes on the property.

- If an assignor is a lender in a trust deed, promissory note, or mortgage, the value of the property transferred would be one-half the balance owing under the trust deed, or mortgage.

- If an assignor is a person buying land on a trust deed or mortgage, the value of the property transferred would be one-half the difference between the market value of the property (what the assignor could sell the property for) and what the assignor still owes on the trust deed, note, or mortgage.

- If an assignor is a landlord in a rental agreement, the value of the interest transferred would be one-half the difference between balance owing on the lease.

- If an assignor is a renter in a rental agreement, the value of the interest transferred would be one-half the difference between market value of the lease (what the renter could sell the lease for) and what the assignor still owes on the lease.

- If an assignor is a seller in a personal property sales contract, the value of the property transferred would be one-half of the balance owing to the assignor under the contract.

- If an assignor is a buyer in a personal property sales contract, the value would be one-half the the market value of the property (what the assignor could sell the property for) and what the assignor still owes on the property.

Date, signatures, attestation, and acknowledgment of the assignment. Every assignment must include the date that the assignor signs it and the proper signature of the assignor. Some states require that assignments be witnessed, sometimes called *attested*, by one or two witnesses. In those states, assignments must include the signatures of the witnesses in whose presence the assignor signed the assignment.

Almost all states require that an assignment be acknowledged before it can be recorded. An acknowledgment is the assignor's statement, to a notary public, that he or she signed the assignment and is the same person named as the assignor in the assignment.

In the sample, the word "SEAL" is next to the signature of the assignor. In the past, many states required the assignor to imprint his or her seal on the assignment. Most states have eliminated that requirement. In the states that retain the requirement, typing the word "SEAL" next to the signature of the assignor satisfies the requirement.

Delivery of the assignment. You may have heard the expression "signed, sealed, and delivered." This chapter has already discussed signing and sealing an assignment. The assignor must also deliver an assignment to the assignee. If the assignor keeps the assignment after signing it, the assignment may not be a valid transfer of the property to the assignee.

An assignor delivers an assignment by handing or mailing it to the assignee. An assignor can also deliver an assignment by other, more complicated means, such as escrow accounts. Those methods are beyond the scope of this book. The forms in this book are for use by an assignor who is directly handing or mailing an assignment to an assignee.

Recording of the assignment. Once an assignor delivers an assignment to an assignee, the assignee should record the assignment if it relates to real property. An assignee should record assignments of interests in real estate contracts, trust deeds, mortgages, leases that are recorded, and sales contracts that are recorded. An assignee records an assignment by taking the assignment to the recorder's office for the county where the property is located. The recorder's office is in the same building as the county clerk's office. There will be a recording fee of $1.00 or $2.00 per page. The recorder makes a copy of the assignment and places the copy in the records of the county clerk's office or county commissioner's office. After recording the assignment, the recorder will return the original assignment to the assignee.

A recorder will indicate on an assignment when and where the recorder recorded the assignment. In counties that organize deed books by book and page numbers, the recorder will indicate the book and page numbers where the recorder recorded the assignment. In counties that organize deed records by recorder's fee numbers, the recorder will indicate the recorder's fee number for the assignment.

By recording an assignment, an assignee gives notice to the world that he or she owns an interest in the property described in the assignment. Any person who searches the title to that property will discover the assignee's interest in the property.

See the state laws section of Chapter 10 for further guidance on recording documents.

The name and address of the person who prepared the assignment. Some states require assignments to state the name and address of the person who prepared the assignment. An assignment should state this even in states that do not require it. If there are questions about the assignment, whoever prepared the assignment may have valuable information regarding the assignment.

A statement of the amount of transfer taxes owed. Some states impose transfer taxes when one person transfers property to another person. These taxes are based upon the amount of consideration involved, or the value of the property transferred, and vary from state to state. To determine whether or not there will be a transfer tax on an assignment, call or visit the county clerk's office in your county. Show the assignment to the clerk. Ask the clerk to compute the amount of any transfer taxes you owe as a result of the assignment.

Fig. 6-2. Assignment Creating Joint Ownership with Right of Survivorship. (Sample). *Page 1 of 3*

After recording return to:
John M. Jones and
Mary L. Jones
222 Third Street
Waynecastle, Pennsylvania
County of Burr, 17294

Assignment Creating Joint Ownership With Right of Survivorship

This assignment is from John M. Jones, a married man, whose address is 222 Third Street, Waynecastle, Pennsylvania, County of Burr, 17294, hereafter called assignor, to Mary L. Jones, a married woman, whose address is 222 Third Street, Waynecastle, Pennsylvania, County of Burr, 17294, hereafter called assignee.

In consideration of the payment of Five Dollars ($5.00) to assignor by assignee, receipt of which is hereby acknowledged, and in consideration of love and affection (assignor and assignee are husband and wife), assignor hereby grants, conveys, assigns, transfers, and sets over to assignee an undivided one-half interest in assignor's right, title, and interest as a seller in that certain contract for the sale of real estate, in all payments to be received under said contract, and in the property that is sold in said contract, which contract is dated January 5, 1988, and recorded in the Office of the Clerk of the County Court of Burr County, Pennsylvania, in Miscellaneous Record Book 444, at Page 222. Assignee's undivided one-half interest shall be held with assignor's remaining undivided one-half interest in said contract, payments, and property, jointly with right of survivorship, not as tenants in common. Upon the death of either assignor or assignee, the survivor shall automatically own the entire interest in said contract, payments, and property, without probate.

The present unpaid balance on said contract is Five Thousand Two Hundred Dollars ($5,200.00), with interest paid until January 1, 1990. The unpaid balance accrues interest at the rate of ten percent (10%) per year.

The tax assessor should send all tax statements regarding this property to the assignor and assignee at the address listed above for the assignor.

This instrument will not allow use of the property described in this instrument in violation of applicable land use laws and regulations. Before signing or accepting this instrument, the person acquiring fee title to the property should check with the appropriate city or county planning department to verify approved uses.

The undersigned assignor hereby declares that the true value of the property transferred in this assignment is $2,600.00.

IN WITNESS WHEREOF, I have signed this assignment this 5th day of January, 1990, at 1201 9th Street, Waynecastle, Pennsylvania, 17294.

_____ (SEAL)

John M. Jones, Assignor

We, Allen M. Johnson and Frederick L. Roth, hereby acknowledge that we witnessed John M. Jones, who is known to us personally, sign the above assignment on January 5, 1990, in our presence, and that John M. Jones acknowledged to us and it appeared to us that he signed said assignment freely and voluntarily. We signed our names as witnesses in the presence of and at the request of said John M. Jones.

Dated this 5th day of January, 1990.

_____

Allen M. Johnson, Witness
555 6th Street
Waynecastle, Pennsylvania 17294

_____

Frederick L. Roth, Witness
777 8th Street
Waynecastle, Pennsylvania 17294

COMMONWEALTH OF
PENNSYLVANIA   )
) ss.

COUNTY OF BURR   )

Fig. 6-2 (Cont'd). *Page 3 of 3* **79**

I, Wanda C. Twobucks, a resident of and notary public in and for the commonwealth and county named above, who am duly commissioned and sworn and legally authorized to administer oaths and affirmations, hereby certify that on January 5, 1990, John M. Jones, who is known to me personally to be the signer of the above assignment, appeared before me and, after being first duly sworn by me under penalty of perjury, swore on his oath to the truth of the facts in the above assignment, and signed and acknowledged said assignment in my presence, of his own free will, and for the purposes explained in said assignment.

Subscribed and sworn to before me this 5th day of January, 1990.

_____

Wanda C. Twobucks
Notary Public
(SEAL)   My Commission Expires: 2/09/91

This instrument was prepared by Max M. Mumfee, attorney at law, whose address is 694 W. 5th Street, Waynecastle, Pennsylvania, 17294.

COMMONWEALTH OF
PENNSYLVANIA   )
)
COUNTY OF BURR   ) ss.
)
CITY OF WAYNECASTLE   )

I certify that the above assignment was recorded in my office on the 5th day of January, 1990, at 2:13 o'clock, P.M., and is duly recorded in Book 267, at Page 422, of the Miscellaneous Records of the above state, county, and city.

_____

Recorder for Burr County, Pennsylvania

By: _____
Deputy

Transfer Fee: $0.00

Instructions for Blank Forms

This chapter includes two blank forms. Figure 6-3 is a joint property affidavit creating joint ownership with right of survivorship. Figure 6-4 is an assignment creating joint ownership with right of survivorship.

Each form has blank spaces with a number under each blank. Before filling in any of the blanks, make several photocopies of the form. Use one copy as a work copy, one as an original, and the rest for future work copies or originals. Fill out a work copy first and be sure it is correct, then type or print in the blanks on your original form.

Blank Affidavit of Joint Ownership   The following numbered instructions match the numbers under the blanks in FIG. 6-3:

(1) Enter the name of the state where the affiants sign the affidavit.

(2) Enter the name of the county where the affiants sign the affidavit.

(3) Enter the names and addresses of all the affiants.

(4) Enter a description of the property that the affiants wish to own jointly with right of survivorship. If the affiants want to own all their present and future property jointly with right of survivorship, use the language from the sample affidavit in this chapter. If the signers only want to own specific property jointly with right of survivorship, list and accurately describe the property. If Blank 4 does not have enough room for your list, put "See Exhibit A, attached here to and incorporated herein by this reference" in Blank 4. Prepare a list of the property on a separate sheet of paper, mark it "Exhibit A", and staple it to the affidavit.

(5) Enter the address where the affiants sign the affidavit.

(6) Enter the date that the affiants sign the affidavit.

(7) The affiants should sign their full names above these lines in the presence of a notary public. Under their signatures, print or type their names. After they sign the affidavit, the notary public should ask the affiants to raise their right hands and solemnly swear upon their oaths and under penalty of perjury that they are the people referred to in the affidavit, that the facts in the affidavit are true, that they signed the affidavit of their own free will and for the purposes explained in the affidavit, and that they acknowledge signing their names to the affidavit.

The following items should be completed by a notary public:

(8) Enter the name of the notary public.

(9) Enter the date that the affiants sign the affidavit.

(10) Enter the names of the affiants.

(11,12,13) Enter the day, month, and year that the affiants sign the affidavit.

(14) The notary public should sign his or her full name here. Under the notary public's signature, print or type the name of the notary public.

(15) The notary public should put the date that his or her commission expires here.

(16) The notary public should affix his or her seal to the affidavit.

After the affiants and notary public sign the affidavit, the affiants should keep the original affidavit with their other important papers. The affiants may want to sign several original affidavits if they need to give original affidavits to certain persons or institutions.

Blank Assignment Creating Joint Ownership with Right of Survivorship (FIG. 6-4)   The following numbered instructions match the numbers under the blanks in FIG. 6-4.

(1) Enter the name(s) and address where the recorder should send the assignment after recording.

(2) Enter the full name(s) of the assignor(s). State the marital status of the assignor(s).

(3) Enter the full address(es) of the assignor(s).

(4) Enter the full name(s) of the assignee(s). State the marital status of the assignee(s).

(5) Enter the full address(es) of the assignee(s).

(6) Enter a description of the consideration that the assignee is giving to the assignor for the property. If the consideration is money, enter the amount of money in words and in numbers. If the consideration is love and affection, indicate that. If the consideration is something other than money or love and affection, describe the consideration and state the value of the consideration in terms of money. If the consideration is love and affection, state in parentheses whether or not the assignor and assignee are blood relatives, and if so, their relationship.

(7) If there is only one assignee, enter "assignee an undivided one-half interest". If there are two assignees, enter "each assignee an undivided one third interest". If there are three assignees, enter "each assignee an undivided one-fourth interest", etc.

(8) Enter a description of the property that the assignor is assigning to the assignee. Review the explanation of the sample assignment to be sure that you include all the necessary information regarding the property.

(9) If the property transferred has an unpaid balance, enter the amount of the unpaid balance in words, and then in numbers within the parentheses. If the property does not have an unpaid balance, put "not applicable" in this blank. Interests in promissory notes, real estate contracts, trust deeds, mortgages, personal property sales contracts, and leases will have unpaid balances owing.

(10) If the property transferred has an unpaid balance with interest paid to a certain date, enter the date to which the interest is paid. If this is not applicable, put "not applicable" in the blank. Interests in promissory notes, real estate contracts, trust deeds, mortgages, and personal property sales contracts will usually have dates to which interest is paid.

(11) If the property transferred has interest accruing on it at a certain rate per year, enter the annual interest rate. If this is not applicable, put "not applicable" or "N/A" in the blank. Interests in promissory notes, real estate contracts, trust deeds, mortgages, and personal property sales contracts will usually have interest rates.

(12) Enter the value of the property the assignor is transferring to the assignee. See the explanation earlier in this chapter to determine how to value the property.

(13,14,15) Enter the day, month, and year that the assignor(s) sign the assignment.

(16) Enter the address where the assignor(s) sign the assignment.

(17) The assignor(s) should sign their full names in the presence of two witnesses and a notary public. Under the signatures, print or type the name(s) of the assignor(s).

(18,19,20) Enter the day, month, and year that the spouse(s) of the assignor(s) signed the assignment. If the assignor(s) has no spouse(s), put "not applicable" or "N/A" in the blanks.

(21) The spouse(s) of the assignor(s) should sign here. Under each signature, print or type the name(s) of the spouse(s) who signed the assignment. If the assignor(s) has no spouse(s), put "not applicable" in these blanks.

(22) Enter the names of two witnesses to the assignment.

(23) Enter the name(s) of the assignor(s).

(24) Enter the date that the assignor(s) signed the assignment.

(25) Enter the name(s) of the assignor(s).

(26,27,28) Enter the day, month, and year that the assignor(s) signed the assignment.

(29) The witnesses should sign their full names on the top lines. Under the signatures, print or type their names. Put their addresses on the lines below.

The following items should be completed by a notary public:

(30) Enter the name of the state where the assignor(s) signed the assignment.

(31) Enter the name of the county where the assignor(s) signed the assignment.

(32) Enter the name of the notary public who is notarizing the assignment.

(33) Enter the date that the assignor(s) signed the assignment.

(34) Enter the name(s) of the assignor(s) and of any spouse(s) of the assignor(s) who signed the assignment.

(35,36,37) Enter the day, month, and year that the notary public is notarizing the assignment.

(38) The notary public should ask the assignor(s) and any spouse(s) of the assignor(s) who signed the assignment to raise their right hands and swear on their oaths to the truth of the facts in the assignment, and to the fact that they signed and acknowledged the assignment of their own free will and for the purposes explained in the assignment. The notary public should sign on this line. Under the signature, print or type the name of the notary public.

(39) The notary public should indicate the date his or her commission expires.

(40) The notary public should affix his or her seal to the assignment.

(41) Enter the name of the person who prepared the assignment.

(42) Enter the address of the person who prepared the assignment.

(The recorder will fill out the information in the remaining blanks of the form.)

After the assignment is signed, witnessed, and notarized, the assignor must deliver the assignment to the assignee by handing or mailing the assignment to the assignee. The assignee should record the assignment as explained earlier in this chapter.

Fig. 6-3. Affidavit of Joint Ownership (Blank). *Page 1 of 2* **83**

Affidavit of Joint Ownership

STATE OF _____)

(1)

) ss.

COUNTY OF _____)

(2)

We, the undersigned, whose names and addresses are _____

(3)

_____

_____

_____

_____,

being first duly sworn, upon our oaths do solemnly swear under penalty of perjury that:

1. We are making this affidavit for the purpose of creating joint ownership with right of survivorship of untitled personal property owned by us to avoid probate of that property in the event of the death of one of us.

2. We hereby declare that we own the following property:

_____

(4)

_____

_____

_____,

each as to an equal undivided interest, jointly with right of survivorship, not as tenants in common. Upon the death of any one of us, the survivor or survivors shall own the property automatically, without necessity of probate of said property.

Signed at _____

(5)

_____,

on _____ .

(6)

_____   _____

(7)   (7)

_____   _____

(7)   (7)

I, _____ ,
                                    (8)

a resident of and notary public in and for the state and county named above, who am
duly commissioned and sworn and legally authorized to administer oaths and affirm-

ations, hereby certify that on _____ ,
                                                          (9)

_____
                                    (10)

_____ ,

who are known to me personally to be the affiants in the above affidavit, appeared before
me and, after being first duly sworn by me under penalty of perjury, swore on their oaths
to the truth of the facts in the above affidavit, and signed and acknowledged said affidavit
in my presence, of their own free will, and for the purposes explained in said affidavit.

Subscribed and sworn to before me this _____ day of _____ ,
                                                           (11)   (12)

_____ .
  (13)

_____
                                                                                    (14)

Notary Public
(SEAL)   My Commission Expires: _____
 (16)   (15)

Assignment Creating Joint Ownership With Right of Survivorship

This assignment is from _____
(2)

_____ ,

whose address(es) is/are _____
(3)

_____

_____

_____ ,

hereafter called assignor, to _____
(4)

_____

_____ ,

whose address(es) is/are _____
(5)

_____

_____

hereafter called assignee. Even if there is more than one assignor or assignee, the parties will be referred to in the singular for the rest of this assignment.

In consideration of the payment of Five Dollars ($5.00) to assignor by assignee, receipt of which is hereby acknowledged, and in consideration of assignee giving

assignor _____
(6)

_____

_____

_____

_____

_____ , assignor hereby grants, conveys, assigns, transfers, and sets

over to _____
(7)

_____ in that certain property described as

_____
(8)

_____

_____

_____

_____

_____

_____.

Assignee's undivided interest shall be held

_____

_____

_____

_____

If said property has an unpaid balance owing on it, the present unpaid balance

on said property is _____
(9)

_____ ($),

with interest paid until _____.
(10)

The unpaid balance accrues interest at the rate of _____ per year.
(11)

If this assignment involves any interest in real property, the tax assessor should send tax statements for said real property to the assignor and assignee at the address listed above for the assignor.

This instrument will not allow use of the property described in this instrument in violation of applicable land use laws and regulations. Before signing or accepting this instrument, the person acquiring fee title to the property should check with the appropriate city or county planning department to verify approved uses.

The undersigned assignor hereby declares that the true value of the property

transferred in this assignment is _____
(12)

_____.

IN WITNESS WHEREOF, I/we have signed this assignment on this _____
(13)

day of _____, _____, at _____
(14)   (15)   (16)

_____.

Assignor _____ (SEAL)
(17)

Assignor _____ (SEAL)
(17)

Assignor _____ (SEAL)
(17)

Fig. 6-4. (Cont'd). *Page 3 of 5* **87**

The undersigned spouse of the assignor, or spouses of the assignors if there is more than one assignor, for the consideration stated in the assignment above, hereby give up his/her/their right, title, interest, separate estate, dower and right of dower, or curtesy, as the case may be, and hereby give up any homestead, community property, or other rights he/she/they may have in the above property.

Dated this _____ day of _____, _____.
       (18)   (19)   (20)

_____
         Spouse   (21)

_____
         Spouse   (21)

_____
         Spouse   (21)

We, _____
             (22)

_____,

hereby acknowledge that we witnessed _____
            (23)

_____

_____,

who is/are known to us personally, sign the above assignment on _____
            (24)

in our presence and that _____
            (25)

_____

acknowledged to us and it appeared to us that he/she/they signed said assignment freely and voluntarily. We signed our names as witnesses in the presence of and at the request of said assignor(s).

Dated this _____ day of _____, _____.
(26)   (27)   (28)

_____
                                                      (29)
Witness

_____

_____

_____

_____
                                                      (29)
Witness

_____

_____

_____

STATE OF _____)
                              (30)
) ss.

COUNTY OF _____)
                              (31)

I, _____,
                                              (32)
a resident of and notary public in and for the state and county named above, who am duly commissioned and sworn and legally authorized to administer oaths and affirmations, hereby certify that on _____,
                                                                   (33)

_____,
                           (34)

who is/are known to me personally to be the signer(s) of the above assignment, appeared before me and, after being first duly sworn by me under penalty of perjury, swore on his/her/their oaths to the truth of the facts in the above assignment, and signed and

Fig. 6-4. (Cont'd). *Page 4 of 5* **89**

acknowledged said assignment in my presence, of his/her/their own free will and for the purposes explained in said assignment.

Subscribed and sworn to before me this _____ day of _____,
(35)   (36)

_____ .
(37)

_____
(38)

Notary Public

(SEAL)   My Commission Expires: _____
(40)   (39)

This instrument was prepared by _____
(41)

_____, whose address is

_____
(42)

_____ .

STATE OF _____)

) ss.

COUNTY OF _____)

I certify that the above assignment was recorded in my office on the following date:

_____ at _____

_____ .M., and is duly recorded in Book _____ at Page _____,

(or as recorder's fee number _____), of the _____

records of the above state and county.

_____

Recorder

By: _____

Deputy

Transfer Fee: $_____

Chapter 7

Living Will

A living will is a document that expresses one's desire to be allowed to die a natural death.

Medical technology now enables doctors and hospitals to keep people alive by artificial means. Some people do not want to be kept alive by these artificial means. A living will directs your doctor, family, and others not to keep you alive by artificial means.

The person who makes a living will is known as a *declarant*.

State Laws on Living Wills (FIG. 7-1)

Thirty-eight states and the District of Columbia have passed *natural death acts*, which discuss living wills. Natural death acts cover subjects such as how often you have to renew a living will, how binding a living will is on a doctor, whether a living will is valid during pregnancy, whether a minor can sign a living will, how to revoke a living will, and other matters.

In states that do not have natural death acts, a living will is not binding on anyone. In most states with natural death acts, a living will signed before a diagnosis of terminal illness is not binding on a doctor or family member, but a living will signed after a diagnosis of terminal illness is binding on them. For that reason, if you sign a living will before a diagnosis of terminal illness, and then your doctor diagnoses you as terminally ill, you should sign another living will.

Even if a living will is not binding, it is still useful. If you sign a living will before a diagnosis of terminal illness and then become terminally ill and sign another living will, the first living will shows that you signed the second living will voluntarily. It shows that you did not sign the second living will because you were depressed by the diagnosis of terminal illness.

Another reason for signing a living will, even if it is not binding, is that it tells your family and doctors how you feel about artificial means of keeping you alive. A doctor or family member may still honor the living will, even though not legally bound to do so.

Most natural death acts include living will forms that are approved by the state legislature. Natural death acts refer to these forms in three different ways. Some states say a living will *may* be in the form provided by the legislature. Some states say a living will *must* or *shall* be substantially in the form provided by the legislature. Still others say that a living will shall be substantially in the form provided by the legislature, but can include additional provisions that are not inconsistent with the provisions in the form provided by the legislature.

Figure 7-1 lists the states which have natural death acts, and gives the following information:

- A reference to the specific state laws that contain the natural death act
- Whether or not the state's natural death act provides a living will form
- Whether the state's law says that a living will may or must be in the form provided by the legislature
- How long a living will remains valid
- How many witnesses are required for a living will
- How old the declarant and witnesses have to be to sign a living will

Figure 7-1 also gives detailed notes about the laws of those states that have requirements different from most other states.

The references to state laws in FIG. 7-1 allow you to find and read your state's natural death act. Your county courthouse will have a set of your state's laws. You can find your state's natural death act in the volume and section number referred to in FIG. 7-1.

Anyone preparing a living will would benefit from reading the natural death act in his or her state. People living in a state in which the natural death act says a living will must or shall be substantially in the form provided by the legislature should definitely read the state's natural death act.

Figure 7-1 is based on 1987 and 1988 laws. The state legislatures of the 50 states meet at different times. Some legislatures only meet once every two years. When a state legislature passes a law, the legislature or a publishing company publishes that law at a later time. Several months can pass before the legislature or publisher sends that law to the libraries around the country. As you read these words, months or years will have also passed from the time this book was edited, printed, and distributed. For these reasons, this book, like all legal books, cannot be absolutely current.

Figure 7-1 indicates whether the information for a particular state is based on the 1987 or 1988 laws of that state. If you want to confirm whether or not your state has changed its laws, go to a law library in your state and read the most current version of the law referred to in FIG. 7-1. If the law has changed, the new law will usually have the same number as the old law. Check what are known as the "pocket parts" of your state's laws. Pocket parts are supplements which contain the latest revisions of a state's laws.

You can obtain more up-to-date information regarding living wills and state laws on living wills by writing to: Concern For Dying, 250 West 57th Street, New York, New York, 10019. Concern For Dying is a non-profit organization that provides information regarding living wills. Upon request, Concert For Dying will send you a living will form for use in your state. Concern For Dying will not charge for the form, but it will accept donations to enable it to continue to provide its services.

Sample Living Will (FIG. 7-2)

Figure 7-2 is a sample living will. The following explanation is numbered to match the numbered paragraphs of the sample.

Paragraph 1   A living will should explain to whom the declarant is directing the living will. The sample uses broad language to make it clear that the living will is directed to anyone who is or might be responsible for decisions about the declarant's care.

Paragraph 2   A living will should describe the declarant's full name, current address, and social security number. It should explain that the purpose of the living will is to give instructions for the care of declarant if the declarant is not able to take part in decisions about his or her care. If the declarant is able to take part in those decisions, the declarant can make those decisions without the living will.

	Living Will Valid Until Revoked	Number of Witnesses Required	Minimum Age of Witnesses	Minimum Age of Declarant	Form Included in Act	Compliance Required with Form in Act	Statutory Reference	Year of Update
Alabama*	Y	2	19	18	Y	S	22-8A-1 through -10	1987
Alaska	Y	2	18	18	Y	M	18-12-.010 through .100	1987
Arizona	Y	2	18	18	Y	S[1]	36-3201 through -3210	1988
Arkansas	Y	2	18	18	Y	M	20-17-201 through -218	1987
California*	Y or 5 yrs.[2][3]	2	18	18	Y	F	7185 through 7195	1988
Colorado	Y	2	18	18	Y	M	15-18-101 through -113	1987
Connecticut*	Y	2	18	18	Y	F	19a-570 through -575	1987
Delaware*	Y	2[4]	18	18	Y	F	16-2501 through -2509	1987
District of Columbia	Y	2	18	18	Y	F[1]	6-2421 through -2430	1988
Florida	Y	2	18	18	Y	M	765.01 through .15	1988
Georgia*	Y	2[5]	18	18	Y	S	31-32-1 through -12	1988
Hawaii	Y	2	18	18	Y	M	327D-1 through -7	1987
Idaho*	Y	2	18	18	Y	F[6]	39-4501 through -4508	1988
Illinois	Y	2	18	18	Y	M	110½-701 through -710	1988
Indiana	Y	2	18	18	Y	F[1]	16-8-11-1 through -22	1988
Iowa	Y	2	18	18	Y	M	144A.1 through .11	1988
Kansas	Y	2	18	18	Y	F[1]	65-28,101 through -28,109	1987
Louisiana	Y	2	18	18	Y	M	40:1299.58.1 through .10	1988
Maine	Y	2	18	18	Y	M	22-2921 through -2931	1987
Maryland	Y	2	18	18[7]	Y	F[1]	5-601 through -614	1987
Mississippi*	Y	2	18	18	Y	F[8]	41-41-101 through -121	1987
Missouri	Y	2	18	18	Y	M	459.010 through .055	1988
Montana	Y	2	18	18	Y	M	50 9-101 through -104, -111, -202 through -206	1987
Nevada*	Y	2	18	18	Y	F[9]	449.540 through .690	1987
New Hampshire	Y	2	18	18	Y	M	137-H:1 through :16	1988
New Mexico	Y	2	21	21	N[9]	—	24-7-1 through -11	1987
North Carolina*	Y	2	18	18	Y	F[11]	90-320 through -322	1987
Oklahoma*	Y	2	21	21	Y	F	63-3101 through -3111	1988
Oregon*	Y	2	18	18	Y	F[12]	97.050 through .090	1987
South Carolina*	Y	3	18	18	Y	F[13]	44-77-10 through -160	1987
Tennessee	Y	2	18	18	Y	F[1]	32-11-101 through -110	1987
Texas	Y	2	18	18	Y	M	Health and Safety Code, Art. 4590h	1988
Utah*	Y	2	18	18	Y	F	75-2-1101 through -1118	1988
Vermont	Y	2	21	21	Y	M	18-5251 through -5262, 13-1801	1988
Virginia	Y	2	18	18	Y	M	54-325.8:1 through :13	1988
Washington	Y	2	18	18	Y	F[1]	70.122.010 through .905	1988
West Virginia	Y	2	18	18	Y	F[1]	16-30-1 through -10	1988
Wisconsin*	Y	2	18	18	Y	F[14]	154.01 through .15	1988
Wyoming	Y	2	18	18	Y	M	35-22-101 through -109	1987

The following states do not have natural death acts (as of the year indicated): Kentucky (1987), Massachusetts (1987), Michigan (1988), Minnesota (1988), Nebraska (1987), New Jersey (1988)[10], New York (1988), North Dakota (1987), Ohio (1988), Pennsylvania (1988), Rhode Island (1987), South Dakota (1988).

Key:

F— Living will shall (or must) be in the form provided by the state.

M— Living will may be in the form provided by the state.

N— No.

S— Living will shall substantially comply with the form provided by the state.

Y— Yes.

Notes:

[1] But may include additional provisions not inconsistent with the form provided.

[2] Whichever occurs first.

[3] If declarant is a patient in a skilled nursing home, one of the two witnesses must be a patient advocate or ombudsman designated by the State Department of Aging.

[4] Additional provisions: Each witness shall state in writing that the witness is not prohibited under Subsection (b) of Section 2503 from being a witness under this chapter. If the declarant is a resident of a rest home or other similar facility, one witness must be a person designated by the Division of Aging or the Public Guardian.

[5] Additional requirements: If a living will is signed in a hospital or skilled nursing facility, a third witness is required, who shall be the medical director of the skilled nursing facility or the chief of the hospital medical staff.

[6] Additional requirements: Living wills shall be in the form of durable powers of attorney. The declarant must describe the condition that the declarant has been diagnosed as having. The living will must describe itself as a durable power of attorney.

[7] Additional requirements: Declarant in a living will must have the same qualifications as a person making a will. Those qualifications are that the declarant be of sound mind, lawful age (18), and not be acting under duress or undue influence.

[8] Additional requirements: Three physicians must certify the terminal condition of the declarant, one of whom must be the declarant's attending physician. All living wills shall be filed with the Bureau of Vital Statistics of the State Board of Health. Any revocation of a living will must also be filed with the Bureau of Vital Statistics of the State Board of Health.

[9] Additional requirements: Living wills must be signed like wills. The form at the end of this chapter meets the requirements for signing a will in this state.

[10] The New Jersey legislature created a commission to study this issue and may pass a natural death act in the near future.

[11] Additional requirements: Living wills must be "proved" as described in the natural death act. Notary public must certify that he or she is satisfied as to the genuineness and due execution of the declaration.

[12] Additional requirements: Witnesses must state that they understand that if they have not witnessed the living will in good faith, they may be responsible for any damages that arise out of giving the living will its intended effect. If the declarant is a patient in a long-term care facility, one of the witnesses must be an individual designated by the Department of Human Resources.

[13] Additional requirements: If the declarant is a patient in a hospital or skilled or intermediate care facility, one of the three witnesses must be an ombudsman designated by the State Ombudsman Office of the Governor. No more than one of the witnesses can be an employee of a health care facility. State law requires certain statements to be in capital letters in the living will.

[14] Additional requirements: State law requires the Department of Health and Social Services to prepare a form for living wills.

*Author strongly recommends reading the state natural death act and using the form provided by the state.

Paragraph 3   This paragraph explains when the declarant intends the living will to be used. If death is both inevitable and imminent without artificial or extreme medical procedures, the declarant does not want to be kept alive by those means.

The purpose of a living will is to avoid artificial medical procedures that only prolong a death that is inevitable and imminent. All of our deaths are inevitable, but not all of our deaths are imminent. That is, not all deaths are sure to occur within a very short period of time. A living will says, "If I am sure to die very soon, let me die."

Different states have different requirements regarding certifications by physicians that a declarant has a terminal condition. Some states require that one of the physicians be the declarant's attending physician. Most states define an attending physician as the doctor who is charged with the primary responsibility for the declarant's care and treatment. Mississippi requires a certification by the declarant's attending physician and two other physicians. Many states require that the physicians must have physically examined the declarant. (Figure 7-1 includes state requirements regarding certifications by physicians.)

The sample explains that the declarant understands that life-sustaining procedures do not include medication and sustenance for comfort and care. This informs the declarant's doctor and family that the declarant wants to be given food and water, and medication to alleviate pain. The sample also explains that the declarant wants medication to alleviate suffering, even if the medication hastens the moment of death. This sentence does not have to be included in a living will. If a declarant does not want his or her doctors to administer medication that would ease pain but might hasten death, the declarant should explain that in the living will.

Paragraph 4   This paragraph explains that the declarant expects her family, physician, attorney, and others to follow the instructions in the living will. It states that the declarant is exercising her legal right to make decisions about her medical care, and that the declarant accepts the responsibility for those decisions. By accepting the responsibility for her own medical care, the declarant relieves family members and others of the guilt they might feel if they were to make the decision to withdraw life-support systems. Also, the declarant's accepting legal responsibility helps protect medical personnel from liability for following the instructions in the living will.

Paragraph 5   This paragraph only makes sense where the declarant is a woman. If the declarant is a woman who is pregnant when (or becomes pregnant after) signing the living will, this paragraph explains that the declarant does not want the living will honored during pregnancy. Many states require this clause in a living will.

Paragraph 6   This paragraph only applies where at least two physicians have reached a diagnosis that the declarant has a terminal condition. If the declarant has been so diagnosed, the living will should give the names, addresses, and telephone numbers of the doctors who made the diagnosis, and the date(s) when the doctors informed the declarant of the diagnosis.

Paragraph 7   This paragraph absolves anyone who follows the instructions in the living will from any legal liability for doing so. This paragraph makes it easier for physicians, hospitals, or others to honor a living will.

Paragraph 8   This paragraph states that the declarant knows what he or she is doing, and makes the living will because he or she wants to, not because he or she is being forced to do so. A living will is not valid if the declarant does not understand the meaning of the living will or if anyone forces him or her to sign it. Including this paragraph does not mean that the living will is automatically valid, but it is some evidence that the declarant understood the living will and signed it voluntarily.

This paragraph also states that the declarant is at least 18 years of age. Most states require that in order to make a living will, a declarant must be at least 18 years old. See FIG. 7-1 to find out the age requirement in your state.

Paragraph 9   The sample provides that the living will remains effective until the declarant revokes it. After signing a living will, a declarant may decide that he or she does not want to have a living will, or may want to change the original living will. If so, the declarant should revoke the original living will. This chapter includes a sample and form for revoking a living will. California law states that a living will is only valid for five years, so in that state you must sign a new living will every five years. In all other states, a living will is valid until you revoke it.

This paragraph explains that the living will is governed by the laws of the State of Iowa. Because states have different laws regarding living wills, every living will should indicate which state law governs it. That state should be the state where the declarant resides and signs the living will, which should be the same state.

Paragraph 10   All living wills should indicate when and where they are signed.

Signature of Declarant   A declarant should sign a living will in front of at least two witnesses and a notary public. Figure 7-1 describes how many witnesses each state requires.

Statement of Witnesses   There are strict requirements as to who can witness a living will. A witness must be at least 18 years old (19 or 21 in some states—see FIG. 7-1) and know the declarant personally. A witness cannot be someone who is related to the declarant by blood or marriage, who has any claim on the estate of the declarant, who is entitled to any portion of the declarant's estate by will or otherwise, who is a physician attending the declarant, who is a person involved with the declarant's medical care, who is an employee of the declarant's attending physician, who is an employee of a health care facility in which the declarant is a patient, who is a patient in a health care facility in which the declarant is a patient, or who signed the declarant's signature to the living will for or at the direction of the declarant.

The above requirements rule out many potential witnesses. The best witness would be a friend of the declarant who is not named in the declarant's will, who does not have any claims against the declarant (is not owed money or property by the declarant), who does not live in the same health care facility as the declarant, and who is not a relative of the declarant. See FIG. 7-1 for specific requirements for witnesses in certain states.

The witnesses should sign their full names, list their addresses and social security numbers, and indicate the date they witnessed the living will.

Some states require that declarants acknowledge living wills in the presence of a notary public. Acknowledging a living will ensures that the person who signs the living will is the same person that the living will names as the declarant. Some states also require that a living will be signed like a regular will. The blank living will at the end of this chapter meets the requirements for signing a will in those states.

After the living will is signed, the declarant should keep the original, make 5–10 copies of the original, and have the notary public certify that the copies are true copies. The declarant should give a certified copy to his or her physician and ask the physician to put it in the declarant's medical file. The declarant should also give a certified copy of the living will to his or her attorney and to any family member who may need to use the living will. The declarant should discuss the living will with each of the people who receive a certified copy.

The declarant should not keep the original living will in a safe deposit box. It may be difficult to get into that box if the declarant becomes incapacitated. The declarant should keep the living will in a safe place and tell his or her family members where the original is. The declarant should keep a record of how many copies there are and where those copies are. If the declarant revokes the living will, he or she will want to have those copies returned.

Fig. 7-2. Living Will (Sample). *Page 1 of 3* **97**

Living Will

1. TO: My family, my physician, my attorney, to any medical facility in whose care I happen to be, and to any individual who may become responsible for my health, welfare, or affairs.

2. If the time comes when I, Mary Ellen Jones, presently residing at 222 Endive Street, Dirtrens, Iowa, 50311, County of Hoover, social security number 123-45-6789, can no longer take part in decisions for my own future, this statement, made willfully and while I am of sound mind and emotionally and mentally competent to make this living will, shall stand as my instructions regarding my physical care.

3. If at any time I should have an incurable injury, disease, or illness that at least two physicians who have examined me personally, one of whom is my attending physician, certify to be a terminal condition as defined in my state's laws, and those physicians also certify that the use of life-sustaining, artificial, or extreme medical or surgical procedures or means would only artificially prolong the moment of my death, and certify that my death is imminent if such artificial or extreme procedures are not used, I direct that such procedures be withheld or withdrawn, and that I be permitted to die naturally. I understand that life-sustaining procedures do not include administration of medicine and sustenance for comfort and care. I direct that medication be mercifully administered to me to alleviate suffering, even though this may hasten the moment of my death.

4. I intend that my family, physicians, attorney, and others shall honor this living will as the final expression of my legal right to refuse medical or surgical treatment. I accept the consequences of such a refusal.

5. If I have been diagnosed as pregnant, this living will is not intended to be honored during the course of my pregnancy.

6. I have been diagnosed as having a terminal condition caused by disease, illness, or injury by Dr. Richard E. Wilson and Dr. Robert L. Smith, whose business addresses are, respectively, 444 Endive Street, Dirtrens, Iowa, 50311, County of Hoover, and 777 Belgian Rd., Spooner, Iowa, 51103, County of Hoover, and whose telephone numbers are, respectively, (712) 555-3333 and (712) 555-9999, who informed me of such condition, respectively, on January 13, 1989, and February 13, 1989.

7. I, my estate, and my legal successors will hold harmless from any liability any person or institution that suffers any loss as a result of following the instructions in this living will.

8. I understand what this living will means. I am making this living will freely and voluntarily because it is what I want to do, not because of physical or mental duress. I am making this living will when I am at least 18 years of age.

9. This living will shall be effective unless and until I revoke it, and shall be governed by the laws of the State of Iowa. I understand that I can revoke this living will at any time, and I reserve the right to give current medical directions to my physician or other medical people as long as I am able, even if those directions conflict with this living will.

10. IN WITNESS WHEREOF, I have signed this living will this 10th day of March, 1989, at 222 Endive Street, Dirtrens, Iowa, 50311, County of Hoover.

_____

Mary Ellen Jones

Statement of Witnesses

We hereby declare that on March 10, 1989, we witnessed Mary Ellen Jones, as declarant, sign the above living will in our presence, that we know the declarant personally and believe she is of sound mind and that she signed said living will freely and voluntarily, that we witnessed said living will at her request and signed this statement at her request, that as far as we know we are not prohibited from being witnesses to this living will under the laws of the State of Iowa, that we are at least 18 years of age, that we did not sign declarant's signature to the above living will for or at the direction of declarant, that we are not related to declarant by blood or marriage, that we do not have any claim on the estate of declarant and are not entitled to any portion of her estate by will or otherwise, and that neither or us is a physician attending the declarant, nor a person involved with her medical care, nor an employee of her attending physician, nor an employee of a health care facility in which she is a patient, nor a patient in a health care facility in which she
is a patient.

Dated: March 10, 1989.

_____

Frank L. Johnson, Witness
444 Escarole Street
Dirtrens, Iowa, 50311
County of Hoover
SS# 987-65-4321

_____

Mary M. Johnson, Witness
444 Escarole Street
Dirtrens, Iowa, 50311
County of Hoover
SS# 876-54-3210

Fig. 7-2. (Cont'd). *Page 3 of 3* **99**

STATE OF IOWA   )
) ss.
COUNTY OF HOOVER)

I, Anita C. Myafee, a resident of and a notary public in and for the state and county named above, who am duly commissioned and sworn and legally authorized to administer oaths and affirmations, hereby certify that on March 10, 1989, Mary Ellen Jones, who is known to me personally to be the declarant in the above living will, appeared before me, acknowledged signing the above living will, and, after being first duly sworn by me under penalty of perjury, swore on her oath to the truth of the facts in the above living will, declared said document to be her living will, and declared that she signed it freely and voluntarily. I further certify that she signed said living will in my presence, of her own free will, and for the purposes explained in said living will. I further certify that the above witnesses, who are known to me personally to be the witnesses in the above living will, appeared before me, acknowledged signing the above living will as witnesses, and, after being first duly sworn by me under penalty of perjury, swore on their oaths that at the request of and in the presence of the above declarant and in the presence of each other, they witnessed declarant sign the above living will, signed their names as witnesses to said living will, declarant declared the above document to be her living will, and said witnesses further swore that the facts they attested to in the above statement of witnesses are true.

Subscribed and sworn to before me this 10th day of March, 1989.

_____

Notary Public

(SEAL)   My Commission Expires: 2/09/91

Sample Revocation of a Living Will (FIG. 7-3)

After signing a living will, a declarant may change his or her mind about the living will and want to revoke the living will.

Figure 7-3 is a sample revocation of a living will. It includes the following that all revocations of living wills should include:

- The full name of the declarant, the declarant's address at the time of signing the original living will, and the date the declarant signed the original living will.

- The names of the people or institutions to whom the declarant directed the original living will.

- A copy of the original living will, attached to the revocation as an exhibit and incorporated into the revocation.

- A description of where the declarant kept the original living will and a list of all the people or institutions who received copies of the living will.

- A statement by the declarant revoking the original living will and making the original living will null and void from a certain date on.

- The current address and social security number of the declarant.

- The date when, and the place where, the declarant signed the revocation.

- The signature of the declarant.

- Attestations by at least two witnesses, similar to the attestations on the original living will. The witnesses do not have to be the same witnesses as in the original living will, although they can be.

- A notarization, similar to the notarization in the original living will.

After the declarant signs the revocation, the declarant should obtain all copies of the original living will from the people who received copies. The declarant should destroy the original and the copies of the living will, except for the copy that he or she attaches to the revocation. The declarant should ask his or her physician and attorney to keep a copy of the revocation in the declarant's medical and legal files.

Fig. 7-3. Revocation of Living Will (Sample). *Page 1 of 2* **101**

Revocation of Living Will

On March 10, 1989, I, Mary Ellen Jones, whose address at the time was 222 Endive Street, Dirtrens, Iowa, 50311, signed a living will directed to my family, my physician, my attorney, to any medical facility in whose care I happened to be, and to any individual who may have become responsible for my health, welfare, or affairs. A copy of that living will is attached hereto, marked Exhibit "A", and incorporated into this revocation by this reference.

After signing the attached living will, I kept the original in my possession and gave certified copies to my physicians, Dr. Richard E. Wilson and Dr. Robert L. Smith, to my attorney, Jeffrey L. Barnes, to my husband, John M. Jones, to my daughter, Susan M. Laird, and to my brother, Joseph P. Smith.

After careful thought and being of sound mind, I hereby voluntarily and freely revoke the above-described living will and declare it to be null and void from this date on.

I am now living at 222 Endive Street, Dirtrens, Iowa, 50311. My social security number is 123-45-6789.

IN WITNESS WHEREOF, I have signed this revocation of a living will on May 4, 1990, at 222 Endive Street, Dirtrens, Iowa, 50311.

_____

Mary Ellen Jones

Statement of Witnesses

We hereby declare that on May 4, 1990, we witnessed Mary Ellen Jones, as declarant, sign the above revocation of a living will in our presence, that we know the declarant personally and believe she is of sound mind and that she signed said revocation freely and voluntarily, that we witnessed said revocation at her request and signed this statement at her request, that as far as we know we are not prohibited from being witnesses to this revocation under the laws of the State of Iowa, that we are at least 18 years of age, that we did not sign declarant's signature to the above revocation for or at the direction of declarant, that we are not related to declarant by blood or marriage, that we do not have any claim on the estate of declarant and are not entitled to any portion of her estate by will or otherwise, and that neither of us is a physician attending the declarant, nor a person involved with her medical care, nor an employee of her attending physician, nor an employee of a health care facility in which she is a patient, nor a patient in a health care facility in which she is a patient.

Dated: May 4, 1990.

Frank L. Johnson, Witness

444 Escarole Street

Dirtrens, Iowa, 50311

County of Hoover

SS# 987-65-4321

Mary M. Johnson, Witness

444 Escarole Street

Dirtrens, Iowa, 50311

County of Hoover

SS# 876-54-3210

STATE OF IOWA   )

) ss.

COUNTY OF HOOVER)

I, Anita C. Myafee, a resident of and a notary public in and for the state and county named above, who am duly commissioned and sworn and legally authorized to administer oaths and affirmations, hereby certify that on May 4, 1990, Mary Ellen Jones, who is known to me personally to be the declarant in the above revocation of a living will, appeared before me, acknowledged signing the above revocation, and, after being first duly sworn by me under penalty of perjury, swore on her oath to the truth of the facts in the above revocation, declared said document to be her revocation of a living will, and declared that she signed it freely and voluntarily. I further certify that she signed said revocation in my presence, of her own free will, and for the purposes explained in said revocation. I further certify that the above witnesses, who are known to me personally to be the witnesses of the above revocation, appeared before me, acknowledged signing the above revocation as witnesses, and, after being first duly sworn by me under penalty of perjury, swore on their oaths that at the request of and in the presence of the above declarant, and in the presence of each other, they witnessed the declarant sign the above revocation, signed their names as witnesses to said revocation, declarant declared the above document to be her revocation of a living will, and said witnesses further swore that the facts they attested to in the above statement of witnesses are true.

Subscribed and sworn to before me this 4th day of May, 1990.

(SEAL)

Notary Public

My Commission Expires: 2/09/91

Instructions for Blank Forms

This chapter includes blank forms for a living will and a revocation of a living will. Each form has blank spaces with a number under each blank. Before filling in any of the blanks, make several photocopies of the form. Use one copy as a work copy, one as an original, and the rest for future work copies or originals. Fill out the work copy first and be sure it is correct, then type or print in the blanks on your original form.

Blank Living Will (FIG. 7-4) The following numbered instructions match the numbers under the blanks in FIG. 7-4:

(1) Enter the full name of the declarant.

(2) Enter the current address of the declarant.

(3) Enter the social security number of the declarant.

(4) If the declarant does not want pain medication that may hasten death, *cross out* the word "do". If the declarant does want this medication, *cross out* the words "do not". The declarant, witnesses, and notary public should initial the cross-outs.

(5) Enter the names of at least two physicians who have diagnosed the declarant as having a terminal condition the declarant has been so diagnosed. In some states, one of the physicians must be the declarant's attending physician. Also, some states require more than two doctors to certify the terminal condition (See FIG. 7-1) If no physician has diagnosed the declarant as having a terminal condition, put "not applicable" here.

(6) Enter the addresses of the physicians who have diagnosed the declarant as having a terminal illness. List the addresses in the same order as the names in Blank 5. If no physician has diagnosed the declarant as having a terminal condition, put "not applicable" here.

(7) Enter the telephone numbers of the physicians who have diagnosed the declarant as having a terminal condition. List the telephone numbers in the same order as the names listed in Blank 5. If no physician has diagnosed the declarant as having a terminal condition, put "not applicable" here.

(8) Enter the date(s) that any physicians informed the declarant that the declarant had a terminal condition. List the dates in the same order as the names listed in Blank 5. If no physician has diagnosed the declarant as having a terminal condition, put "not applicable" here.

(9) Enter the minimum age required by the declarant's state for making living wills. Obtain that age from FIG. 7-1.

(10) Enter the name of the state where the declarant resides, which should be the same state where the living will is signed.

(11,12,13) Enter the day, month, and year that the the living will is signed.

(14) Enter the address where the living will is signed.

(15) The declarant should sign his or her full name in front of at least two witnesses and a notary public for the state in which the living will is signed. See FIG. 7-1 for the number of witnesses the state requires.

(16) Enter the date the declarant signed the living will.

(17) Enter the full name of the declarant.

(18) Enter the state's minimum age for witnesses. See FIG. 7-1 to obtain this age.

(19) Enter the date the witnesses sign their names.

(20) The first witness should sign here. On the lines under the signature, print or type the witness's full name, address (including the county), and social security number.

(21) Complete similar information for the second witness.

(22) If the state requires more than two witnesses, complete similar information for the third witness. If the state requires only two witnesses, put a large "X" through the blanks numbered 22.

The following items should be completed by a notary public:

(23) Enter the name of the state where the declarant signed the living will.

(24) Enter the name of the county where the declarant signed the living will.

(25) Enter the name of the notary public.

(26) Enter the date that the declarant signed the living will.

(27) Enter the full name of the declarant.

(28,29,30) Enter the day, month, and year that the declarant signed the living will.

(31) The notary public should sign on this line.

(32) Enter the date the notary's commission expires.

(33) The notary should affix his or her seal to this document.

After the living will is signed, witnessed, and notarized, make 5–10 copies of the original. Have the notary public certify the copies as true copies of the original. Give a copy of the living will to the declarant's family members, doctors, and lawyer, and discuss it with them. The declarant should keep the original living will in a safe place, but not in a safe deposit box. The declarant should tell one or more family members where the living will is.

Fig. 7-4. Living Will (Blank). *Page 1 of 4* **105**

Living Will

1. TO: My family, my physician, my attorney, to any medical facility in whose care I happen to be, and to any individual who may become responsible for my health, welfare, or affairs.

2. If the time comes when I, _____
(1)

_____,

presently residing at _____
(2)

_____,

Social Security number _____–_____–_____, can no longer take part in
(3)

decisions for my own future, this statement, made willfully and while I am of sound mind and emotionally and mentally competent to make this living will, shall stand as my instructions regarding my physical care.

3. If at any time I should have an incurable injury, disease, or illness that at least two physicians who have examined me personally, one of whom is my attending physician, certify to be a terminal condition as defined in my state's laws, and those physicians also certify that the use of life-sustaining, artificial, or extreme medical or surgical procedures or means would only artificially prolong the moment of my death, and certify that my death is imminent if such artificial or extreme procedures are not used, I direct that such procedures be withheld or withdrawn, and that I be permitted to die naturally. I understand that life-sustaining procedures do not include administration of medication and sustenance for comfort and care. I (do) (do not) want medication
(4)

to be mercifully administered to me to alleviate suffering, even though this may hasten the moment of my death.

4. I intend that my family, physicians, attorney, and others shall honor this living will as the final expression of my legal right to refuse medical or surgical treatment. I accept the consequences of such a refusal.

5. If I have been diagnosed as pregnant, this living will is not intended to be honored during the course of my pregnancy.

6. I have been diagnosed as having a terminal condition caused by disease, illness, or injury by _____
(5)

_____,

whose business addresses are, respectively, _____
(6)

_____

_____

_____,

and whose telephone numbers are, respectively, _____
(7)

_____,

who informed me of such condition, respectively, on _____
(8)

_____.

If I have indicated "not applicable" in the blanks in this paragraph, I understand that I am indicating that I have not been diagnosed as having a terminal condition at the time of signing this living will.

7. I, my estate, and my legal successors will hold harmless from any liability any person or institution that suffers any loss as a result of following the instructions in this living will.

8. I understand what this living will means. I am making this living will freely and voluntarily because it is what I want to do, not because of physical or mental duress. I am making this living will when I am at least _____ years of age.
(9)

9. This living will shall be effective unless and until I revoke it, and shall be governed by the laws of the State of _____.
(10)

I understand that I can revoke this living will at any time, and I reserve the right to give current medical directions to physicians or other medical people as long as I am able, even if those directions conflict with this living will.

10. IN WITNESS WHEREOF, I have signed this living will on this _____
(11)

day of _____, _____, at _____
(12)   (13)   (14)

_____.
(15)

     Declarant

Statement of Witnesses

We hereby declare that on _____,
(16)

we witnessed _____,
(17)

as declarant, sign the above living will in our presence, that we know the declarant personally and believe that declarant is of sound mind and that declarant signed said living will freely and voluntarily, that we witnessed said living will at declarant's request and signed this statement at declarant's request, that as far as we know we are not prohibited from being witnesses to this living will under the laws of the above named state, that we are at least _____ years of age, that we did not sign declarant's
(18)

signature to the above living will for or at the direction of declarant, that we are not related to declarant by blood or marriage, that we do not have any claim on the estate of declarant and are not entitled to any portion of declarant's estate by will or otherwise, and that none of us is a physician attending the declarant, nor a person involved with

Fig. 7-4. (Cont'd). *Page 3 of 4* **107**

declarant's medical care, nor an employee of declarant's attending physician, nor an employee of a health care facility in which declarant is a patient, nor a patient in a health care facility in which declarant is a patient.

Dated: _____
(19)

_____
(20)
Signature of First Witness

_____
Name

_____
Address

_____

_____
SS#

_____
(21)
Signature of Second Witness

_____
Name

_____
Address

_____

_____
SS#

_____
(22)
Signature of Third Witness

_____
Name

_____
Address

_____

_____
SS#

STATE OF _____)
                    (23)
) ss.

COUNTY OF _____)
                       (24)

I, _____, a resident of and a
                                  (25)
notary public in and for the state and county indicated above, who am duly commissioned
and sworn and legally authorized to administer oaths and affirmations, hereby certify

that on _____,
                                          (26)
_____, who is known to
                              (27)
me personally to be the declarant in the above living will, appeared before me,
acknowledged signing the above living will, and, after being first duly sworn by me under
penalty of perjury, swore on his/her oath to the truth of the facts in the above living
will, declared said document to be his/her living will, and declared that he/she signed
it freely and voluntarily. I further certify that the declarant signed said living will in my
presence, of his/her own free will, and for the purposes explained in said living will.
I further certify that the above witnesses, who are known to me personally to be the
witnesses of the above living will, appeared before me, acknowledged signing the above
living will as witnesses, and, after being first duly sworn by me under penalty of perjury,
swore on their oaths that at the request of and in the presence of the above declarant
and in the presence of each other, they witnessed the above declarant sign the above
living will, signed their names as witnesses to said living will, declarant declared the
above document to be the declarant's living will, and said witnesses further swore that
the facts they attested to in the above statement of witnesses are true.

Subscribed and sworn to before me this _____ day of _____,
                                                            (28)   (29)
_____.
    (30)

_____
                                                                (31)
Notary Public
(SEAL)   My Commission Expires: _____
(33)   (32)

Blank Revocation of Living Will (FIG. 7-5)   The following numbered instructions match the numbers under the blanks in FIG. 7-5:

(1) Enter the date that the declarant signed the original living will.

(2) Enter the full name of the declarant in the original living will.

(3) Enter the full address of the declarant at the time he or she signed the original living will.

(4) List the names and addresses of the people or institutions who received certified copies of the original living will, including the relationship of those people or institutions to the declarant.

(5) Enter the current address of the declarant.

(6) Enter the social security number of the declarant.

(7) Enter the date that the declarant signs the revocation.

(8) Enter the location where the declarant signs the revocation.

(9) The declarant should sign the revocation in front of at least two witnesses and a notary public. If a state requires three witnesses to sign a living will, have three people witness any revocation of that living will. Figure 7-1 tells which states require three witnesses for living wills.

(10) Enter the date the declarant signed the revocation.

(11) Enter the full name of the declarant.

(12) Enter the minimum age for witnesses to a revocation of a living will. This will be the same age as the minimum age for witnesses to a living will, which FIG. 7-1 describes.

(13) Enter the date that the declarant signed the revocation.

(14) The first witness should sign here. On the lines under the first witness's signature, print or type the witness's full name, address (including the county), and social security number.

(15) Complete similar information for the second witness.

(16) Complete similar information for the third witness, if the state requires three witnesses for a revocation of a living will. If the state only requires two witnesses for a living will, it does not require more than two witnesses to revoke a living will, so put a large "X" through the blanks numbered 16.

The following items should be completed by a notary public:

(17) Enter the name of the state where the declarant signed the revocation.

(18) Enter the name of the county where the declarant signed the revocation.

(19) Enter the name of the notary public.

(20) Enter the date that the declarant signed the revocation.

(21) Enter the full name of the declarant.

(22,23,24) Enter the day, month, and year that the declarant signed the revocation.

(25) The notary should sign his or her name above this line.

(26) The notary should enter the date his or her commission expires.

(27) The notary should affix his or her seal to the revocation.

The declarant should make a copy of the original living will, mark that copy Exhibit "A" at the top or bottom of the copy, and staple it to the revocation of the living will.

After the revocation is signed, witnessed, and notarized, the declarant should keep the original revocation. The declarant should have the notary public certify 5–10 copies of the revocation as true copies of the original. The declarant should give a certified copy of the revocation to each of the people to whom the declarant gave a copy of the original living will. The declarant should ask anyone who received a copy of the original living will to return that copy. The declarant should then destroy the original living will and all copies of it, except for the copy attached to the revocation of the living will.

Fig. 7-5. Revocation of Living Will (Blank). *Page 1 of 4* **111**

Revocation of Living Will

On _____, I,_____

_____,
(1)   (2)

whose address at the time was _____
(3)

_____,

signed a living will directed to my family, my physicians, my attorney, to any medical facility in whose care I happened to be, and to any individual who may have become responsible for my health, welfare, or affairs. A copy of that living will is attached hereto, marked Exhibit "A", and incorporated into this revocation by this reference.

After signing the attached living will, I kept the original in my possession and gave certified copies to the following people:

Name	Relationship	Address
_____(4)_____	_____	_____
_____(4)_____	_____	_____
_____(4)_____	_____	_____
_____(4)_____	_____	_____
_____(4)_____	_____	_____

After careful thought and being of sound mind, I hereby voluntarily and freely revoke the attached living will and declare it to be null and void from this date on.

I am now living at _____
(5)

_____

My social security number is _____-_____-_____.

IN WITNESS WHEREOF, I have signed this revocation of a living will on

_____ at _____
(7)   (8)

_____.

_____
(9)
Declarant

Statement of Witnesses

We hereby declare that on _____,
(10)

we witnessed _____,
(11)

as declarant, sign the above revocation of a living will in our presence, that we know declarant personally and believe declarant is of sound mind and that declarant signed said revocation freely and voluntarily, that we witnessed said revocation at declarant's request and signed this statement at declarant's request, that as far as we know we are not prohibited from being witnesses to this revocation under the laws of the above-named state, that we are at least _____ years of age, that we did not sign declarant's
(12)
signature to the above revocation for or at the direction of declarant, that we are not related to declarant by blood or marriage, that we do not have any claim on the estate of declarant and are not entitled to any portion of declarant's estate by will or otherwise, and that none of us is a physician attending the declarant, nor a person involved with declarant's medical care, nor an employee of declarant's attending physician, nor an employee of a health care facility in which declarant is a patient, nor a patient in a health care facility in which declarant is a patient.

Dated:_____
(13)

_____
(14)
Signature of First Witness

_____
Name

_____
Address

_____

_____
SS#

_____
(15)
Signature of Second Witness

_____
Name

_____
Address

_____

_____
SS#

Fig. 7-5. (Cont'd). *Page 3 of 4* **113**

_____ (16)

Signature of Third Witness

_____

Name

_____

Address

_____

_____

SS#

STATE OF _____)
                   (17)   ) ss.

COUNTY OF _____)
                   (18)

I, _____, a resident of and a notary
                (19)

public in and for the state and county named above, who am duly commissioned and
sworn and legally authorized to administer oaths and affirmations, hereby certify
that on _____, who is known to me personally to be the declarant in
        (20)

_____,
                         (21)

the above living will, appeared before me, acknowledged signing the above living will,
and, after being first duly sworn by me under penalty of perjury, swore on his/her oath
to the truth of the facts in the above living will, declared said document to be his/her
living will, and declared that he/she signed it freely and voluntarily. I further certify that
the declarant signed said living will in my presence, of his/her own free will, and for
the purposes explained in said living will. I further certify that the above witnesses, who
are known to me personally to be the witnesses of the above living will, appeared before
me, acknowledged signing the above living will as witnesses, and, after being first duly
sworn by me under penalty of perjury, swore on their oaths that at the request of and
in the presence of the above declarant and in the presence of each other, they witnessed
the above declarant sign the above living will, signed their names as witnesses to said
living will, declarant declared the above document to be the declarant's living will, and
said witnesses further swore that the facts they attested to in the above statement of
witnesses are true.

    Subscribed and sworn to before me this _____ day of _____,
                                       (22)   (23)

_____.
   (24)

_____ (25)

Notary Public

(SEAL)   **My Commission Expires:** _____

revocation, appeared before me, acknowledged signing the above revocation as witnesses, and, after being first duly sworn by me under penalty of perjury, swore on their oaths that at the request of and in the presence of the above declarant, and in the presence of each other, they witnessed the declarant sign the above revocation, signed their names as witnesses to said revocation, declarant declared the above document to be his/her revocation of a living will, and said witnesses further swore that the facts they attested to in the above statement of witnesses are true.

Subscribed and sworn to before me this _____ day of _____,
                                              (22)   (23)
_____.
   (24)

_____
                                           (25)
                  Notary Public
   (SEAL)   My Commission Expires: _____
    (27)   (26)

Chapter 8

Residential Rental Agreement

A residential rental agreement is an agreement in which a landlord, for a fee, allows a renter to temporarily use, as the renter's home, a house or apartment owned by the landlord. Some states allow oral rental agreements for a residence if the rental agreement is for less than one year. Most states require that if a rental agreement is for more than one year, it must be in writing. Some states have special requirements for rental agreements that will last more than one year. The blank rental agreement at the end of this chapter does *not* meet all those special requirements. You should *not* use it for agreements for more than one year. A landlord and tenant can prepare a new rental agreement each year if they want to use the form in this book for longer than one year.

Even though some oral rental agreements are valid, you should have a written rental agreement which explains the rights of the landlord and the renter. There should be two original rental agreements, one kept by the landlord and one kept by the renter. Both original agreements should be dated and signed by the landlord and the renter.

Before entering into a rental agreement, a landlord should check with his or her insurance agent regarding any adjustments in the landlord's homeowners policy in light of the landlord's intention to rent property. The landlord should check the rental property to be sure there are no safety hazards, and install a fire extinguisher, smoke alarms, dead-bolt locks, and secure window latches. The landlord should photograph each side of the house and the rooms inside the house. If the landlord intends to rent an apartment, the landlord should take photographs that show the condition of the apartment prior to renting. If the rental agreement includes furniture, the landlord should photograph the rental furniture to show its condition prior to renting.

At the beginning of the rental agreement, the tenant should photograph any damaged or worn rental furniture and any other damage in the house or apartment at the time the tenant takes possession. The tenant should send the landlord a certified letter soon after moving in, listing any damage to furniture or damage on the property. This letter will avoid confusion in the future as to whether or not the tenant caused the damage.

Sample Residential Rental Agreement (FIG. 8-1)

Figure 8-1 is a sample residential rental agreement. The numbered paragraphs below match the numbered paragraphs of the sample.

1. Duration. Every rental agreement should describe the duration of the agreement. The sample agreement is a month-to-month rental agreement. A month-to-month rental agreement continues month after month until one of the parties terminates the agreement. If the agreement is for a fixed period of time (e.g., six months or one year), the rental agreement should describe the beginning and the end of the time period.

2. Parties. Every rental agreement should describe the full names of the parties. If there are two landlords or two renters, the agreement should make it clear what happens if one of the landlords or renters dies before the end of the agreement. Most husbands and wives want the survivor to receive all the interest in the rental agreement without going through a probate court if one of them dies before the end of the agreement (a probate court manages a deceased person's affairs). The sample rental agreement contains wording to allow the surviving landlord or renter to continue to make or receive payments without having to go through a probate court. That wording is, "jointly with right of survivorship, not as tenants in common". The parties do not want a *tenancy in common* as their form of joint ownership. When one joint owner dies in a tenancy in common, a probate court manages the deceased person's one-half interest in the property.

3. Description. Every agreement should include the address of the rental property and list any furniture or personal property that is rented with the residence.

4. Rent. Every agreement should state the amount of rent, the date it is due, and where it is due. If the agreement is more than a month-to-month tenancy, it should describe the total amount of rent for the entire agreement and the amount of any monthly or other regular payments. For instance, if the rental agreement is for one year, with $200.00 rent payable each month, the rental agreement should state, "The amount of rent shall be $2,400.00, payable $200.00 each month, payable on the first day of each month, in advance, beginning on May 1, 1989, and continuing until and including April 1, 1990."

5. Liens and encumbrances. Every rental agreement should state that the renter cannot allow any liens or other encumbrances to attach to the property. An encumbrance is any right or interest of someone other than the landlord or tenant in the property, such as a construction lien or bank loan.

6. Occupants and pets. Every rental agreement should describe how many adults, children, and pets can live on the property. If the landlord allows pets, the rental agreement should state what type of pets are allowed.

7. Violation of laws. Every rental agreement should state that the renter cannot violate any laws on or about the property.

8. Subletting. Every rental agreement should describe whether the renter can sublet or assign the lease. *Assignment* means that the renter transfers all the renter's rights in the rental agreement to someone else. *Subletting* means the renter transfers less than all the renter's rights in the rental agreement to someone else. Most landlords do not want the renter to be able to sublet or assign without the landlord's prior written consent to the transfer. This consent gives the landlord the right to refuse to rent to anyone whom the landlord does not wish to rent the property to.

9. Termination. Every rental agreement should describe how either party can terminate the agreement. In a month-to-month agreement, either party is usually allowed to terminate the agreement by giving the other party one month's written notice of termination. In a longer rental agreement, more notice may be necessary. Figure 8-3 includes a table that lists each state's laws regarding notice of termination of a tenancy. Read that table carefully, and follow the rules for your state for notice of termination of a tenancy.

A rental agreement should provide a method to terminate the agreement quickly if either party breaches the agreement. Different states have different requirements as to how to terminate a rental agreement when one party breaches the agreement. A rental agreement should provide that if one party breaches the agreement, the other party has all the rights allowed by state law. In order to be sure the non-breaching party complies with local law, the non-breaching party should consult a local attorney when the other party breaches the agreement.

10. Maintenance. Every rental agreement should require the renter to maintain the property in good condition and return the property to the landlord at the end of the rental agreement in as good a condition as when received, except for ordinary wear and tear. If the rental agreement is for a house that has a lawn, the rental agreement should explain who is responsible for removing snow and ice from the driveway and sidewalks, and who is responsible for mowing the lawn and keeping the landscaping in a neat and healthy condition.

11. Representations and utilities. Every rental agreement should state that the landlord has the right to rent the property. It should state that during the rental agreement the landlord will provide the renter with the quiet enjoyment of the property. The landlord should represent that the property is *habitable*, which means that the property is livable and safe. Many states have laws that require a landlord to provide a house that is habitable.

A rental agreement should describe who is responsible for supplying electricity, plumbing, and heating to the property, and who is responsible for paying for specific utilities. The landlord may be responsible for supplying a utility, but not for paying for it.

A rental agreement should explain which party is responsible for repairs. If one party is responsible for all repairs, the agreement should say so. If each party is responsible for certain repairs, the agreement should describe who is responsible for what repairs.

12. Liability for damages. Every rental agreement should state that the renter will assume all liability for damages caused by the renter or by people the renter invites onto the property.

13. Expenses. A rental agreement should explain that if one party incurs expenses to enforce any provision of the agreement, the other party must pay those expenses.

14. Owner. Some states require that the name, address, and telephone number of the owner and manager of the property be listed in the rental agreement. Some states also require that the rental agreement include a telephone number for emergencies. Every rental agreement should list the addresses that the parties should use for notices they send to each other under the agreement.

15. Mortgages. A rental agreement should state that the landlord is not breaching the rental agreement by having a mortgage on the property, or by applying for a mortgage on the property during the term of the rental agreement. On the other hand, a rental agreement should not allow these mortgages to interfere with the renter's use of the property.

16. Access. A rental agreement should allow a landlord access to the property to inspect it and to make repairs. On the other hand, a rental agreement should not allow a landlord to use this right of access unreasonably. For that reason, a rental agreement should require that a landlord give a renter reasonable notice before inspecting the property.

17. Insurance on personal property. A rental agreement should state who is responsible for insuring the renter's personal property. Usually, the landlord is not responsible for doing so.

18. Destruction—eminent domain. A rental agreement should explain what happens if the majority of the property is destroyed by fire or other loss or taken by *eminent domain*. Eminent domain is the government's right to force an owner to sell property to the government. A fair rental agreement will provide that destruction of the majority of the property entitles either party to terminate the rental agreement.

19. Complete agreement. Every rental agreement should state that it is the complete and final agreement of the parties and that it replaces any other written or oral agreements that the parties may have regarding the property.

20. Security deposit. A security deposit is different from a cleaning deposit. Some rental agreements provide for a nonrefundable cleaning deposit to reimburse the landlord for cleaning the property before the renter moves in or when the renter moves out.

A security deposit is refundable. It gives the landlord money to repair any damage done to the property by the renter. Many states require the landlord to return any unused portion of the security deposit to the renter within a short period of time after termination of the tenancy, and to provide the renter with an itemization of any deductions from the security deposit. Some states also require the landlord to keep the security deposit in an interest-bearing account and pay the tenant interest that accrues on the security deposit.

A tenant can sometimes sue a landlord for more than the amount of the security deposit if the landlord fails to comply with state law regarding security deposits. For that reason, a landlord should use extreme care in dealing with security deposits.

Because state laws governing security deposits vary greatly, the next section of this chapter includes a table which lists each state's laws regarding security deposits. If a landlord is going to require a security deposit, the landlord must check FIG. 8-2 to find out which laws govern security deposits in his or her state.

21. Additional provisions. The sample and the blank form at the end of this chapter leave spaces for any additional provisions that a landlord or tenant may wish to include in the rental agreement.

22. Satisfaction with property. A renter should inspect the property thoroughly before moving in. A rental agreement should state that the renter is satisfied with the property at the time of signing the agreement. If there is any damage to the property at the time the renter moves in, the parties should list the damage in the additional provisions section of the rental agreement and state who will repair the damage, if the parties agree to repair the damage.

Both parties should read the rental agreement and the agreement should state that both parties have done so.

23. Execution of the rental agreement. Every rental agreement should include the date that the parties sign it. Both parties should sign two originals, and each party should keep one original.

Fig. 8-1. Residential Rental Agreement (Sample). *Page 1 of 3* **119**

Residential Rental Agreement

1. Duration. This rental agreement begins at 12:01 A.M. on May 1st, 1989, and continues as a month-to-month agreement until terminated as described in this agreement.

2. Parties. This agreement is between John Francis Smith and Mary Jane Smith, jointly with right of survivorship, not as tenants in common, their heirs, successors, and assigns, referred to as "landlord", and Frederick Allen Jones and Susan Anne Jones, jointly with right of survivorship, not as tenants in common, their heirs, successors, and assigns, referred to as "renter".

3. Description. Landlord agrees to rent, to renter and renter agrees to rent from landlord, the residence described as Apartment –8, 517 North Main Street, Waynecastle, Pennsylvania, 17294. The property is rented without furniture. A refrigerator and cooking stove are presently on the property and are part of this rental agreement.

4. Rent. The amount of the rent shall be FIVE HUNDRED DOLLARS ($500.00) each month, payable on the first day of each month, in advance, beginning with May 1, 1989, and continuing until this agreement is terminated as described below. Rent is payable to the landlord at 542 North Madison Avenue, Waynecastle, Pennsylvania, 17294.

5. Liens and encumbrances. Renter agrees that renter will not allow any liens or encumbrances to attach to the property during the term of this agreement.

6. Occupants and pets. No more than two adults and two children shall occupy the property. Pets are not allowed. Renters shall use the property as a residence only.

7. Violation of laws. Renter shall not violate any city ordinance, state law, or other law on or about the property.

8. Subletting. Any attempt by renter to sublet, assign, or in any way transfer the property, any part of the property, or the renter's rights in this agreement without the landlord's prior written consent is void.

9. Termination. Either party may terminate this agreement by giving the other party not less than thirty (30) days notice in writing prior to the date set in the termination notice as the date for ending the tenancy. If, however, either party breaches any provision of this agreement, the non-breaching party shall have the right to terminate this rental agreement as provided by state law and pursue any legal remedies allowed by law. Upon termination of this tenancy, the renter agrees to promptly and peacefully surrender the premises to the landlord.

10. Maintenance. Renter shall maintain the property in a clean and sanitary condition at all times. Renter shall not do anything on the property that will make voidable or increase landlord's insurance on the property. Renter shall not make any alterations to the property or change any locks on the property without the prior written consent of the landlord. At the termination of the tenancy, renter shall surrender the property to landlord in as good a condition as when received, except for ordinary wear and tear.

11. Representations and utilities. Landlord represents to renter that landlord owns the property landlord is renting and has the right to rent this property to renter. Landlord also represents that renter shall have the quiet enjoyment of the property during the period of this rental agreement, and that the property the landlord is renting is habitable. Landlord further agrees to supply utilities capable of producing hot and cold running water and adequate heating for the property. Renter shall pay for all heating facilities, electricity, telephone service, and other utilities, except that the landlord shall pay for all water, garbage, and sewer service. Except for repairs caused by renter's misuse, waste, or negligence, the landlord shall pay for all repairs costing more than $100. Renter shall pay for all repairs under $100, and shall pay for all repairs caused by the renter's misuse, waste, or neglect.

12. Liability for damages. Renter agrees to assume all liability for, and hold landlord harmless from, all damages to people or property caused by renter, renter's family, or renter's guests on any part of the property. "Damages" includes any costs and attorney's fees that the landlord incurs in defending any lawsuit or other action.

13. Expenses. If either party incurs any expenses to enforce any provision of this agreement, including reasonable attorney's fees, either before or after either party begins an action in a court, the losing party in the suit or action, or the party defaulting on this agreement if there is no suit or action, shall pay the other party's expenses and reasonable attorney's fees, including attorney's fees at trial and on any appeal of any suit or action.

14. Owner. The owners of this property are John Francis Smith and Mary Jane Smith, whose address is 542 North Madison Avenue, Waynecastle, Pennsylvania, 17294, and whose telephone number is (717) 555-6542. Renter can call this telephone number in an emergency. The managers are the same people at the same address. All notices required by this agreement shall be valid if sent to landlord at this address. All notices required by this agreement shall be valid if sent to renter at Apartment #8, 517 North Main Street, Waynecastle, Pennsylvania, 17294, or such other address as renter shall provide landlord notice of in writing.

15. Mortgages. Renter agrees that this rental agreement is subordinate to all existing mortgages and other encumbrances on this property at the time of signing this rental agreement. Renter also agrees that during the term of this rental agreement the landlord may place mortgages or other encumbrances on the property, as long as they do not interfere with renter's use of the property.

16. Access. Renter shall allow landlord reasonable access to the rented property to inspect the property or to repair any portion of the property. Landlord must exercise this right of access reasonably, and shall not use it to harass the renter in any way. Landlord must give the renter reasonable notice prior to exercising this right of inspection.

17. Insurance on personal property. Renter acknowledges that landlord is not responsible for insuring any of renter's personal property.

18. Destruction—eminent domain. Landlord and renter agree that in the event more than half of the property being rented is destroyed by fire or other loss, or is taken by eminent domain, this rental agreement, at the option of either the landlord or the renter, shall become void.

Fig. 8-1. (Cont'd). *Page 3 of 3* **121**

19. Complete agreement. This is the complete and final agreement of the parties regarding rental of the property described in this agreement. This agreement replaces any prior written or oral agreements regarding this property.

20. Security deposit. Renter hereby gives landlord an amount equal to one month's rent, FIVE HUNDRED DOLLARS ($500.00), receipt of which landlord hereby acknowledges, as a security deposit. Landlord shall use this security deposit only as compensation for damage or repair of damage to the rented property caused by the renter or the renter's family or guests. Landlord shall not use this security deposit for repair of or compensation for ordinary wear and tear of the property. Landlord shall keep this security deposit in an interest-bearing bank account established specifically for renters' security deposits, and shall notify renter of the name and address of the bank where the account is located and of the number of the bank account. Landlord shall not commingle any of landlord's private funds with the funds in said account. Landlord agrees that within ten (10) days after the renter has vacated the rented premises after termination of this agreement, landlord will return this security deposit, with accrued interest, to renter. Landlord shall pay renter accrued interest on this security deposit at least once a year. If landlord has made any deductions from this security deposit, landlord shall, within ten (10) days of renter's vacating the rented property, provide renter with an itemized statement detailing those deductions and the reasons for those deductions. At the time renter vacates the property, renter must provide landlord with an address for return of this security deposit or accounting.

21. Additional provisions. None.

22. Satisfaction with property. Renter agrees that renter has personally inspected the property and finds it satisfactory at the time of signing this agreement. The parties agree that they have both read all the provisions contained in this agreement. The parties agree that they have not made any promises that this agreement does not contain.

23. Execution of the rental agreement. The parties have signed two originals of this agreement on May 1, 1989, at 542 North Madison Avenue, Waynecastle, Pennsylvania, 17294. By signing this agreement, each party acknowledges that he or she has received one original agreement.

Dated this 1st day of May, 1989.

John Francis Smith	Frederick Allen Jones
Landlord	Renter
Mary Jane Smith	Susan Anne Jones
Landlord	Renter

State Laws on Security Deposits (FIG. 8-2)

Figure 8-2 lists all 50 states and the District of Columbia, and refers to the sections of each state's laws that discuss security deposits. You can find these laws by going to a law library in your state. One is located at your county courthouse. Ask the librarian to help you find the laws FIG. 8-2 refers to. Your state real estate commission or local consumer protection office may also be able to provide you with these laws.

Figure 8-2 indicates which states have special provisions regarding security deposits. Unless FIG. 8-2 indicates otherwise, a state's laws do not require more than the following:

- All security deposits should be refundable.
- No security deposit should be in an amount greater than one month's rent.
- A security deposit should be kept in a separate, interest-bearing account, and not commingled with the landlord's private funds.
- No security deposit should be used for repair of, or compensation for, ordinary wear and tear of the property, or to compensate the landlord for a tenant's other breaches of the rental agreement.
- No security deposit should be used for nonpayment of rent.
- Within ten (10) days after termination of the rental agreement, the landlord should return the security deposit to the renter, with accrued interest, with an accounting of the amounts of, and reasons for, any deductions from the security deposit, all of which should be sent by certified mail, return receipt requested.
- When the landlord sells or transfers the property, the landlord shall transfer the security deposit to whomever he or she transfers the property to, shall notify the renter of the name and address of the new owner, and shall require the new owner to honor all the terms of the agreement regarding the security deposit.

Figure 8-2 is based on 1987 and 1988 laws. The state legislatures of the 50 states meet at different times. Some legislatures only meet once every two years. When a state legislature passes a law, the legislature or a publishing company publishes that law at a later time. Several months can pass before the legislature or publisher sends that law to the libraries around the country. As you read these words, months or years will also have passed from the time this book was edited, printed, and distributed. For these reasons, this book, like all legal books, cannot be absolutely current.

Figure 8-2 indicates whether the information for a particular state is based on the 1987 or 1988 laws of that state. If you want to confirm whether or not your state has changed its laws, go to a law library in your state and read the most current version of the law referred to in FIG. 8-2. If the law has changed, the new law will usually have the same number as the old law. Check what are known as the "pocket parts" of your state's laws. Pocket parts are supplements which contain the latest revisions of a state's laws. Or, again, contact your state real estate commission or local consumer protection office.

Fig. 8-2. State Laws on Security Deposits. **123**

Alabama—None found (1987 Update).

Alaska—34.03.070 (1987 Update).

Arizona—33-1321 (1988 Update). Landlord must pay at least 5% interest on any security deposits, paid each year or compounded each year. Compounding means that the landlord must take the interest from a previous year and add it to the bank account, so that the new balance will earn interest on the principal plus the previous year's interest.

Arkansas—18-16-304 and -305 (1987 Update).

California—Civil Code, 1950.5 (1988 Update). Special requirements exist for landlords regarding security deposits when a landlord transfers ownership of the property to someone else.

Colorado—38-12-101 to -103, 38-12-207 (1987 Update).

Connecticut—47a-21(a), (b), (c), (d), (h), (i) (1987 Update). Landlord must pay 5% interest on all security deposits, to be paid annually or credited to the rent annually.

Delaware—25-5511 (1987 Update).

District of Columbia—None found (1988 Update).

Florida—83.49 (1988 Update). A landlord must pay interest on a security deposit as follows: 5% interest or three-quarters of the annual interest rate on the account that contains the security deposit. Florida laws contain numerous other requirements regarding security deposits.

Georgia—44-7-30 to -36 (1988 Update). If a landlord requires a security deposit, the landlord and tenant must inspect the property before the landlord receives the security deposit and make a list of all the repairs that the property needs. Georgia laws also contain numerous other requirements regarding security deposits.

Hawaii—521-44 (1987 Update).

Idaho—6-321 (1988 Update).

Illinois—S.H.A. 80-101, -121, -218 (1988 Update). Special rules apply to landlords with more than ten rental units.

Indiana—None found (1988 Update).

Iowa—562A.12 (1988 Update). Iowa law allows a landlord to keep the interest on security deposits for the first five years. After five years of holding a security deposit, a landlord must give the interest to the tenant. A landlord must put security deposits in a bank, savings and loan, or credit union insured by an agency of the federal government.

Kansas—58-2550 (1987 Update).

Kentucky—383.580 (1987 Update). If a landlord requires a security deposit, the landlord and tenant must inspect the property before the landlord receives the security deposit and make a list of all repairs that the property needs. Kentucky laws also have numerous other requirements regarding security deposits.

Louisiana—9:3251 (1988 Update).

Maine—14-6032, -6033 (1987 Update).

Maryland—Real Property, 8-203 (1987 Update). Maryland law includes many requirements for landlords who require security deposits.

Massachusetts—186-15B (1987 Update). A landlord must pay the tenant at least 5% interest on security deposit accounts. Massachusetts laws also have numerous other requirements regarding security deposits.

Michigan—26.1138(2), (3), (4)-(16) (1988 Update). Michigan law includes many requirements for landlords who require security deposits.

Minnesota—504.20 (1988 Update). A landlord must pay a tenant 5½% simple interest on security deposits.

Mississippi—None found (1987 Update).

Missouri—535.300 (1988 Update). A landlord must give reasonable notice to a tenant or his or her representative in writing, in person, or at the tenant's last known address of a date and time when the landlord will inspect the property to determine if the landlord will refund the security deposit. The tenant has the right to be present at the inspection.

Montana—70-25-201 to -203, -206 (1987 Update). Before landlords can charge a security deposit to a new tenant, landlords must give tenants a written statement of the conditions of the property and any damages a previous tenant caused.

Nebraska—76-1416 (1987 Update).

Nevada—118A.240, .242, .244, .250 (1987 Update).

New Hampshire—540A:5 to :8 (1988 Update). New Hampshire has special requirements regarding inspection of the property, repairs needed for the property, and the duties of a landlord if the landlord sells the property during the rental agreement.

New Jersey—46:8-19, -19.1, -20, -21, -21.1, -21.2, -21.3, -22, -23 (1988 Update). New Jersey laws have special requirements regarding security deposits, such as the duties of a landlord if a landlord sells the property during the rental agreement.

New Mexico—47-8-18 (1987 Update).

New York—General Obligations Law, 7-103, -105, -107, and -108 (1988 Update). New York has special requirements regarding security deposits, such as complex rules regarding interest on security deposits.

North Carolina—42-50 to -53, -56 (1987 Update). North Carolina requires landlords to keep security deposits in an insured bank or savings institution in North Carolina and to notify tenants of the location of security deposits within 30 days of the beginning of the tenancy. Landlords cannot require more than two weeks rent as security deposit if the tenancy is a week-to-week tenancy. Landlords must hold security deposits at least six months if a tenant's address is unknown after a tenant moves out.

North Dakota—47-16-07.1 and 47-16-07.2 (1987 Update). To require a security deposit, North Dakota requires that a landlord give a written statement to the tenant describing the condition of the facilities in and about the premises to be rented at the time of entering into the rental agreement. This statement must be signed by the landlord and the tenant. Landlords must keep security deposits in federally insured institutions, in interest-bearing savings or passbook accounts established only for security deposits.

Ohio—5321.16 (1988 Update). If a tenant is in possession for more than six months, a landlord must compute and pay 5% annual interest to the tenant on a security deposit.

Oklahoma—41-115 (1988 Update). Oklahoma law contains many requirements for security deposits.

Oregon—91.760 (1987 Update).

Pennsylvania—68 PS 250.511 (a)(b), 512 (1988 Update). Interest on security deposits must be paid annually. Once a tenant is in possession more than five years, a landlord cannot raise the security deposit when the landlord raises the rent.

Rhode Island—34-18-19 (1987 Update).

South Carolina—27-40-410 (1987 Update). A landlord must read and follow the requirements of this section if he or she rents more than four adjacent dwelling units on the same premises and imposes different security deposit standards among the tenants.

South Dakota—43-32-6.1, 43-32-24 (1988 Update).

Tennessee—66-28-301 (1987 Update). Tennessee has special requirements regarding security deposits, such as requiring a landlord to allow a tenant to verify a landlord's list of damages, and providing a court procedure for a tenant to challenge a landlord's list of damages.

Texas—Property Code 92.102 to .109 (1988 Update).

Utah—57-17-1 to -5 (1988 Update).

Vermont—9-4461 (1988 Update).

Virginia—55-248.11 and 55-248.11.1 (1988 Update) Virginia has special requirements regarding security deposits, such as inspections of the property by the tenant, records that the landlord must keep, notices a landlord must give, and other requirements.

Washington—59.18.260 to .280 (1988 Update). Washington has special requirements regarding security deposits, such as a written checklist which landlords must fill out concerning the condition of the property.

West Virginia—None found (1988 Update).

Wisconsin—134.03 and .06 (1988 Update). Wisconsin laws require that a landlord give a tenant a written receipt for a security deposit and that a landlord must allow a tenant seven days after entry onto property to inspect the property and give to the landlord a list of the damages.

Wyoming—None found (1987 Update).

State Laws on
Notice of Termination of a Tenancy (FIG. 8-3)

Figure 8-3 lists the sections of state laws that discuss notice of termination of a tenancy. Again, you can find these laws by going to a law library in your state (ask the librarian to help you find the laws), or your state real estate commission or local consumer protection office may be able to provide you with these laws.

Figure 8-3 indicates which states have special requirements regarding notice of termination of a tenancy. Some states have requirements for notice of termination for some types of tenancies, but not for all tenancies. If FIG. 8-3 does not list any requirements for a certain type of tenancy in a particular state, the author found no requirements in that state's laws for notice of termination of that type of tenancy. In those cases, the agreement of the parties would control what notice is required. Unless otherwise indicated, the notice requirements in FIG. 8-3 apply equally to landlords and renters. The following definitions will help you understand FIG. 8-3:

Tenancy for a definite term (also called a *tenancy for years*). A tenancy with a definite beginning date and a definite ending date. The laws of most states provide that these tenancies end on the date set in the rental agreement, without any need for either party to notify the other party of intent to terminate the tenancy at that ending date. However, tenants sometimes continue to occupy rental property after the ending date of a tenancy for a definite term. If the landlord agrees to such occupancy and the landlord and tenant do not enter into another agreement for a definite term, the type of tenancy that results is usually a periodic tenancy, depending on the intent of the parties and how often rent is paid. Periodic tenancies are explained below.

Periodic tenancy. An agreement between a landlord and a tenant that does not fix a definite ending date for the tenancy, but which continues from one period to another, such as week-to-week, month-to-month, or quarter-to-quarter. The period is determined by the agreement of the parties or by when rent is due (e.g., if rent is due once a month, the tenancy is a month-to-month tenancy). A periodic tenancy is automatically renewed at the end of a period for another full period, unless either party gives the other party the notice of termination required by state law (or required by the rental agreement if state law sets no requirements).

Tenancy at will. A tenancy with no definite ending date, which continues based on the joint will of the landlord and the tenant. A tenancy at will ends whenever either party wishes, as long as the party that wishes to terminate the tenancy follows any state requirements for notice of termination of tenancies at will. As you will see from FIG. 8-3, many states have requirements for notice of termination of tenancies at will.

Both periodic tenancies and tenancies at will have no definite ending date. For that reason, you cannot always distinguish between the two if the parties do not state which type of tenancy they have in a written rental agreement. Paying rent in regular intervals usually results in a periodic tenancy. However, six states—Florida, Georgia, Iowa, Kansas, North Dakota, and Oklahoma—define tenancies at will to include periodic tenancies. Those states provide rules for notice of termination of tenancies at will, but not for periodic tenancies. Those six states' rules for tenancies at will apply to periodic tenancies. The other states and the District of Columbia either do not clearly define tenancies at will or define them as indefinite tenancies that are not periodic tenancies (these are rare). Some of these states have the same rules for notice of termination of tenancies at will and periodic tenancies, so it does not matter how those states define those tenancies. A few states have confusing definitions and rules for termination of tenancies at will. Follow these rules in the following states:

- *California*—give at least 30 days notice before terminating any tenancy for less than one year.
- *Colorado*—give 3 months notice to terminate a tenancy at will, which is rare because Colorado defines tenancies at will to be indefinite tenancies that are not periodic tenancies.
- *Connecticut*—give at least 8 days notice to terminate any tenancy.
- *Idaho*—give at least 30 days notice to terminate any tenancy.
- *Maryland*—give at least 30 days notice to terminate a tenancy at will, which is rare because Maryland defines tenancies at will to be indefinite tenancies that are not periodic tenancies.
- *New Hampshire*—you must read the statutes referred to in FIG. 8-3. New Hampshire notice requirements are complicated and go on for several pages.

Tenancy at sufferance—A tenancy where a tenant stays in possession after the tenant's right to possession ends. Most states do not require landlords to give tenants at sufferance any notice to terminate this type of tenancy.

Figure 8-3 is based on 1987 and 1988 laws. The earlier comments regarding the updating of FIG. 8-2 apply to FIG. 8-3 as well.

Fig. 8-3. State Laws on Notice of Termination of Tenancy.

Alabama—35-9-3, -4, -5, -6, -8 (1987 Update). Ten (10) days written notice is required to terminate tenancy at will, month-to-month tenancy, or tenancy for less than one year. If tenancy was for a specific period and the period expires, no notice is required. If a lease is breached, 10 days notice is required and the statute includes a form to send. Notices must be delivered to tenant or left with a person over 18 years of age residing on premises. 35-9-4 contains rules for termination of lodging or dwelling houses.

Alaska—34.03.290(a) and (b) (1987 Update). Thirty (30) days written notice is required to terminate a month-to-month tenancy, but 14 days written notice is required to terminate a week-to-week tenancy.

Arizona—33-341, -1476 (1988 Update). When rent is not paid when due, no notice is required to terminate. Ten (10) days notice is required to terminate a month-to-month tenancy. A year-to-year tenancy can be terminated when the year ends. 33-1476 contains special rules for mobile home tenancies.

Arkansas—18-16-101 and -106 (1987 Update). Ten (10) days notice is required to terminate all tenancies except tenancies for years, for which 30 days notice after expiration of the tenancy is required.

California—Civil Code, Section 789 (1988 Update). Tenancy at will can be terminated by 30 days written notice.

Colorado—13-40-107 and 38-12-202 (1987 Update). If a lease is for a specific period of time, no notice is required to terminate the tenancy on the date set for the end of the term. If the time period has not expired, 3 days notice is required for a tenancy of 1 week to 1 month, 10 days notice for a tenancy of 1 month to 6 months, 1 month notice for a tenancy of 6 months to 1 year, and 3 months notice for a tenancy of 1 year or more. 38-12-202 contains rules for mobile home tenancies.

Connecticut—47a-23 (1987 Update). If the time period of a lease ends or if a lease is breached, 8 days notice is required to terminate the tenancy. The statute contains a form for such notice.

Delaware—25-5107, -5509 (1987 Update). If a tenancy is for a definite term, no notice is required to terminate the tenancy on the date set for the end of the term. If a tenancy does not specify a date when it ends, it can be terminated by 60 days notice, unless

Fig. 8-3. (Cont'd). 127

it is a farm tenancy. A tenant may terminate a lease on 30 days notice if the tenant must move because of the death or illness of a tenant or a resident family member, or because of reasons related to the tenant's job.

District of Columbia—45-1401 to -1406, 1561 (1988 Update). If a tenancy is for a definite term, no notice is required to terminate the tenancy on the date set for the end of the term. If a tenancy is a tenancy at sufferance, a month-to-month tenancy, a quarter-to-quarter tenancy, or a tenancy at will, 30 days notice is required. 45-1561 contains special notice requirements for evictions.

Florida—83.03 and .56 (1988 Update). Three (3) months notice is required to terminate a year-to-year tenancy, 45 days notice to terminate a quarter-to-quarter tenancy, 15 days notice to terminate a month-to-month tenancy, and 7 days notice to terminate a week-to-week tenancy.

Georgia—44-7-7 (1988 Update). A landlord must give 60 days notice to terminate a tenancy at will, while a tenant only has to give 30 days notice to do so.

Hawaii—666-1, -2, -3 (1987 Update). 666-1 requires 10 days notice to terminate an oral tenancy. 666-2 contains special notice requirements to terminate a tenancy when the tenant creates a nuisance. 666-3 requires 25 days notice to terminate a periodic tenancy.

Idaho—55-208 (1988 Update). One (1) month notice is required to terminate a tenancy at will.

Illinois—110-9-205 to -207, -210, -213 (1988 Update). If a tenancy is for a definite term, no notice is required to terminate the tenancy on the date set for the end of the term. A landlord must give ten (10) days notice to terminate a lease because a tenant breached the lease. Seven (7) days notice is required to terminate a week-to-week tenancy. Thirty (30) days notice is required to terminate a tenancy for a period of less than one year. Sixty (60) days notice is required to terminate a year-to-year non-farm lease, and 4 months notice to terminate a year-to-year farm lease.

Indiana—32-7-1-1 and 32-7-1-3 (1988 Update). Three (3) months notice is required to terminate a year-to-year tenancy, and the statute gives a form for such notice. One (1) month notice is required to terminate a tenancy at will.

Iowa—562.4 (1988 Update). Thirty (30) days notice is required to terminate a tenancy at will. If rent is payable in time periods of less than 30 days, the tenancy can be terminated by notice equal to those time periods.

Kansas—58-2504, -2505, -2506, -2509, -2570 (1987 Update). These sections of Kansas law contain numerous requirements for terminating tenancies.

Kentucky—383.695(1), (2), (3) (1987 Update). If a tenant fails to pay rent, no notice is required to terminate a tenancy. If a written lease for the tenancy expired, but the tenancy continued, the landlord can give ten (10) days notice to terminate the tenancy. Thirty (30) days notice is required to terminate a month-to-month tenancy, and seven (7) days notice is required to terminate a week-to-week tenancy.

Louisiana—Civil Code Art. 2686 (1988 Update). If a lease is for a definite term, no notice is required to terminate the tenancy on the date set for the end of that term, unless the lease provides for notice. If no duration is set for a lease, 10 days notice is required to terminate a month-to-month tenancy.

Maine—14-6002 and -6002(1) (1987 Update). Thirty (30) days notice is required to terminate a tenancy at will. 14-6002(1) requires only seven (7) days notice to terminate a tenancy for special reasons, such as failure to pay rent or damage to the property.

Maryland—Real Property Code 8-402(b)(1) and (b)(4)(iii) (1988 Update). One (1) week notice is required to terminate a week-to-week tenancy. One (1) month notice is required to terminate a month-to-month tenancy. Three (3) months notice is required to terminate a year-to-year tenancy. Montgomery County requires two (2) months notice to terminate certain tenancies, as detailed in 8-402(b)(4)(iii).

Massachusetts—186-12 (1987 Update). If rent is paid more frequently than once every three months, thirty (30) days notice is required to terminate a tenancy at will. Three (3) months notice is required to terminate a tenancy at will where rent is paid once every three (3) months or less frequently.

Michigan—26.1104 (1988 Update). If rent is not paid when due, seven (7) days notice is required to terminate a tenancy. One (1) month notice is required to terminate a tenancy at will. One (1) year notice is required to terminate a year-to-year tenancy.

Minnesota—504.06 (1988 Update). Fourteen (14) days notice is required to terminate a tenancy when rent is not paid when due. Three (3) months notice is required to terminate a tenancy at will where rent is payable once every three (3) months or less frequently. When rent is payable more frequently than once every three (3) months, a tenancy at will may be terminated by notice equal to the interval between rent payments.

Mississippi—89-7-23 (1987 Update). If a lease is for a definite term, no notice is required to terminate the lease on the date set for the end of the term. Two (2) months notice is required to terminate a year-to-year tenancy. One (1) month notice is required to terminate a tenancy for a quarter or one-half year. One (1) week notice is required to terminate a month-to-month or week-to-week tenancy.

Missouri—441.050, .060, .070 (1988 Update). If a lease is for a definite term, no notice is required to terminate the lease on the date set for the end of the term. Sixty (60) days notice is required to terminate a year-to-year tenancy. One (1) month notice is required to terminate a tenancy for less than one year, a tenancy at will, and a tenancy at sufferance.

Montana—70-24-441 and 70-27-104 (1987 Update). Thirty (30) days notice is required to terminate a tenancy at will. Notice equal to the interval between rent periods is required to terminate a periodic tenancy, such as a week-to-week or month-to-month tenancy.

Nebraska—76-1437(1) and (2) (1987 Update). Thirty (30) days notice is required to terminate a month-to-month tenancy. Seven (7) days notice is required to terminate a week-to-week tenancy.

Nevada—118A.370, .380, .390, .400, .430; 118B.190 (1987 Update). These statutes contain numerous requirements for notices to terminate tenancies.

New Hampshire—540:1(a), :2, :3, :5, :11; 205-A:3 (1988 Update). New Hampshire rules are probably the most complicated in the entire country. Landlords and tenants must read these statutes to understand New Hampshire notice requirements. These statutes go on for several pages.

New Jersey—46:8-9, 2A:18-56 (1988 Update). Three (3) months notice is required to terminate a tenancy at will or a year-to-year tenancy. Any other tenancy may be terminated by giving notice equal to the term of the tenancy, such as one (1) month notice for a month-to-month tenancy and one (1) week notice for a week-to-week tenancy.

New Mexico—47-8-37 (1987 Update). Thirty (30) days notice is required to terminate a month-to-month tenancy. Seven (7) days notice is required to terminate a week-to-week tenancy.

New York—Real Property Law 228; 232-a, -b (1988 Update). Thirty (30) days notice is required to terminate a tenancy at will or a tenancy at sufferance. One (1) month notice is required to terminate a month-to-month tenancy. In New York City, a landlord is required to give thirty (30) days notice to terminate a month-to-month tenancy.

North Carolina—42-14 (1987 Update). Thirty (30) days notice is required to terminate a mobile-home-space tenancy, regardless of the other rules that follow. One (1) month notice is required to terminate a year-to-year tenancy, seven (7) days notice to terminate a month-to-month tenancy, and two (2) days notice to terminate a week-to-week tenancy.

North Dakota—47-17-01 (1987 Update). One (1) month notice is required to terminate a tenancy at will.

Ohio—5321.11, .17 (1988 Update). Thirty (30) days notice is required to terminate a month-to-month tenancy. Seven (7) days notice is required to terminate a week-to-week tenancy. If a landlord wants to terminate a tenancy because of a tenant's breach of the lease, the landlord must give the tenant thirty (30) days from receipt of a notice that the tenant has breached the lease to cure the breach or to have the lease terminated.

Oklahoma—41-5 (1988 Update). Thirty (30) days notice is required to terminate a tenancy at will, three (3) months notice to terminate a year-to-year tenancy, and seven (7) days notice to terminate a tenancy for less than month-to-month.

Oregon—91.050, .060, .070, .080; 105.120 (1987 Update). If a tenancy is for a definite term, no notice is required to terminate the tenancy on the date set for the end of the term. Thirty (30) days notice is required to terminate a month-to-month tenancy, sixty (60) days notice to terminate a year-to-year tenancy, ninety (90) days notice to terminate an agricultural lease.

Pennsylvania—68-250.501 (1988 Update). If a tenancy is for a definite term, no notice is required to terminate the tenancy on the date set for the end of the term. Three (3) months notice is required to terminate leases for one year or more. Thirty (30) days notice is required to terminate a tenancy for less than one year, or a tenancy that does not have a specific term.

Fig. 8-3. (Cont'd). **129**

Rhode Island—34-18-3, -4 (1987 Update). Three (3) months notice is required to terminate a year-to-year tenancy. For a tenancy of less than one year, notice of at least one-half the term of the lease, not to exceed three (3) months notice, is required to terminate.

South Carolina—27-35-100, -110, -120, -130, -140 (1987 Update). Unless it specifies otherwise, a farm tenancy automatically terminates on December 31 of each year. If a tenancy is for a definite term, no notice is required to terminate the tenancy on the date set for the end of the term. Thirty (30) days notice is required to terminate a month-to-month tenancy. Twenty (20) days notice is required to terminate a tenancy at will. If the tenant fails to pay rent when due, no notice is required to terminate a tenancy for a term, for years, month-to-month, or at will.

South Dakota—43-32-13, -18 (1988 Update). Thirty (30) days notice is required to terminate a month-to-month tenancy, but a landlord can terminate any lease before the date set for the end of the lease if the tenant uses the property in breach of the lease or fails to make necessary repairs.

Tennessee—66-28-512(a) and (b) (1987 Update). Thirty (30) days notice is required to terminate a month-to-month tenancy. Ten (10) days notice is required to terminate a week-to-week tenancy.

Texas—Property Code 91.001 (1988 Update). If a lease specifies the length of notice required to terminate the tenancy, that time period controls. If a lease does not specify that time period, the statute indicates when the tenancy will terminate, depending on when the notice of termination is given during the rent period. Rather than rely on the statutory procedure, the parties should simply agree in the lease how much notice is required to terminate the tenancy.

Utah—57-16-4 (1988 Update). This statute details rules for terminating mobile home tenancies. Otherwise, no requirements for notice of termination of tenancies were found in Utah.

Vermont—9-4467 (1988 Update). A landlord is required to give thirty (30) days notice to terminate a month-to-month tenancy, and seven (7) days notice to terminate a week-to-week tenancy. A tenant is required to give notice of termination equal to one rental pay period before the date set in the notice of termination.

Virginia—55-222 (1988 Update). Thirty (30) days notice is required to terminate a month-to-month tenancy, and three (3) months notice to terminate a year-to-year tenancy, but 120 days notice is required for any tenancy if the termination is due to rehabilitation of the property or change in use of the building, if the building contains at least 4 rental units.

Washington—59.04.020, .030, .040, .050 (1988 Update). If a tenancy is for a definite term, no notice is required to terminate the tenancy on the date set for the end of the term. Thirty (30) days notice is required to terminate a period-to-period tenancy, such as a month-to-month or week-to-week tenancy. A tenancy is automatically terminated ten (10) days after a landlord gives a tenant notice of nonpayment of rent if the tenant does not pay the rent within that ten (10) days. No notice is required to terminate a tenancy at sufferance.

West Virginia—37-6-5 (1988 Update). Three (3) months notice is required to terminate a year-to-year tenancy. The length of one payment period is the required notice to terminate a periodic tenancy, such as a month-to-month or week-to-week tenancy.

Wisconsin—704.19 (1988 Update). The parties to a lease can agree in writing to a time period for notice of termination that is different from the time periods contained in this statute. Rather than follow the procedure set out in this statute, the parties should agree in their written rental agreement how much time each must give the other to terminate the lease.

Wyoming—(1987 Update). No laws were found requiring notice to terminate tenancies. The written agreement of the parties would therefore control how much notice each party needs to give the other.

Instructions For Blank Residential Rental Agreement (FIG. 8-4)

Figure 8-4 is a blank residential rental agreement. The form has blank spaces with a number under each blank. Before filling any of the blanks, make several photocopies of the form. Use one or more copies as work copies, two as originals, and the rest for future work copies or originals. Fill in a work copy first and be sure it is correct, then enter in the blanks on your final two original agreements.

The following numbered instructions match the numbers under the blanks in the form:

(1) Enter the date the rental agreement begins.

(2) Enter the duration of the agreement. If the agreement is from month-to-month, enter "month-to-month" in this blank. If the duration is from a particular date to another particular date, enter the exact dates and times of day that the agreement begins and ends.

(3) Enter the full name(s) of the landlord(s). Explain what happens if one of the landlords dies before the agreement ends. This was discussed in the explanation of the sample.

(4) Enter the full name(s) of the renter(s). Explain what happens if one of the renters dies before the agreement ends. This was also discussed in the explanation of the sample.

(5) Describe the property being rented. Include a list of any furniture or other personal property the landlord is renting. If this space is not large enough for all the furniture or property, put "See Exhibit A" in this blank, and attach a page to the rental agreement which lists all the personal property. Label the page "Exhibit A" by entering that at the top or bottom of the page. The landlord and renter should sign and date the exhibit.

For a house or land, the description of the property should include the address of the house or land and the legal description of the property if possible. You can obtain the legal description from the landlord's deed to the property. If the space provided is not large enough for the legal description, attach an "Exhibit A" (or "Exhibit B" if "Exhibit A" is a list of furniture) with the legal description on it. Have both parties sign and date the exhibit.

Staple all exhibits to the rental agreement.

(6) Enter the total amount of the rent for the entire agreement in words, and then in numbers within the parentheses. After describing the total rent, describe the amounts of any monthly or other regular payments, including when regular payments are due. See the sample and explanation of the sample for wording that you can use in this space.

(7) Enter the address where the renter should pay rent.

(8) Enter the number of adults allowed to occupy the property.

(9) Enter the number of children allowed to occupy the property.

(10) Enter the number of pets allowed to occupy the property. If no pets are allowed, put "none" in this blank.

(11) Enter the type of pets allowed, if applicable.

(12) Describe the requirements for termination of the agreement. Refer to FIG. 8-3 to determine whether or not your state has special requirements for notices of termination of the type of tenancy involved in your agreement.

(13) Explain who is responsible for paying each utility. Explain who is responsible for making and paying for repairs. See the sample for an example of wording that you can use here.

(14) Enter the name(s) of the owner(s) of the rental property.

(15) Enter the address(es) of the owner(s).

(16) Enter the telephone number(s) of the owner(s).

(17) Enter the address where the renter should send notices to the landlord.

(18) Enter the name(s) of the manager(s) of the rental property. If the manager(s) is (are) the landlord(s), put the name(s) of the landlord(s) here.

(19) Enter the address(es) of the manager(s). If the manager(s) is (are) the landlord(s), put the address(es) of the landlord(s) here.

(20) Enter the telephone number(s) of the manager(s). If the manager(s) is(are) the landlord(s), put the telephone number(s) of the landlord(s) here.

(21) Enter a telephone number the renter can call in case of an emergency.

(22) Enter the correct mailing address of the renter.

(23) Enter the provisions for a security deposit, if there are any. If there are none, enter "none" in this blank. See the sample, the explanation of the sample, and FIG. 8-2 for a full discussion of security deposits.

(24) Enter any additional provisions of the rental agreement. If there are none, put "none" in this blank.

(25) Enter the date that the parties sign the two original rental agreements.

(26) Enter the address where the agreements are signed.

(27) The landlord(s) should sign their full name(s) on both originals on these lines.

(28) The renter(s) should sign their full name(s) on both originals on these lines.

After the rental agreement is completed, signed, and dated, and the exhibits attached (if any), the landlord should keep one original rental agreement, and the renter should keep the other.

Fig. 8-4. Residential Rental Agreement (Blank). *Page of 1 of 4* **133**

Residential Rental Agreement

1. Duration. This rental agreement begins at 12:01 A.M. on _____
(1)

_____ and continues as follows: _____
(2)

_____

_____

_____.

2. Parties. This agreement is between _____
(3)

_____

_____,

referred to as "landlord", and _____
(4)

_____

_____,

referred to as "renter". Even if there is more than one landlord or renter, the parties will be referred to in the singular.

3. Description. Landlord agrees to rent to renter, and renter agrees to rent from landlord, the residence described as _____
(5)

_____

_____

_____

_____.

4. Rent. The total amount of the rent for this rental agreement shall be

_____
(6)

_____ ($_____),
(6)   (6)

payable as follows: _____
(6)

_____

_____

_____

_____.

Rent is payable to the landlord at _____
(7)

_____.

5. Liens and encumbrances. Renter agrees not to allow any liens or encumbrances to attach to the property during the term of this agreement.

6. Occupants and pets. No more than _____ adults, and _____
₍₈₎ ₍₉₎

children shall occupy the property. No more than _____ _____
₍₁₀₎ ₍₁₁₎

_____ shall occupy the property as pets. The renter shall use the rented
property as a residence only.

7. Violation of laws. Renter shall not violate any city ordinance, state law, or
other law in or about the property.

8. Subletting. Any attempt by renter to sublet, assign, or in any way transfer the
property, any part of the property, or the renter's rights in this agreement without the
landlord's prior written consent is void.

9. Termination. Either party may terminate this agreement as follows:

_____
(12)

_____

_____

_____

_____.

If, however, either party breaches any provision of this agreement, the non-breaching
party shall have all the rights allowed by state law, including the right to terminate this
rental agreement if allowed by state law, and pursue any remedies allowed by law. Upon
termination of this tenancy, the renter agrees to promptly and peacefully surrender the
premises to landlord.

10. Maintenance. Renter shall maintain the property in a clean and sanitary
condition at all times. Renter shall not do anything on the property that will make voidable,
or increase the premium for, landlord's insurance on the property. Renter shall not make
any alterations to the property or change the locks on the property without the prior
written consent of the landlord. At the termination of the tenancy, renter shall surrender
the property to landlord in as good a condition as when received, except for ordinary
wear and tear.

11. Representations and utilities. Landlord represents to renter that landlord owns
the property being rented and has the right to rent this property to renter. Landlord also
represents that renter shall have the quiet enjoyment of the property during the period
of this rental agreement, and that the property is habitable. Landlord further agrees
to supply utilities capable of producing hot and cold running water and adequate heating
for the property. The parties will pay for utilities and repairs as follows:

_____
(13)

_____

_____

_____.

12. Liability for damages. Renter agrees to assume all liability for, and hold
landlord harmless from, all damages to people or property caused by renter, renter's
family, or renter's guests on any part of the property. "Damages" includes any costs
and attorney's fees that the landlord incurs in defending any lawsuit or other action.

Fig. 8-4. (Cont'd). *Page 3 of 4* **135**

13. Expenses. If either party incurs any expenses to enforce any provision of this agreement, including reasonable attorney's fees, either before or after either party begins an action in a court, the losing party in the suit or action, or the party defaulting on this agreement if there is no suit or action, shall pay the other party's expenses and reasonable attorney's fees, including attorney's fees at trial and on any appeal of any suit or action.

14. Owner. The owner(s) of this property is/are _____
(14)

_____

_____,

whose address(es) is/are _____
(15)

_____

_____,

and whose telephone number(s) is/are _____
(16)

_____.

The address to be used for sending notices to the landlord required by this agreement is

_____
(17)

_____.

The manager(s) of the property is/are _____
(18)

_____,

whose address(es) is/are _____
(19)

_____

_____,

and whose telephone number(s) is/are _____
(20)

_____.

Renter can call the following telephone number in case of an emergency:

_____
(21)

The address to which the landlord should send notices to the renter is _____
(22)

_____

_____.

15. Mortgages. Renter agrees that this rental agreement is subordinate to all existing mortgages and other encumbrances on this property at the time of signing this rental agreement. The renter also agrees that during the term of this rental agreement the landlord may place mortgages or other encumbrances on the property, as long as they do not interfere with renter's use of the property.

16. Access. Renter shall allow landlord reasonable access to the rented property to inspect the property or to repair any portion of the property. Landlord must exercise this right of access reasonably, and shall not use it to harass the renter in any way. Landlord shall give the renter reasonable notice before inspecting or repairing the property.

17. Insurance on personal property. Renter acknowledges that landlord is not responsible for insuring any of renter's personal property.

18. Destruction—eminent domain. Landlord and renter agree that in the event more than half of the property being rented is destroyed by fire or other loss, or is taken by eminent domain, this rental agreement shall become void at the option of either the landlord or the renter.

19. Complete agreement. This is the complete and final agreement of the parties regarding rental of the property described in this agreement. This agreement replaces any prior written or oral agreements regarding this property.

20. Security deposit. Landlord and renter make the following agreement regarding

a security deposit: _____
(23)

_____

_____

_____

_____

_____

_____.

21. Additional provisions. _____
(24)

_____

_____

_____.

22. Satisfaction with property. Renter agrees that renter has personally inspected the property and finds it satisfactory at the time of signing this agreement. The parties agree that they have both read all the provisions contained in this agreement. The parties agree that they have not made any promises that this agreement does not contain.

23. Execution of rental agreement. The parties have signed two originals of this

agreement on _____ at _____
(25)   (26)

_____.

By signing this agreement, each party acknowledges receipt of one original agreement.

_____   _____
(27)   (28)
Landlord   Renter

_____   _____
(27)   (28)
Landlord   Renter

Chapter 9
Personal Property Rental Agreement

A rental agreement for personal property is an agreement in which the owner of personal property, for a fee, allows a renter to temporarily use the owner's property.

Personal property includes goods and movable objects, such as cars, boats, and lawn mowers. Personal property does not include real property, such as land or buildings attached to land.

An owner should use a written personal property rental agreement to protect himself or herself against the renter not living up to his or her agreement with the owner, and against the renter injuring someone or damaging property while using the rented property. A renter should have a written rental agreement because it is the renter's proof that he or she has the right to use the property.

This chapter covers rental agreements where the owner and renter intend the renter to return the property at the end of the rental agreement. Some rental agreements are really sales of property. They provide that, at the end of the agreement, the renter owns the property without paying any more money for the property. This chapter does not cover such "rent-town" agreements.

This chapter provides samples and forms for personal property rental agreements where the owner is not normally in the business of renting personal property. Certain federal and state laws apply to personal property rental agreements where the owner is regularly in the business of renting personal property. These laws are complicated and beyond the scope of this book.

PRECAUTIONS

If a renter hurts someone or damages property while using rented property, the injured party may have the right to sue and recover damages from the owner of the property. In some states, the owner can be held responsible for these damages unless the owner used extraordinary care, not just ordinary care, in maintaining the personal property.

Owners can do three things to protect themselves in these situations. First, an owner should have adequate insurance. Liability insurance is insurance for injuries to people and their property from the renter's use of the property. Adequate liability insurance should be at a minimum $100,000 per injured person and $300,000 per accident. But the more, the better. If you can afford the premiums, $1,000,000 coverage per accident adequately protects most people.

Adequate insurance for damage to the rented property means insurance on the property for its full replacement value or full insurable value. Full replacement value insurance means that if the renter destroys the property, the insurance company will pay to replace the property, not just pay the value of the property at the time of destruction. The replacement value is usually higher than the value at the time of destruction. Full insurable value means insurance equal to the market value of the property. If an insurance company will not issue a replacement value insurance policy for property, the property should be insured for at least its full insurable value. The owner can obtain this insurance himself and/or require the renter to obtain it. See Paragraph 6 of the explanation of the sample, on page 139.

The second thing an owner can do to protect against lawsuits involving rented property is to keep detailed maintenance records for the property. The owner should have a separate file for each vehicle or other major item of personal property. In that file, the owner should keep receipts from mechanics or other specialists who repaired or performed maintenance work on the property. The file should also include a maintenance checklist which shows who did maintenance on the property and when and what maintenance was done.

The third thing an owner can do to protect against lawsuits involving rented property is to have the renter and a mechanic or other specialist certify in writing that the property is in good condition at the time the rental agreement is signed. If it is not practical to have a mechanic certify the condition of the property, the owner and renter should inspect the property and certify that it is in good condition.

The renter and owner might want to photograph the property at the time the renter takes possession of it. This could avoid future arguments about the condition of the property at the time the rental agreement began.

Sample Personal Property Rental Agreement (FIG. 9-1)

The numbered paragraphs below match the numbered paragraphs of the sample personal property rental agreement (FIG. 9-1).

1. Date and parties. Every rental agreement should state the date that the parties sign it, the names of all the parties to the agreement, and what happens if one of the parties dies before the agreement ends. Most husbands and wives want the survivor to continue to make or receive payments under the agreement when one of them dies, without having to go through a probate court. A probate court manages a deceased person's affairs.

The sample agreement contains wording to allow the survivor of one of the owners or renters to continue to make or receive payments without having to go through a probate court. That wording is "as joint tenants, to be held jointly with right of survivorship, not as tenants in common". The parties do not want a *tenancy in common*. When one joint owner dies in a tenancy in common, a probate court manages the deceased person's interest in the agreement. The probate court will transfer that interest to whomever is named to receive it in the deceased person's will. If the deceased person has no will, the probate court will transfer the interest to whomever is entitled to it under state law.

2. Property. A rental agreement should describe the property that the owner is renting, including the year, make, and model, and any serial, identification, model, and license numbers that the property may have. If the property does not have any serial or other numbers, the description should give enough identifying information to avoid any confusion as to what property the owner is renting.

3. Duration. Every rental agreement should describe the duration of the agreement. The sample agreement is a one-year agreement. Whatever the duration, the agreement should describe the exact times and dates that the agreement begins and ends.

4. Rent. The agreement should state the total amount of rent to be paid under the agreement, the amount of any monthly or other regular payments, the date or dates when regular payments, the date or dates when regular payments are due, and where rent is due. The agreement should describe the amount of rent in words and in numbers.

5. Deposit. A security deposit is a refundable sum of money that the renter gives the owner to repair any damage that the renter does to the property. The owner should keep the deposit in a separate interest-bearing account, especially when the rental agreement will last for several months or more. The owner should give the renter a written accounting of any sums deducted from the security deposit, and give the reasons for those deductions.

6. Insurance and damages. A rental agreement should require the renter to adequately insure the property. Adequate insurance was discussed earlier in this chapter. For vehicles, the agreement should require adequate comprehensive, liability, and collision insurance. For other personal property, the agreement should require adequate insurance against damage to the property and adequate liability insurance. If the renter has adequate collision insurance or insurance against damage to the property, the renter will have insurance money to repair the property or to pay the owner in full for the property if the renter damages the property. Adequate liability insurance protects the owner and renter against lawsuits for injuries to people and property that result from the renter's use of the property.

By requiring that insurance policies name the owner as a loss payee, the owner ensures that the owner will receive any insurance money for damage to the property. The insurance check will have the owner's name on it. The renter cannot cash the check without the owner's signature.

A personal property rental agreement should provide a method by which the owner can demand that the renter prove to the owner that the renter has the insurance required by the contract. The sample agreement contains language to accomplish this. It requires the renter to give the original policy to the owner. The sample rental agreement also provides that the owner can obtain adequate insurance for the property, and charge the renter for it, if the renter fails to obtain the insurance.

By providing that the owner must receive ten days written notice before any insurance policy is cancelled, the sample agreement ensures that the owner will know if the renter's insurance is about to be cancelled. This gives the owner an opportunity to contact the renter and demand that the renter obtain adequate insurance. This also gives the owner the opportunity to obtain adequate insurance if the renter does not.

7. Use of property. This paragraph protects the owner against the renter's misuse of the property. Every rental agreement should explain what the parties do and do not intend the property to be used for. Also, every rental agreement should explain where the property is or is not to be used.

8. Maintenance. The agreement should require the renter to maintain the property in good condition and to repair any damage to the property. The agreement should prohibit the renter from changing the property in any way, other than to repair it.

9. Inspection. This paragraph gives the owner the right to make sure that the renter is keeping the property in good condition and using it for the purposes that the renter is supposed to be using it for. By saying the owner's access must be reasonable, this paragraph prevents the owner from using this right to harass the renter.

10. Return of property. The agreement should describe when and where the renter should return the property.

11. Termination. Paragraph 3 tells when the normal termination of the agreement is. In addition, the rental agreement should provide a method of terminating the agreement quickly if either party breaches the agreement. Different states have different requirements as to how to terminate a rental agreement when one party breaches the agreement. The agreement provides that if one party breaches it, the other party has all the rights allowed by state law. The non-breaching party should consult a local attorney when the other party breaches the agreement. Do not try to represent yourself in a situation where another party has breached an agreement with you.

If the renter breaches the agreement, the sample allows the owner to repossess the property if the owner does not "breach the peace." Before any owner tries to repossess property, the owner should consult a local attorney to make sure that the owner does not "breach the peace" in doing so. An owner who "breaches the peace" in repossessing property can be sued for money damages by the renter.

12. Taxes and fees. There may be sales, personal property, or other taxes, or license and other fees owed on the property during the term of the agreement. By making it clear who is to pay for these, the agreement avoids any future dispute about such taxes and fees.

13. Assignment. Every rental agreement should describe whether the renter can sublet or assign the lease. *Assignment* means that the renter transfers all of the renter's rights in the rental agreement to someone else. *Subletting* means the renter transfers less than all of the renter's rights in the rental agreement to someone else. If the rental agreement does not prohibit the renter from subletting or assigning, the renter can sublet or assign his or her rights in the property and in the agreement. Most owners would not want the renter to be able to sublet or assign the property or the agreement without the owner's prior written consent. This consent gives the owner the right to refuse to rent to anyone the owner does not wish to rent the property to.

14. Liens and encumbrances. Every rental agreement should require that the renter not allow any liens or other encumbrances to attach to the property. An *encumbrance* is someone else's right or interest in the property (i.e., someone other than the owner or renter). For instance, a mechanic who performed work on the property could have a mechanic's lien on the property, which is one type of encumbrance on property. A bank loan on property is another type of encumbrance.

15. Complete agreement. A rental agreement should state that it is the complete and final agreement of the parties. It should replace any other written or oral agreements that the parties may have regarding the property. Often the parties will say things about the property that are not in the written agreement. A person may find it difficult to prove what someone else said. For that reason, put in the written agreement all the terms of the agreement between the parties.

16. Attorney's fees. A rental agreement should state that if one party incurs expenses to enforce any provision of the agreement, including attorney's fees, the other party should have to pay those expenses and attorney's fees. Without this clause, a person who has to pay an attorney to force the other party to abide by the agreement usually cannot force the other party to pay for the attorney's fees.

17. Condition of property. The renter wants the owner to represent that the property is in good, safe working condition. If the owner is going to make this representation, the owner should be sure that it is accurate. As explained earlier in this chapter, the owner should have records showing the maintenance and repair work performed on the property. Also, the owner should require the renter to acknowledge that the renter has had an opportunity to inspect the property, has inspected it, and is satisfied that it is in good working condition at the beginning of the rental agreement.

The least expensive way to satisfy the needs of the owner and renter as to the condition of the property is for them to share the expense of having an expert inspect the property before it is rented. This gives the renter the best insurance as to the condition of the property, and it shows the owner's care in providing safe property to the renter.

18. Registration and title. If an owner rents property that has a certificate of title and registration, such as the automobile in the sample agreement, the owner should keep the certificate of title in the owner's name and possession. The owner should keep the registration in the owner's name, but should leave the registration in the automobile. The renter should keep the original rental agreement in the vehicle. If a police officer questions the renter's right to operate the automobile, the renter can show the officer the original agreement as proof of the renter's right to possession of the automobile.

19. Additional provisions. This paragraph is for any additional provisions that the owner or renter may wish to include.

20, 21. Execution of the rental agreement. A rental agreement should describe the date and place of its signing. All parties should sign two originals, so each party can keep one original. The parties should sign the agreements in the presence of a notary public for the state where the owner lives, which should be the same state where the parties sign the agreement.

Personal Property Rental Agreement

1. Date and parties.   This agreement is entered into on the 4th day of June 1989, by John M. Jones and Mary J. Jones, husband and wife, as joint tenants, to be held jointly with right of survivorship, not as tenants in common, as owners and lessors, whose address is 222 Third Street, Waynecastle, Pennsylvania, 17294, and Robert L. Williams and Jane F. Williams, husband and wife, as joint tenants, to be held jointly with right of survivorship, not as tenants in common, as renters, whose address is 612 W. Fourth Street, Waynecastle, PA 17294. Even though there is more than one lessor and renter, the parties will be referred to in the singular.

2. Property.   Owner hereby rents to renter, and renter hereby rents from owner, a 1984 Ford Squire Stationwagon automobile, Serial No. 1234, Vehicle ID No. 61984, License No. AJ416.

3. Duration.   This rental agreement shall begin on June 4, 1989, at 6:00 P.M., and shall end on June 3, 1990, at 11:59 P.M.

4. Rent.   As consideration for owner renting this property to renter, renter shall pay to owner the total sum of One Thousand Two Hundred Dollars ($1,200.00), to be paid as follows: One Hundred Dollars ($100.00) each month, payable on or before the fourth day of each month, beginning with the month of June, 1988, and continuing until the end of this agreement. Renter shall make payments at or send payments to owner's address listed above, unless owner notifies renter in writing to make the payment at a different address.

5. Deposit.   Renter hereby gives owner Five Hundred Dollars ($500.00), receipt of which owner hereby acknowledges, as a security deposit. Owner shall use this security deposit only as compensation for damage or for the repair of damage to the rented property caused by renter or renter's business guests, social guests, agents or family members cause. Owner shall keep this deposit in an interest-bearing account, and shall notify renter of the name and address of the bank where the account is located. Owner agrees that within ten (10) days after the renter returns the rented property, owner will return this deposit to renter, with accrued interest. If owner has made any deductions from this deposit, owner shall, within ten (10) days of renter's return of the property, give renter an itemized statement detailing those deductions and the reasons for those deductions.

6. Insurance and damages.   Renter shall at all times keep the property fully insured, by an insurance company acceptable to owner, with comprehensive, liability, and collision insurance. Collision insurance shall be in an amount equal to the full replacement value of the vehicle. If full replacement value insurance is not available, collision insurance shall be in an amount equal to the full insurable value of the vehicle. Liability insurance shall be not less than $100,000 per person and $300,000 per accident. The policy of insurance must contain a loss payee clause naming the owner as loss payee, and must require at least ten (10) days written notice to owner before any insurance required by this agreement can be cancelled.

Fig. 9-1. (Cont'd). *Page 2 of 4* **143**

Renter shall deliver to owner an original policy for the above insurance. If renter does not do so, owner shall be entitled to declare a default of this agreement and/or obtain insurance as required by this contract and charge the renter for the cost of that insurance.

Renter shall indemnify owner for any and all damages to the rental property that occur during this rental agreement, except for damage caused by defects in the property not caused by renter's failure to properly maintain the property.

7. Use of property.   Renter shall use the rented property in a careful manner and shall not violate any laws, rules, or regulations regarding the property. Renter shall not use the property in any illegal, dangerous, racing, or competitive manner, or for commercial purposes, or for any purpose for which the property was not built or designed such as towing another vehicle. Renter shall not allow the property to be used by anyone other than renter without owner's written consent. Renter shall not remove the property from the states of Pennsylvania, New York, New Jersey, or Connecticut without owner's written consent, and shall not remove any equipment from the property without owner's written consent.

8. Maintenance.   Renter shall be responsible for maintaining the rented property and keeping it in good repair and good working order. Renter shall not alter the property in any way except to keep it in good repair and maintenance.

9. Inspection.   Renter shall allow owner reasonable access to the property to inspect it.

10. Return of property.   Renter shall return the property to owner at 222 Third Street, Waynecastle, Pennsylvania 17294, on or before the date set for the end of this agreement.

11. Termination.   This agreement shall end when described above, or sooner, at the option of the non-breaching party, if either party breaches any of the terms of this agreement. If there is such a breach, each party shall have the rights provided by the laws of the Commonwealth of Pennsylvania Owner's rights shall include the right to immediately take possession of the rented property without notice or demand, as long as owner does so without "breaching the peace".

12. Taxes and fees.   Renter shall be responsible for any sales, personal property, or other taxes, and for any license or other fees owed on the rented property during the term of this agreement.

13. Assignment.   Any attempt by renter to sublet, assign, or in any way transfer the property or renter's rights in this agreement without owner's prior written consent shall be void.

14. Liens and encumbrances.   Renter agrees that renter will not allow any liens or encumbrances to attach to the property during the term of this agreement.

15. Complete agreement.   This agreement is the complete and final agreement of the parties regarding rental of the property described above. This agreement replaces and makes void any prior oral or written agreements regarding this property.

16. Attorney's fees.   If either party incurs any expenses to enforce any provision of this agreement, including reasonable attorney's fees, either before or after an action is begun in a court, the losing party in the court action, or the party defaulting on this agreement if there is no lawsuit, shall pay the other party's expenses, including reasonable attorney's fees at trial and upon appeal of any trial.

17. Condition of property—warranties.   Owner represents that the property rented is in good and safe working condition and that to the best of the owner's knowledge the property has no material defects. Renter acknowledges that renter has had an opportunity to inspect the property and to have an expert mechanic or other specialist inspect the property. Renter has inspected the property and is satisfied that the property is in good and safe working condition. The parties agree that there is no equipment on the property that is not working.

18. Registration and title.   The registration and title of the property will remain in owner's name. Owner will keep the title to the property. Renter will keep the registration to the property in the vehicle at all times.

19. Additional provisions.   None.

20. Date and place of signing.   This agreement is signed on the 4th day of June, 1989, at 2:30 P.M., at 222 Third Street, Waynecastle, Pennsylvania 17294.

21. Signatures and notary.

John M. Jones, Owner   Robert L. Williams, Renter

Mary J. Jones, Owner   Jane F. Williams, Renter

COMMONWEALTH OF PENNSYLVANIA   )

) ss.

COUNTY OF BURR   )

I, Wanda C. Twobucks, a resident of and notary public in and for the commonwealth and county named above, who am duly commissioned and sworn and legally authorized to administer oaths and affirmations, hereby certify that on June 4, 1989, John M. Jones, Mary J. Jones, Robert L. Williams and Jane F. Williams, who are known to me personally to be the signers of the above rental agreement, appeared before me and, after being

Fig. 9-1. (Cont'd). *Page 4 of 4* **145**

first duly sworn by me under penalty of perjury, swore on their oaths to the truth of the facts in the above agreement, and signed and acknowledged said agreement in my presence, of their own free will, and for the purposes explained in said agreement.

Subscribed and sworn to before me this 4th day of June, 1989.

_____

Notary Public
My commission expires: 02/09/90

(SEAL)

Instructions for Blank Personal Property Rental Agreement (FIG. 9-2)

Figure 9-2 is a blank rental agreement for personal property. The form has blank spaces with a number under each space. Before filling in any of the blanks, make several photocopies of the form. Use one copy as a work copy, two as originals, and the rest for future work copies or originals. Fill in the work copy first and be sure it is correct, then type or print in the blanks on your two original agreements.

The following numbered instructions match the numbers under the blanks in the form:

(1,2,3) Enter the day, month, and year that the owner and renter sign the agreement.

(4) Enter the full name(s) of the owner(s) of the property. If there is more than one owner, use the appropriate wording to create joint ownership with right of survivorship, if the owners desire that. See the sample and explanation of the sample for wording to create this type of joint ownership.

(5) Enter the address(es) of the owner(s).

(6) Enter the full name(s) of the renter(s). Again, use the appropriate wording for joint ownership if the renters desire that.

(7) Enter the address(es) of the renter(s).

(8) Enter a full and accurate description of the property rented. Include any model, title, serial, and license numbers, the year of manufacture, the brand name, any equipment or attachments included with the property, and any other information necessary to make it clear beyond doubt what property the agreement refers to.

(9) Enter the date the agreement begins.

(10, 11) Enter the hour when the agreement begins, including whether the hour is A.M. or P.M.

(12) Enter the date the agreement ends.

(13,14) Enter the hour when the agreement ends, including whether the hour is A.M.SIZE or P.M.

(15) Enter, in words and numbers, the total amount of rent due for the entire rental agreement.

(16) Enter the amount of any regular or monthly payments due, and when the rent is due. If rent is due each month, describe what day of each month it is due, and what month is the first month it is due. See the sample rental agreement for wording you can use for monthly payments. Enter the amount of rent in words and in numbers.

(17) Enter in words and then in numbers any security deposit the owner requires, and describe the agreement of the parties regarding use and return of that security deposit. See the sample and explanation of the sample for a discussion of this. If the owner is not requiring any security deposit, put "none" in this blank.

(18) Enter the amount of liability insurance per person that is required by the owner. If none is required, put "none".

(19) Enter the amount of liability insurance per accident that is required by the owner. If none is required, put "none".

(20) Enter the name(s) of the state(s) where the renter must keep the property.

(21) Enter the address or location where the renter is to return the property at the end of the rental agreement.

(22) Enter the name of the state where the agreement is signed, which should be the same state where the owner resides.

(23) Enter any additional provisions that the parties agree to include in the agreement, such as a registration and title section, if applicable. If there are no additional provisions, enter "none" in this blank.

(24,25,26) Enter the day, month, and year that the agreement is signed.

(27,28) Enter the hour when the agreement is signed, including whether the hour is A.M. or P.M..

(29) Enter the address where the agreement is signed.

(30) The owner(s) should sign their full name(s) on these lines on each of two original agreements in the presence of a notary public.

(31) The renter(s) should sign their full name(s) on these lines on each of two original agreements in the presence of a notary public.

The following items should be complete by a notary public:

(32) Enter the state where the notary public is authorized to notarize documents.

(33) Enter the county where the notary public is authorized to notarize documents.

(34) Enter the name of the notary public.

(35) Enter the date the parties sign the agreement.

(36) Enter the name(s) of the owner(s) and renter(s).

(37,38,39) Enter the day, month, and year that the parties sign the agreement.

(40) The notary public should sign his or her name here.

(41) The notary public should indicate the date his or her commission expires.

(42) The notary public should affix his or her seal to the agreement next to his or her signature.

After the parties sign two original agreements, the owner(s) should keep one original agreement. The renter(s) should keep the other. The owner(s) should give the renter(s) possession of the personal property at the same time that the parties sign the agreements.

Personal Property Rental Agreement

1. Date and parties. This agreement is entered into on the _____ day of
(1)

_____, _____, by _____
(2) (3) (4)

_____

_____

_____,

as owner(s) and lessor(s), whose address(es) is/are _____
(5)

_____,

_____

and _____
(6)

_____

_____,

as renter(s), whose address(es) is/are _____
(7)

_____

_____.

Even if there is more than one owner or renter, the parties will be referred to in
the singular.

2. Property. Owner hereby rents to renter, and renter hereby rents from owner,

_____
(8)

_____

_____

_____.

3. Duration. This rental agreement shall begin on _____,
(9)

at _____, _____ .M., and shall end on _____
(10) (11) (12)

at _____, _____ .M.
(13) (14)

4. Rent. As consideration for owner renting this property to renter, renter shall

pay to owner the total sum of _____ (\$ _____)
(15)

to be paid as follows: _____
(16)

_____

_____

_____

_____.

Renter shall make payments at or send payments to owner's address listed above, unless owner notifies renter in writing to make payments at a different address.

5. Deposit. The parties make the following agreement regarding a security deposit:

_____
(17)
_____
_____
_____
_____
_____
_____
_____.

6. Insurance and damages. Renter shall at all times keep the property fully insured; by an insurance company acceptable to owner, with comprehensive and liability coverage, and coverage for damage to the property. Insurance against damage to the property shall be in an amount equal to the full replacement value of the property. If full replacement value insurance is not available for the property, such insurance should be in an amount equal to the full insurable value of the property. Liability insurance shall be not less than \$_____
(18)
per person, and \$_____ per accident. Insurance
(19)
policies must contain a loss payee clause naming the owner as loss payee, and must require at least ten (10) days written notice to owner before any insurance required by this agreement can be cancelled.

Renter shall deliver to owner an original policy for the above insurance. If renter does not do so, owner shall be entitled to declare a default of this agreement and/or obtain insurance as required by this contract and charge the renter for the cost of that insurance.

Renter shall indemnify owner for any and all damages to the rented property that occur during this rental agreement, except for damage caused by defects in the property not caused by renter's failure to properly maintain the property.

7. Use of property. Renter shall use the rented property in a careful manner and shall not violate any laws, rules, or regulations regarding the property. Renter shall not use the property in any illegal, dangerous, racing, or competitive manner, or for commercial purposes, or for any purpose for which said property was not built or designed, such as towing another vehicle if the rented property is a vehicle. Renter shall not allow the property to be used by anyone other than renter without owner's written consent. Renter shall not remove the property from the states of

_____
(20)
_____

without owner's written consent, and shall not remove any equipment from the property without owner's written consent.

Fig. 9-2. (Cont'd). *Page 3 of 5* **149**

8. Maintenance.   Renter shall be responsible for maintaining the rented property and keeping it in good repair and good working order. Renter shall not alter the property in any way except to keep it in good repair and maintenance.

9. Inspection.   Renter shall allow owner reasonable access to the property to inspect it.

10. Return of property.   Renter shall return the property to owner at _____
(21)

on or before the date set for the termination of this agreement.

11. Termination.   This agreement shall end when described above, or sooner, at the option of the non-breaching party, if either party breaches any of the terms of this agreement. If there is such a breach, each party shall have the rights

provided by the laws of the State of _____ Owner's rights shall include
(22)

the right to immediately take possession of the rented property without notice or demand, as long as owner does so without "breaching the peace".

12. Taxes and fees.   Renter shall be responsible for any sales, personal property, or other taxes, and for any license or other fees owed on the rented property during the term of this agreement.

13. Assignment.   Any attempt by renter to sublet, assign, or in any way transfer the property or renter's rights in this agreement without owner's prior written consent shall be void.

14. Liens and encumbrances.   Renter agrees that renter will not allow any liens or encumbrances to attach to the property during the term of this agreement.

15. Complete agreement.   This agreement is the complete and final agreement of the parties regarding rental of the property described above. This agreement replaces and makes void any prior oral or written statements regarding this property.

16. Attorney's fees.   If either party incurs any expenses to enforce any provision of this agreement, including reasonable attorney's fees, either before or after an action is begun in a court, the losing party in the court action, or the party defaulting on this agreement if there is no lawsuit, shall pay the other party's expenses, including reasonable attorney's fees at trial and upon appeal of any trial.

17. Condition of property—warranties.   Owner represents that the property rented is in good and safe working condition and that to the best of the owner's knowledge the property has no material defects. Renter acknowledges that renter has had an opportunity to inspect the property and to have an expert mechanic or other specialist inspect the property. Renter has inspected the property and is satisfied that the property is in good and safe working condition. The parties agree that there is no equipment on the property that is not working.

18. Additional provisions. _____
(23)

_____

_____

_____

_____

_____

_____

_____

_____

_____

19. Date and place of signing. This agreement is signed on the _____ day (24)

of _____, _____, at _____ o'clock, _____ .M., at
(25)   (26)   (27)   (28)

_____
(29)

_____

Signatures and notary.

_____ Owner (30)	_____ Renter (31)
_____ Owner (30)	_____ Renter (31)
_____ Owner (30)	_____ Renter (31)

Fig. 9-2. (Cont'd). *Page 5 of 5* **151**

STATE OF _____)
                   (32)

) ss.

COUNTY OF _____)
                   (33)

I, _____ , _____
                (34)

a resident of and notary public for the state and county named above, who am duly commissioned and sworn and legally authorized to administer oaths and affirmations, hereby certify that on _____
                                                        (35)

_____
                  (36)

_____

who are known to me personally to be the signers of the above agreement, appeared before me and, after being first duly sworn by me under penalty of perjury, swore on their oaths to the truth of the facts in the above agreement, and signed and acknowledged said agreement in my presence, of their own free will, and for purposes explained in said agreement.

Subscribed and sworn to before me this _____ day of _____
                                              (37)   (38)

_____.
  (39)

_____
                                   (40)
Notary Public
My Commission Expires: _____

(SEAL)   (41)
(42)

Chapter 10
Deed

A deed is a document that transfers ownership of real property from one person to another. Owning real property is sometimes known as having *title* to the property. The person who signs a deed is the *grantor*. The person receiving a deed is the *grantee*. You cannot transfer title to real estate without a written deed. Written deeds protect grantors and grantees by showing who owns a piece of real estate.

PRECAUTIONS

A grantor gives a deed to a grantee when the grantor sells or gives property to the grantee. The grantee should know whether or not the grantor has the right to transfer the property, and whether or not there are any liens, mortgages, or other *encumbrances* on the property. An encumbrance is the right of someone other than the grantor or grantee in the property. A bank loan on property is an encumbrance. Easements for electric or telephone lines are encumbrances.

The grantee can determine the grantor's right to transfer property and whether or not there are any encumbrances on property by a *title search*. A title search is a search of the public records in the county where the property is located. The search determines the *chain of title*. The chain of a title consists of the links between the present owner of the property and previous owners, going back 30 or more years. Attorneys can search titles, and in some states, title insurance companies search titles.

After an attorney or title company does a title search, a buyer can purchase a title insurance policy which insures that the attorney or title company properly searched the title. If it was not properly searched, the buyer can make a claim against the insurance company for his or her loss, up to the amount of the policy limits. Title insurance companies issue title insurance policies.

When you hire an attorney or title company to search a title and issue a title policy, one of them usually prepares the deed to transfer title. If you decide to prepare your own deed, this chapter will help you prepare a valid deed. A valid deed is not a substitute for a title search and a title insurance policy. A buyer should always have a title search done and purchase a title insurance policy when the buyer is unfamiliar with the seller and the property. In transfers between family members or co-owners of property, a title search and title insurance are not always necessary. Family members or co-owners may know who owns the property and whether or not there are any encumbrances against the property. Sometimes a search of title has been done very recently.

A grantee needs to understand that accepting or buying property without a title search and a title insurance policy involves some risk. The grantee has to consider that risk in deciding whether or not to hire an attorney to search the title and whether or not to purchase a title insurance policy. The risk will be less if the buyer is familiar with the grantor, the property, and the history of the property.

WARRANTIES IN DEEDS

Warranty deeds, special warranty deeds, bargain and sale deeds, grant deeds, and quitclaim deeds are the most common types of deeds. Before you prepare a deed, you have to decide which type of deed you should use for your purposes. In order to do this, you need to understand something about *warranties* of title.

The differences among deeds involve whether or not they include the warranties, sometimes called *covenants*, described below. A covenant or warranty is a statement made by someone that he or she will do or not do certain things or that certain facts exist or do not exist. If a grantor breaks a covenant or warranty, the grantee can sue the grantor for the damages caused by the breach of the covenant or warranty.

Covenant of seisin. Seisin is an Old English word which, loosely translated, means "ownership." When a grantor makes a covenant of seisin, the grantor is saying that he or she owns the interest in the property which he or she is transferring to the grantee.

Covenant of right to convey. This covenant means the grantor has the right to transfer the interest in the property which he or she is transferring to the grantee. This covenant is similar to the covenant of seisin, but not exactly the same. Someone can have the right to convey property without being the owner of the property. For instance, the owner may be incompetent, and the person transferring the property may have the authority to transfer the owner's property.

Covenant against encumbrances. The covenant against encumbrances means that there are no encumbrances against the title of the property. Encumbrances include mortgages, trust deeds, liens, rights of way, easements, and other rights of third parties against the property.

Covenant of quiet enjoyment and covenant of warranty. These two covenants mean the same thing: that the grantor will defend the grantee's right to, and enjoyment of, the property against all lawful claims other people make against the property. For example, if someone tries to claim that he or she obtained a deed to property from the grantor before the grantor gave the grantee a deed to the same property, the grantor will defend the grantee's right to the property against the other person. If necessary, the grantor has to hire an attorney and defend the grantee's right in court.

Covenant for further assurances. The covenant for further assurances means the grantor will do whatever is reasonably necessary to confirm the title of the grantee to the property. For example, if the grantor has to sign other deeds or documents to confirm that the grantee has title to the property, the grantor agrees to sign those documents.

Deeds can contain any combination of the above covenants, or they can contain none of the above covenants.

A *warranty deed* contains all of the above covenants. For that reason, it is to the grantee's advantage to obtain a warranty deed. The more warranties that the grantor makes, the more protection the grantee has.

A *special warranty deed* contains all the above covenants, except it limits the covenant of warranty. In a special warranty deed, the grantor agrees to defend the grantee against claims made by other people who base their claim on something that the grantor did, or something that happened before or while the grantor was owner of the property.

The grantor will not defend the grantee against claims made by someone who bases his or her claim on something that the grantee did, such as give another person an easement across the property.

Special warranty deeds are used when a grantor gives a deed to a grantee under an installment sales contract. In such a case, the grantor gives possession of the property to the grantee when the contract is signed. Because the grantor will not have control over what happens on the property between the signing and the time that the contract is paid in full (which is when the grantor gives the grantee a deed), the grantor does not want to defend the grantee against claims that arise during that period.

The *quitclaim deeds* in this chapter contain none of the above covenants. In a quitclaim deed the grantor says, "I am not saying that I own this property, but if I do own any interest in this property, I will transfer it to this grantee. I will not defend this grantee against claims against this property. I am not saying there are no encumbrances against this property."

Grantors use quitclaim deeds in transfers of property between family members, co-owners, and in resolving disputes about property. Family members and co-owners are often familiar with the property. They may already know who owns the property and whether or not there are any encumbrances against the property. When one party in a dispute agrees to transfer his or her interest in property to another person in settlement of the dispute, the grantor does not want to make warranties about the property. The agreement to settle the dispute may involve the grantor giving up whatever interest he or she may have in the property. In that situation, a quitclaim deed is appropriate.

Grant deeds and *bargain-and-sale deeds* are deeds that have different meanings in different states. Grant deeds and bargain-and-sale deeds contain some of the above warranties, but not all of those warranties. Because of the differences in state laws regarding the meanings of these deeds, this chapter does not provide forms for these deeds. If your situation requires a deed other than a warranty deed, special warranty deed, or quitclaim deed, you should consult an attorney to prepare the deed.

One other warranty that should be mentioned—the warranty as to the condition or quality of the property. A deed should explain what warranties are or are not being made regarding the condition or quality of the property the grantor transfers to the grantee. If a grantor sells or transfers property "as is", the grantor is saying that any problems with the property are the grantee's problems. If the grantor says the property is fit for certain uses, the grantee can hold the grantor to that representation if the property turns out not to be fit for those purposes. If a deed is silent as to the condition of the property, some states imply a warranty that the property is fit for its normal uses.

State Laws on Deeds (FIG. 10-1)

Different states have different laws on how to prepare and record deeds. Figure 10-1 refers to the sections of each state's laws that discuss deeds. You can find these laws by going to a law library in your state. A law library is located at your county courthouse. Ask the librarian to help you find the laws referred to in FIG. 10-1.

Figure 10-1 describes any peculiar requirements a state may have regarding deeds. If no special requirements are mentioned, then the samples and forms in this chapter meet the requirements of a state's laws on deeds.

Different states have different recording requirements that do not affect the validity of the deed. There are so many minor requirements in different states and counties that it is not possible to describe all of those requirements in FIG. 10-1. Employees of recorder's offices are used to helping people add information necessary to record deeds and other documents. Do not be surprised if the employees of the recorder's office in your county have you add additional information or sign additional documents when you record your deed or other documents.

Figure 10-1 is based on 1987 and 1988 laws. The state legislatures of the 50 states meet at different times. Some legislatures only meet once every two years. When a state legislature passes a law, the legislature or a publishing company publishes that law at a later time. Several months can pass before the legislature or publisher sends that law to the libraries around the country. As you read these words, months or years will have passed since this book was edited, printed, and distributed. For these reasons, this book, like all legal books, cannot be absolutely current.

Figure 10-1 indicates whether the information for a particular state is based on the 1987 or 1988 laws of that state. If you want to confirm whether or not your state has changed its laws, go to a law library in your state and read the most current version of the law referred to in FIG. 10-1. Even if the law has changed, the new law will usually have the same number as the old law. Check what are known as the "pocket parts" of your state's laws. Pocket parts are supplements which contain the latest revisions of a state's laws.

Fig. 10-1. State Laws on Deeds.

Alabama—35-4-1, -20, -73, -74, -113 (1987 Update). Special requirements: 35-4-1 requires a person to be at least 19 years of age to sign a deed. 35-4-74 says that if a deed refers to a plat, the deed must have a copy of the plat attached to the deed and incorporate it into the deed.

Alaska—34.15.010 to .350 (1987 Update).

Arizona—33-401 to -513 (1988 Update). Special requirements: 42-1612 requires that a person who records a deed must sign an affidavit including the value of the property the deed transfers, the names and addresses of the sellers and purchasers, the legal description of the property, the date of the sale, the price paid, the amount of any cash down payment, the type of financing if any, the amount of any personal property transferred, the tax code number, and the use and description of the property. You must attach this affidavit to the deed. The recorder's office in your county should have this affidavit.

Arkansas—16-114, 28-919, 49-201 to -203, 49-101 to -115-1, 50-401 to -415, 50-425 (1987 Update). Special requirements: 84-4304 and 84-4305 require that before someone can record a deed, that person must sign a real property affidavit form which he or she can obtain from the county recorder. 84-408-1 requires that a person recording a deed supply a general description of the improvements on land transferred in the deed, if there are any such improvements.

California—Civil Code 1091 to 1134 (1988 Update). Special requirements: A deed must state that it complies with Civil Code Section 1102, which discusses a real estate transfer disclosure statement. People preparing deeds in California should read Civil Code Section 1102. Civil Code 1134 discusses disclosures that a seller must make when selling a unit in a residential condominium, community apartment, or stock cooperative. Such a seller should read Civil Code Section 1134. Civil Code Section 1099 requires that before any transfer of title to property, an expert must prepare a structural pest control inspection report and issue a certification regarding that pest control inspection report. Section 1133 requires a subdivider to give special notices to buyers if the subdivider has a blanket encumbrance on a unit of a subdivision.

Colorado—12-55-201 to -211, 38-30-101 to -168, 38-35-101 to -122 (1987 Update). Special requirement: 38-35-122 requires that a deed include the street address of the property transferred in the deed, immediately before or after the legal description of the property.

Connecticut—1-28 to -41, 47-1 to -36 (1987 Update).

Delaware—25-101 to -174, 25-301 to -312 (1987 Update). Special requirements: 25-313 requires a grantor to make certain disclosures regarding public sewerage and water facilities in the sale of unimproved real estate. A seller in such a sale should read Section 25-313. Section 9-9605(h) (i) requires that a seller of property sign an affidavit of residence and of gain upon selling property. A seller can obtain this affidavit from the recorder's office in the county where the property is located.

Fig. 10-1. (Cont'd). 157

District of Columbia—45-101 to -119, -201 to -223, -305, -402, -501 to -509, -601 to -612, -901 to -944 (1988 Update). Special requirements: 45-502 requires that in a deed signed by a corporation, the corporation must acknowledge signing the deed by appointing an attorney for that purpose. The written authorization appointing an attorney to sign the deed must be attached to and recorded with the deed. 45-508 requires that all conveyances include a statement of the soil characteristics of the property transferred. A seller in Washington, D.C. should read Section 45-508 for details on what that law requires.

Florida—Chapter 689 (1988 Update). Special requirements: 201.022 requires that upon recording a deed, a grantor or grantee must file certain documents with the clerk of the circuit court in the county where the property is located. You can obtain these documents from the recorder's office in your county. 689.02 requires that a deed have a blank space for the property appraiser's identification number.

Georgia—Title 44 in general and 44-5-30 in particular (1988 Update).

Hawaii—Chapter 502 (1987 Update). Special requirements: 502-31 requires that all deeds be on 8½ × 11 inch paper, and that they reserve at least 2½ inches of blank space at the top of the first page of the deed.

Idaho—55-601 to -615, -701 to -817 (1988 Update).

Illinois—30-1 to -39 (1988 Update).

Indiana—32-1-2-1 to -36, 32-1-3-1 and -2, 32-1-9-1 to -3, 32-1-10-1 and -2, 32-2-1-1 to 32-2-6-1 (1988 Update).

Iowa—Chapters 557 and 558 (1988 Update).

Kansas—58-2201 to -2230 (1987 Update). Special requirements: 58-2223(d) contains a certificate of value form for a grantor to sign. The certificate of value must be in the form described in this law. You can obtain this certificate from the recorder's office in your county.

Kentucky—371.010 and .020 (1987 Update).

Louisiana—Civil Code 1839, Revised Statutes 47-2328 (1988 Update). 47-2328 requires that a deed include the municipal or street address of the property transferred.

Maine—33-151 to -480 (1987 Update).

Maryland—Real Property 2-105, -106; 3-101 to -203, -301 to -304; 4-101 to -110, -202(a); 10-101 to -509; 11-101 to -143 (1987 Update). Maryland law states that you must record a deed before it becomes effective. You must pay all taxes owed on property before the recorder will record your deed. You must obtain and complete a form, available from your recorder's office, describing any buildings or improvements on the property that the deed describes. Maryland law contains many specific recording requirements for certain counties, such as Montgomery, Frederick, Prince Georges, Washington, Talbot, and Worcester counties. The recorder's office in your county will tell you these requirements.

Massachusetts—Chapters 183, 183a, 184 (1987 Update). Special requirements: 183-6 and -6b require that the address of the land transferred in the deed be in the margin of the deed.

Michigan—Title 26 (1988 Update). Special requirements: Deeds must certify that someone has paid the real property taxes for the property for the last five years.

Minnesota—Chapter 507 (1988 Update). Special requirements: 507.05 requires that in deeds corporations sign, the corporation must pass a corporate resolution appointing an attorney to convey the real estate. The corporation may record this corporate resolution with the deed. 272.115 and 287.241 require that someone recording a deed file a certificate of value with the tax classification of the property and other information. You can obtain this certificate from the recorder's office in the county where the property is located.

Mississippi—Title 89, Chapters 1, 3, 5, 9 (1987 Update).

Missouri—Chapter 442 (1988 Update).

Montana—Title 70, Chapters 1, 20, and 21 (1987 Update). Special requirements: 15-7-301 to -311 require the filing of a realty transfer certificate when someone transfers property. You can obtain this certificate from the recorder's office in the county where the property is located.

Nebraska—Chapter 76, Articles 1 and 2 (1987 Update). Special requirements: 76.214 requires that a grantee file a statement required by the tax commissioner of Nebraska at the time of recording a deed. This statement includes, among other things, the social security number of the grantee. You can obtain this statement from the tax commissioner's office in Nebraska, or from the recorder's office in the county where the property is located.

Nevada—Title 10 (1987 Update).

New Hampshire—Chapter 477 (1988 Update). Special requirements: Chapter 478 Section 4-A requires that a deed show, in the first line of the legal description of the property, the names of all municipalities in which the property is located.

New Jersey—Title 46 (1988 Update). Special requirements: 46:15-2 says that if a city has Atlas or block maps, you must obtain a certification from the officer responsible for those Atlas or block maps in order to record a deed. The recorder can do this for you if you pay the recorder to do so. New Jersey law also requires that a deed contain references to a property's tax lot and block number.

New Mexico—Chapters 14 and 47 (1987 Update).

New York—Book 49—Real Property Law (1988 Update). Special requirements: Tax Law Article 31-B requires that you obtain a Department of Taxation and Finances statement before you can record a deed. You can obtain that statement from your recorder's office, or from the Department of Taxation and Finance. If a deed refers to a map, you must file a copy of the map when you record the deed. In New York City, if your deed refers to a multiple dwelling, before you can record the deed you have to file a Registration Statement and pay the fees required by 27-2097 of the New York City Administrative Code and the laws that follow it. Ask your county recorder's office about that Statement and those fees. If your deed does not refer to a multiple dwelling, you must sign an affidavit stating that the deed does not refer to a multiple dwelling and that such a Registration Statement is not required. Your recorder's office should have such an affidavit. In order to record a deed in Suffolk County, your deed must have the map designation of the property maps of the real property tax service agency of Suffolk County. Ask the Suffolk County recorder's office how to obtain these map designations.

North Dakota—1-04-01 to -22, and Title 47 (1987 Update).

Ohio—Title 53 (1988 Update). Special requirements: 5301.25 requires that if the property has been surveyed, the deed must include the name of the surveyor. Ohio law also requires that an auditor endorse a deed and show the value of the property in triplicate. You can obtain forms for this from the recorder's office in the county where the property is located.

Oklahoma—Title 16 (1988 Update).

Oregon—Chapter 93 (1987 Update).

Pennsylvania—Title 21 (1988 Update).

Rhode Island—Title 34 (1987 Update).

South Carolina—Titles 26 (Chapter 3), 27, and 30 (1987 Update).

South Dakota—Title 43 (1988 Update). Special requirements: 43-21-1 states that you cannot record a deed describing land by metes and bounds without having the tract platted by a surveyor.

Tennessee—Title 66 (1987 Update). Special requirements: 66-24-113 states that if property is within a metropolitan identification map, the deed must refer to the map's number, or identifying symbol, for the property. Tennessee law also requires that on the first page of the deed, the name and address of the deed's preparer be listed. 66-24-116 lists certain filing and recording restrictions for maps, plats, and surveys. Ask your local recorder's office about these requirements.

Texas—Civil Statutes Articles 1288 to 1301b; Property Code Titles 1, 2, and 3 (1988 Update).

Utah—Title 57 (1988 Update).

Vermont—Title 27 (1988 Update).

Virginia—Title 55 (1988 Update). Special requirements: Virginia law requires that each individual surname in a deed be underscored or capitalized when that name first appears in a deed. Also, Virginia law requires that you number each page of a deed.

Washington—Title 64 (1988 Update).

West Virginia—Chapter 36 (1988 Update). Special requirements: 11-22-6 requires filing a tax commissioner's form upon recording a deed. You can obtain this form from the recorder's office in the county where the property is located.

Wisconsin—Chapter 706.01 to .15 (1988 Update).

Wyoming—Title 34 (1987 Update).

Sample Deeds (FIGS. 10-2) and 10-3)

This section contains two sample deeds. Figure 10-2 is a sample for a general warranty and special warranty deed. It includes all the covenants of title described in the previous section. Figure 10-3 is a sample quitclaim deed. It does not contain any of those covenants.

The following explanation applies to both samples. The numbered paragraphs correspond to the numbered paragraphs in the samples.

1. Parties and date. Every deed must include the date that the grantor signs it. Every deed must describe the parties involved in the deed. Who is transferring the property? Who is receiving the property? Some states require that a deed describe the marital status of the grantor and grantee. A grantor who has changed names during ownership should be identified by all names in the deed.

Quitclaim deeds can be used when one spouse owns property in his or her name and wants to add his or her spouse as an owner of the property. Most husbands and wives want to own their property jointly with right of survivorship, in order to avoid probate. (Probate is the process of managing a deceased person's affairs through a probate court.) In such a case, the spouse who owns the property would be the grantor. The spouse to be added as an owner would be the grantee. Avoiding probate is discussed in detail in Chapter 6 of this book.

If two people own property together, but not with right of survivorship, and are signing a deed to create right of survivorship, both people are the grantors and both are the grantees. If the grantor is married and the grantee is not his or her spouse, make the spouse a grantor, even if that spouse is not an owner of the property.

2. Future tax statements. Some states require deeds to state the name and address where the tax assessor should send future real estate tax statements. Some states require that this information be on the first page of the deed. When a husband or wife signs a quitclaim deed to add his or her spouse as an owner of property, tax statements should be sent to both spouses at their common address. In all other cases, tax statements should be sent to the grantee.

3. Consideration, description of property, words of conveyance, and estate conveyed.
Consideration. Every deed should describe the *consideration* involved in the deed. Consideration is whatever the grantee gives the grantor in exchange for the grantor's transferring the property to the grantee. In the samples, the consideration is $10,000.

Consideration in a deed must be either *good* or *valuable* consideration. Good consideration is consideration that is personal. For instance, transferring property for love and affection is good consideration. Valuable consideration is consideration that has some value. Money is valuable consideration. Cancellation of a debt is valuable consideration. In return for transferring real estate to the grantee, the grantee could forgive a debt owed by the grantor to the grantee. Services or property are also valuable consideration.

When property, services, or cancellation of a debt is the consideration for transfer of property, the deed should state, in terms of money, the value of the property, services, or the cancellation of the debt. In cases where the grantor transfers property to the grantee based on love and affection, the deed should state whether or not the grantor and grantee are blood relatives. Also, some states require that there be some *nominal* consideration in deeds where the consideration is love and affection. Nominal consideration means a small amount of money, such as one dollar.

Description of property. Every deed must describe the property that is being transferred. A deed can refer to a recorded map or plat, or use a description of the property's boundaries from the most recent land survey. If a deed refers to a plat or map, some states require that a copy of the plat or map be attached to the deed and that the deed state when and where the plat was recorded. You can obtain these copies from the clerk's office in your county courthouse. Deeds should include an approximation of the total area of the property, such as "approximately four acres".

Words of conveyance. Every deed must contain some *words of conveyance*. Certain words, such as *convey, grant,* or *quitclaim,* have specific meanings defined by state laws. You must choose the words of conveyance that match the intent of the parties.

In a warranty and special warranty deed, you should use the following words of conveyance: "conveys, grants, gives, bargains, sells, releases, and transfers". These words indicate that the grantor claims to own the property, to have the right to transfer the property, and warrants the property against encumbrances and claims.

You should use the following words of transfer in a quitclaim deed: "releases, transfers, and forever quitclaims". These words indicate that the grantor is not claiming that he or she owns any interest in the property, or has any right to transfer the property.

Estate conveyed. Every deed must describe the *estate* that is transferred. Deeds can transfer present and future ownership of property, or part of the present or future ownership of property. For instance, a *life estate* is ownership of property until death (of the grantor, grantee, or third party, as specified in the deed). A deed giving someone a life estate does not give that person ownership of all of the future interest in the property.

A *fee simple estate* is ownership of all the present and future interest in property.

Estates in land can be very confusing. This chapter will only deal with transfers of fee simples, that is, transfers of all the present and future interest in property. If you need to transfer part of the total ownership of property, you should consult an attorney to prepare the necessary documents.

Every deed should explain what happens if one of the parties involved in the deed dies. Most husbands and wives want the survivor to own property automatically if one of them dies, without having to go through a probate court. The samples contain wording to allow the surviving grantee to own all of the property automatically upon the death of the other grantee, without having to go through a probate court. That wording is "each as to an undivided one-half interest, to be held jointly with right of survivorship, not as tenants in common".

The grantees in both sample deeds do not want a *tenancy in common.* When one joint owner dies in a tenancy in common, a probate court might control the deceased person's interest in the joint property. The probate court may have to transfer the interest in the property to whomever is named to receive it in the deceased person's will. If the deceased person has no will, the probate court may have to transfer the interest to whomever is entitled to it under state law.

When someone is preparing a quitclaim deed to add one other person as a joint owner of property in order to avoid probate upon the death of either person, the estate conveyed is "an undivided one-half interest in the following real property, to be held with grantor's remaining undivided one-half interest jointly with right of survivorship, not as tenants in common". This language should be followed by the description of the property.

When someone is preparing a quitclaim deed to add two other people as joint owners of property in order to avoid probate upon the death of one joint owner, the estate the deed conveys is "each as to an undivided one-third interest in the following real property, to be held with grantor's remaining undivided one-third interest jointly with right of survivorship, not as tenants in common".

When the grantor will not be one of the joint owners after the transfer, or when two people own property together but not with right of survivorship and are signing a deed to create right of survivorship, estate conveyed would be the same as in the sample, "each as to an undivided one-half [or one-third if there are three grantees] interest . . .". If there will only be one owner after the transfer, the deed would read, ". . . transfers to grantee and to grantee's heirs and assigns forever, a fee simple estate in the following real estate:".

Both samples indicate that the deeds transfer the "tenements, hereditaments, and appurtenances belonging to the above property". *Tenements* are houses or buildings on real property. *Hereditaments* are anything someone can inherit, whether real property, personal property, or mixed property. *Appurtenances* are anything belonging to the land and part of the land, such as an easement for a road across property.

4. Covenants. Covenants were explained earlier in this chapter. Figure 10-2 includes all the covenants of title and a covenant as to the condition of the property. Figure 10-3 contains no covenants of title and no covenants as to the condition of the property.

If you are preparing a general warranty deed, you should use the language in Paragraph 4(c) of FIG. 10-2, except for the language that is in the parentheses. The language included in the parentheses only applies to special warranty deeds. If you are preparing a special warranty deed, you should add the wording in the parentheses to the end of the last sentence of Paragraph 4(c) of FIG. 10-2.

The covenant about encumbrances in FIG. 10-2 describes a right-of-way that encumbers the property. Warranty or special warranty deeds should describe all encumbrances against the property that will remain on the property after the deed is signed. The grantor should warrant that there are no encumbrances on the property other than the ones described in the deed. By listing an encumbrance, the grantor makes the grantee aware that the grantee is taking the property subject to that encumbrance, in which case the grantee has to honor the rights of the person who has the encumbrance.

The blank form for a general or special warranty deed (FIG. 10-4) provides space to include utility and other easements and rights-of-way that will remain on the property after transfer of the property from the grantor to the grantee. Do not use the form when a grantee receives property subject to a bank loan or other financing encumbrance. These encumbrances often state that transferring the property without the lender's written consent is a violation of the loan agreement. There may be severe penalties for transfers made without the lender's written consent. If a grantor wants to transfer property that has a financing encumbrance on it, he or she should consult an attorney to review the financing documents, obtain any written consents required, and prepare a deed.

If a grantor wants to transfer property subject to all encumbrances that are recorded, he or she would put in the deed, ". . . subject to all encumbrances of record".

5. Dower, curtesy, homestead, and community property rights. Some states give a husband or wife certain rights in real property owned by his or her spouse. These rights are called *dower rights* on behalf of women, and *curtesy rights* on behalf of men.

In the sample warranty deed, the owner of the property is John M. Jones. His wife is not on the title to the property he is transferring. Even though her name is not on the title, she may have dower rights in the property. The grantees want the wife to release any dower interest she may have in the property so that the wife cannot make a claim against the property after the grantees buy it. For that reason, the wife is listed as a grantor, and has to sign the deed.

Many states have abolished dower and curtesy rights. In the states that still have these rights, a final divorce of the parties that dissolves the marriage of the parties forever will eliminate dower and curtesy rights. For that reason, a grantee only needs to have the present spouse of the grantor give up dower or curtesy rights.

In some states, a husband or wife has homestead, community property, and other rights in his or her spouse's property. A grantee wants the spouse of a grantor to release those rights, so that the spouse of the grantor cannot make a claim against the property based on those rights.

6. *Grantor's source of title.* Some states require deeds to state the name under which the grantor obtained title to the property and a description of the source of the grantor's title. Usually, the grantor obtained title by another deed. In that case, the deed you are preparing should describe the earlier deed, including the name of the preceding grantor, the date it was signed, and the date and place it was recorded.

If the grantor of the new deed obtained title by inheriting property, the new deed should describe from whom and when the grantor inherited the property. It should also describe the manner in which the grantor inherited the property. For instance, if the grantor inherited the property by will, describe the date of the will and the time and place of the will's recording if it is recorded. If the grantor inherited the property from someone who died without a will, describe the date of the court order distributing the property to the grantor and the time and place of the order's recording. If there is no such court order, the new deed should state that the grantor obtained title as the heir of the deceased person, and should state the date, county, and state of the deceased person's death.

7. *Uses of property.* Some states require that deeds tell the grantee to consult local authorities regarding how the grantee may use the property being transferred. A grantee should consult the zoning departments in the city, county, and state where the property is located to find out how the property may and may not be used.

8. *Declaration of value.* Some states require that a deed state the *market value* of the property transferred. Market value is what a willing seller could sell the property for to a willing buyer. This value is usually whatever the consideration for the deed is. That will not necessarily be true in quitclaim deeds prepared to create joint ownership with right of survivorship. See the explanation of the assignment in Chapter 6 for a full discussion of how to value the property transferred in that case.

9. *Date, place, signatures, attestation, and acknowledgment.* Every deed must include the date that the grantor signs it and the signature of the grantor. A deed should describe where it is signed because that may affect which state's laws govern the deed.

Some states require that deeds be witnessed, sometimes called "attested". In those states, deeds must include the signatures of the witnesses in whose presence the grantor signed the deed.

Almost all states require that a deed be *acknowledged* before it can be recorded. An acknowledgment is a statement made under oath by the person signing a deed that he or she is the person the deed names as grantor. An acknowledgment is made before an officer authorized to acknowledge documents, usually a notary public. A deed can be valid without an acknowledgment, but a recorder will not record it without an acknowledgment. Since it is wise to record deeds, as will be explained below, all deeds should be acknowledged.

Individual acknowledgments are different from corporate acknowledgments. An individual acknowledgment is used when the grantor is an individual person. A corporate acknowledgment is used when the grantor is a corporation. The forms at the end of this chapter include both individual and corporate acknowledgments.

In both samples, the word "SEAL" is typed next to the signatures of the grantors. In the past, many states required that a grantor seal his or her signature, which meant that it be imprinted with the seal of the grantor. Most states have eliminated that requirement. Some states retain the requirement, but allow you to meet the requirement by typing the word "SEAL" next to the signature of the grantor.

10. *Delivery and recording.* You may have heard the expression "signed, sealed, and delivered". Paragraph 9, above, discussed signing and sealing a deed. With few exceptions, a grantor must also *deliver* the deed to the grantee with intent to transfer ownership to the grantee. If the grantor keeps the deed after signing it, the deed may not be a valid transfer of the property to the grantee.

Fig. 10-2. General or Special Warranty Deed (Sample). *Page 1 of 3*   **163**

Warranty Deed

1. Parties and date. This warranty deed is made on the 3rd day of January, 1989, by and between John M. Jones and Mary Ellen Jones, husband and wife, whose address is 222 Third Street, Waynecastle, Pennsylvania, 17294, hereafter called "grantors", and Frederick L. Smith and Mary J. Smith, husband and wife, whose address is 333 Fourth Street, Waynecastle, Pennsylvania, 17294, hereafter called "grantees".

2. Future tax statements. Future property tax statements for the property transferred in this deed should be sent to the following names and address: Frederick L. Smith and Mary J. Smith, 333 Fourth Street, Waynecastle, Pennsylvania, 17294.

3. Consideration, description, words of conveyance, and estate conveyed. In consideration of grantees paying grantors the sum of Ten Thousand Dollars ($10,000.00), receipt of which grantors hereby acknowledge, grantors hereby convey, grant, give, bargain, sell, release, and transfer to grantees, each as to an undivided one-half interest, to be held jointly with right of survivorship, not as tenants in common, and to grantees' heirs and assigns forever, a fee simple estate in the following real estate:

"Lot 2, KINGSTON ADDITION to the City of Waynecastle, as referred to and more fully described in the map and plat of said addition, of record in the deed records in the office of the Clerk of the County Court of Burr County, Pennsylvania, in Volume 262, at Page 694, containing approximately 0.20 acres."

To have and to hold the above property by grantees and grantees' heirs and assigns forever, along with all the tenements, hereditaments, and appurtenances belonging to the above property.

4. Covenants. Grantors, for themselves and for their heirs and successors, make the following covenants with grantees and grantees' heirs and assigns:

a) Grantors are the lawful owners of the fee simple estate in the above property and have the right to convey the above property;

b) There are no encumbrances against the above property, except for a right-of-way for a telephone transmission line to Penn West Telephone Company, dated March 6, 1962, and recorded on March 6, 1962, in the office of the above-mentioned clerk in Deed Book 652, at Page 451;

c) Grantors and grantors' heirs and successors will warrant and defend forever the title to the above property against all lawful claims made against the property, (made by anyone claiming by, through, or under grantors);

d) At the expense of grantees or grantees' heirs or assigns, grantors and grantors' heirs and successors will do whatever is reasonably necessary to perfect or confirm the title of grantees or grantees' heirs or assigns to the above property;

e) The above property is fit for the normal uses of such property. All plumbing, heating, electricity, sewer, and other systems on said property are in good working order at the time of transfer of this property.

5. Dower, curtesy, homestead, and community property rights. Mary Ellen Jones, whose address is 222 Third Street, Waynecastle, Pennsylvania, 17294, for the consideration stated above, hereby gives up her right, title, interest, separate estate, dower, and right of dower in the above property, and hereby also gives up any homestead, community property, or other rights she may have in the above property.

6. Grantor's source of title. Grantor John M. Jones acquired the above property under grantor's present name from Joseph A. Johnson, by deed dated May 5, 1974, and recorded in the office of the Clerk of the County Court of Burr County, Pennsylvania, in Deed Book 46, at Page 22.

7. Uses of property. This deed will not allow use of the property it describes in violation of applicable land use laws and regulations. Before signing or accepting this deed, the person acquiring fee title to the property should check with the appropriate city or county planning department to verify approved uses.

8. Declaration of value. The undersigned grantors hereby declare that the true value of the property transferred in this deed is $10,000.00.

9. Date, place, and signatures. IN WITNESS WHEREOF, we have signed this deed on January 3, 1989, at 222 Third Street, Waynecastle, Pennsylvania, 17294.

_____ (SEAL)   _____ (SEAL)

John M. Jones   Mary Ellen Jones

We, Allen M. Johnson and Frederick L. Roth, hereby acknowledge that we witnessed John M. Jones and Mary Ellen Jones, who are both known to us personally, sign the above deed on January 3, 1989, in our presence, and that John M. Jones and Mary Ellen Jones acknowledged to us and it appeared to us that they signed said deed freely and voluntarily.

Dated this 3rd day of January, 1989.

_____   _____

Allen M. Johnson   Frederick L. Roth

555 Sixth Street   777 Eighth Street

Waynecastle, Pennsylvania 17294   Waynecastle, Pennsylvania 17294

Fig. 10-2. (Cont'd). *Page 3 of 3* **165**

COMMONWEALTH OF PENNSYLVANIA

)
) ss.

COUNTY OF BURR   )

I, Wanda C. Twobucks, a resident of and notary public in and for the commonwealth and county named above, who am duly commissioned and sworn and legally authorized to administer oaths and affirmations, hereby certify that on January 3, 1989, John M. Jones and Mary Ellen Jones, who are known to me personally to be the signers of the above deed, appeared before me and, after being first duly sworn by me under penalty of perjury, swore on their oaths to the truth of the facts in the above deed, and signed and acknowledged said deed in my presence, of their own free will, and for the purposes explained in said deed.

Subscribed and sworn to before me this 3rd day of January, 1989.

_____

                           Wanda C. Twobucks
                           Notary Public
    (SEAL)   My commission expires: 2/09/90

This instrument was prepared by Joseph M. Herd, Attorney at Law, whose address is 694 West Fifth Street, Waynecastle, Pennsylvania, 17294.

COMMONWEALTH OF PENNSYLVANIA

)
)
COUNTY OF BURR   ) ss.
)
CITY OF WAYNECASTLE   )

I certify that the above warranty deed was recorded in my office on the 3rd day of January, 1989, at 2:13 o'clock P.M., and is duly recorded in Book 267, at Page 422, of the Deed Records of the above commonwealth, county, and city.

_____

                       Recorder for Burr County, Pennsylvania

By: _____

                       Deputy

Transfer fee: $70.00

Quitclaim Deed

1. Parties and date. This quitclaim deed is made on the 3rd day of January, 1989, by and between John M. Jones, a single man, whose address is 222 Third Street, Waynecastle, Pennsylvania, 17294, hereafter called "grantor", and Frederick L. Smith and Mary J. Smith, husband and wife, whose address is 333 Fourth Street, Waynecastle, Pennsylvania, 17294, hereafter called "grantees".

2. Future tax statements. Future property tax statements for the property transferred in this deed should be sent to the following names and address: Frederick L. Smith and Mary J. Smith, 333 Fourth Street, Waynecastle, Pennsylvania, 17294.

3. Consideration, description, words of conveyance, and estate conveyed. In consideration of grantees paying grantor the sum of Ten Thousand Dollars ($10,000.00), receipt of which grantor hereby acknowledges, grantor hereby releases, transfers, and forever quitclaims to grantees, each as to an undivided one-half interest, to be held jointly with right of survivorship, not as tenants in common, and to grantees' heirs and assigns forever, any and all interest which grantor may have in the following real estate:

"Lot 2, KINGSTON ADDITION to the City of Waynecastle, as referred to and more fully described in the map and plat of said addition, of record in the deed records in the office of the Clerk of the County Court of Burr County, Pennsylvania, in Volume 262, at Page 694, containing approximately 0.20 acres."

To have and to hold the above property by grantees and grantees' heirs and assigns forever, along with all the tenements, hereditaments, and appurtenances belonging to the above property.

4. Covenants. Grantor is not covenanting that grantor is the lawful owner of any estate in the above property, has the right to convey the above property, that there are no encumbrances against the above property, that grantor or grantor's heirs will warrant and defend the property against claims made against the property, or that grantor or grantor's heirs will perfect grantees' title to the property. Grantor is not making any representations as to the condition or quality of the property, which is sold "as is". Grantor and grantees intend this deed to convey to grantees whatever interest grantor may have in the property.

5. Dower, curtesy, homestead, and community property rights. Since grantor is not married, no spouse has any dower, homestead or community property rights in the property transferred herein.

6. Grantor's source of title. Grantor acquired the above property under grantor's present name from Joseph A. Johnson, by deed dated May 5, 1974, and recorded in the office of the Clerk of the County Court of Burr County, Pennsylvania, in Deed Book 46, at Page 22.

Fig. 10-3. (Cont'd). *Page 2 of 3* **167**

7. Uses of property. This deed will not allow use of the property it describes in violation of applicable land use laws and regulations. Before signing or accepting this deed, the person acquiring fee title to the property should check with the appropriate city or county planning department to verify approved uses.

8. Declaration of value. The undersigned grantor hereby declares that the true value of the property transferred in this deed is $10,000.00.

9. Date, place, and signatures. IN WITNESS WHEREOF, I have signed this deed on January 3, 1989, at 222 Third Street, Waynecastle, Pennsylvania, 17294.

(SEAL)

_____

John M. Jones

We, Allen M. Johnson and Frederick L. Roth, hereby acknowledge that we witnessed John M. Jones, who is known to us personally, sign the above deed on January 3, 1989, in our presence, and that John M. Jones acknowledged to us and it appeared to us that he signed said deed freely and voluntarily.

Dated this 3rd day of January, 1989.

Allen M. Johnson	Frederick L. Roth
555 Sixth Street	777 Eighth Street
Waynecastle, Pennsylvania 17294	Waynecastle, Pennsylvania 17294

COMMONWEALTH OF
PENNSYLVANIA   )
) ss.
COUNTY OF BURR   )

I, Wanda C. Twobucks, a resident of and notary public in and for the commonwealth and county named above, who am duly commissioned and sworn and legally authorized to administer oaths and affirmations, hereby certify that on January 3, 1989, John M. Jones, who is known to me personally to be the signer of the above deed, appeared before me and, after being first duly sworn by me under penalty of perjury, swore on his oath to the truth of the facts in the above deed, and signed and acknowledged said deed in my presence, of his own free will, and for the purposes explained in said deed.

Subscribed and sworn to before me this 3rd day of January, 1989.

_____

              Wanda C. Twobucks
              Notary Public
(SEAL)   My commission expires: 2/09/90

This instrument was prepared by Joseph M. Herd, Attorney at Law, whose address is 694 West Fifth Street, Waynecastle, Pennsylvania, 17294.

COMMONWEALTH OF PENNSYLVANIA)
)
COUNTY OF BURR   ) ss.
)
CITY OF WAYNECASTLE   )

I certify that the above quitclaim deed was recorded in my office on the 3rd day of January, 1989, at 2:13 P.M., and is duly recorded in Book 267, at Page 422, of the Deed Records of the above commonwealth, county, and city.

_____

           Recorder for Burr County, Pennsylvania

By: _____

               Deputy

Transfer fee: $70.00

A grantor delivers a deed by handing or mailing it to the grantee. Delivery to one of several grantees, with intent to transfer ownership to all grantees, is valid delivery to all grantees. A grantor can also deliver a deed by other, more complicated means, such as escrow accounts, but those methods are beyond the scope of this book. Only grantors who are directly handing or mailing deeds to grantees should use the forms in this book.

Once a grantor delivers a deed to a grantee, the grantee should *record* the deed. The grantee records the deed by taking it to the recorder's office for the county where the property is located. The recorder's office is in the same building as the county clerk's office. The recorder will charge a recording fee, usually one or two dollars per page. The recorder makes a copy of the deed and places it in the deed records of the county clerk's office or the county commissioner's office.

The recorder will indicate on the deed when and where the deed was recorded. In counties that organize deed records by book and page numbers the recorder will indicate in what book number and at what page the deed is recorded. In counties that organize deed records by recorder's fee numbers, the recorder will indicate the recorder's fee number on the deed.

By recording a deed, a grantee gives notice to the world that he or she owns the property. Any person who searches the title to that property will discover the grantee's deed.

After recording the deed, the recorder will return the original deed to the grantee, so the recorder will want the grantee to list on the first page of the deed the address where the deed should be returned.

Some states require that transfer taxes be paid when property is transferred from one person to another. These taxes are based upon the amount of consideration involved, or on the value of the property if the value is different from the consideration. The amount of these taxes varies from state to state. To determine whether or not a recorder will charge a transfer tax on a deed, visit the county clerk's office in your county. Tell the clerk the value of the property, the consideration that will be given for the property, and the relationship between the grantor and grantee, such as husband and wife. Ask the clerk to compute the amount of any transfer taxes owed. The custom in most parts of the country is for the grantor to pay the transfer taxes.

Both samples describe the name and address of the person who prepared the deed. Some states require this, but a deed should indicate this even if your state's law does not require it. If there are ever questions about the deed, the preparer may have valuable information regarding it.

Instructions for Blank Deeds

This chapter includes two blank forms. Figure 10-4 is a blank general or special warranty deed. Figure 10-5 is a blank quitclaim deed. Each form has blank spaces with a number under each blank. Before filling in any of the blanks, make several photocopies of the form from the book. Use one copy as a work copy, one as an original, and the rest for future work copies or originals. Fill out the work copy first and be sure it is correct, then type or print in the blanks on your original form.

Blank General or Special Warranty Deed (FIG. 10-4) The following numbered instructions match the numbers under the blanks in the form.

(1) Enter the name(s) and the address where the recorder should send the deed after recording. If the grantor and grantee are husband and wife, use their names and their common address. Otherwise, use the grantee's name and address.

(2,3,4) Enter the day, month, and year that the grantor(s) signs the deed.

(5) Enter the full name(s) of the grantor(s). State the marital status of the grantor(s). If property is owned by one spouse, make both spouses grantors. State all the names of any grantor who has changed names during ownership.

(6) Enter the address(es) of the grantor(s).

(7) Enter the full name(s) of the grantee(s). State the marital status of the grantee(s).

(8) Enter the address(es) of the grantee(s).

(9) Enter the name(s) and address where the tax assessor should send future tax statements for the property transferred in the deed. If the grantor and grantee are husband and wife, put their names and their common address. Otherwise, use the name and address of the grantee, as the grantee will normally be paying the taxes after the property is transferred.

(10) Enter the consideration that the grantee is giving to the grantor for the property. If the consideration is money, enter the amount of money in words and in numbers. If the consideration is love and affection, indicate that, indicate whether or not the grantee is a blood relative of the grantor, and describe the relationship between grantor and grantee. If there is some other type of consideration, such as the transfer of property or the cancellation of a debt, describe the consideration and state the value of the consideration in terms of money.

(11) If there is more than one grantee, or if the grantor is only transferring part of his or her interest in the property, enter the necessary language to create joint ownership with right of survivorship, if the grantees desire that. See the explanation of the sample deeds for an explanation of the difference between a tenancy in common and joint ownership with right of survivorship and for an explanation of the wording to use here in different situations.

　　After indicating how the grantees will own the property, enter the legal description of the property being transferred, including any easements, rights-of-way, or other encumbrances that the property is sold subject to. If there are any easements, rights-of-way, or other encumbrances, give the date of the encumbrance, the name of the person or company in whose favor the encumbrance runs, and describe the book and page number (or the recorder's fee number) where the encumbrance is recorded. If the legal description of the property is too long to fit in Blank 11, put "See Exhibit A" in Blank 11, and staple to the deed an "Exhibit A" containing the full legal description of the property. Label the attachment "Exhibit A" by writing that at the top or bottom of the exhibit.

　　If your legal description refers to a plat or map of the property and your state requires you to attach a copy of the plat or map (see FIG. 10-1), attach a copy of the map or plat, label it "Exhibit A" (or "Exhibit B" if you attached your legal description as "Exhibit A"), and staple all exhibits to the deed. You can obtain a copy of the map or plat from your county recorder's office.

(12) If you are preparing a general warranty deed, cross out the words in the parentheses. All people who are signing the deed, including the witnesses and the notary public, should initial the phrase that you crossed out. If you are preparing a special warranty deed, cross out the parentheses only, not the words in the parentheses. All parties who sign the deed should initial the cross outs.

(13) Enter any representations the grantor(s) is/are making about the condition of the property. If the property is being sold "as is", indicate that and state that the grantor(s) is/are making no representations regarding the condition or quality of the property.

(14) Enter the full name of the spouse(s) of the grantor(s), if applicable. If not applicable because the grantors are husband and wife and both own the property, or because the grantor is not married, or because the grantor and grantee are husband and wife, do not complete this blank and Blank 15. Put "not applicable" in these blanks.

(15) Enter the full address(s) of the spouse(s) of the grantor(s).

(16) Enter the name(s) of the grantor(s) when he, she, or they obtained title.

(17) Enter a description of how the grantor(s) obtained title, including the name of the grantor(s) in the preceding deed by which grantor(s) obtained title, the dates that deed was signed and recorded, and the book and page (or recorder's fee numbers) where that deed was recorded. If the grantor(s) obtained title by inheritance, describe from whom and when the grantor(s) inherited the property, and describe the document by which the grantor(s) inherited the property. For instance, if the grantor(s) inherited the property by will, describe the date of the will and the time and place that the will was recorded, if it was recorded. If the grantor(s) inherited the property from a person who died without a will, describe the date when and the place where the person from whom the grantor(s) inherited the property died, and state that the grantor(s) inherited the property as heir(s) of that person. See the explanation of the sample deeds for a full discussion of this.

(18) Enter, in numbers, the market value of the property transferred in the deed.

(19) Enter the date that the grantor(s) sign the deed.

(20) Enter the address where the grantor(s) sign the deed.

(21) The grantor(s) should sign his, her or their name(s) above these lines, in front of two witnesses and a notary public. Under the grantor's signature, enter the name of the grantor, to the left of the word "Grantor". If the grantor is a corporation, enter the name of the corporation above the line for the grantor's signature. Under the name of the corporation, an authorized representative of the corporation should sign his or her name on behalf of the corporation, indicating his or her position in the corporation, such as president, vice president, etc. Under the representative's signature, enter the name of the representative. If the corporation has a corporate seal, affix the corporate seal in the left-hand margin of the deed, next to the signature of the representative.

(22) Enter the full names of the two witnesses.

(23) Enter the full name(s) of the grantor(s).

(24) Enter the date the grantor(s) signed the deed.

(25) Enter the name(s) of the grantor(s).

(26,27,28) Enter the day, month, and year that the grantor(s) signed the deed.

(29) The witnesses should sign their full names above these lines. Under the signatures of the witnesses, to the left of the word "Witness", enter the names of the witnesses. On the lines beneath their signatures the witnesses should put their full addresses.

The following items should be completed by a notary pubic:

(30) If the grantor is signing for himself or herself, not on behalf of a corporation, enter the name of the state where the grantor(s) signed the deed. Put a large "X" through the entire corporate notary section, and follow instructions 31 through 40 in filling out the individual notary section. Then follow instructions 53 and 54. If the grantor is a corporation, fill out the corporate notary section, put a large "X" through the individual notary section, and ignore instructions 31 through 40.

(31) Enter the name of the county where the deed is signed and notarized.

(32) Enter the full name of the notary public who is notarizing the document.

(33) Enter the date the grantor(s) signed the deed.

(34) Enter the name(s) of the grantor(s).

(35,36,37) Enter the day, month, and year that the deed is signed and notarized.

(38) The notary public should sign above this line.

(39) The notary public should enter the date his or her commission expires.

(40) The notary public should affix his or her seal to the deed.

(41) Corporate Notary Section—Enter the name of the state where the deed is signed and notarized.

(42) Enter the name of the county where the deed is signed and notarized.

(43) Enter the name of the notary public.

(44) Enter the date the deed is signed and notarized.

(45) Enter the name(s) of the person(s) who are signing the deed on behalf of the corporation.

(46) Enter the name of the corporation. Indicate the office(s) that the signer(s) of the deed hold(s) in the corporation, such as president, vice president, secretary, etc.

(47,48,49) Enter the day, month, and year that the deed is signed.

(50) The notary public should sign above this line.

(51) The notary public should enter the date his or her commission expires.

(52) The notary public should affix his or her seal to the deed.

(53) Enter the full name of the person who prepared the deed.

(54) Enter the address of the person who prepared the deed.

(The recorder will fill out the remaining blanks on the form.)

After the deed is signed, witnessed, and notarized, the grantor must physically deliver the deed by handing or mailing the deed to the grantee. The grantee should record the deed, as explained earlier.

Blank Quitclaim Deed (FIG. 10-5)   The instructions for FIG. 10-5 are identical to the instructions for FIG. 10-4, above, except Instruction 12 is not applicable to a quitclaim deed, therefore Blank 12 does not appear in FIG. 10-5.

Fig. 10-4. General or Special Warranty Deed (Blank). *Page 1 of 6* **173**

Warranty Deed

1. Parties and date. This warranty deed is made on the _____ day of
(2)

_____, _____, by and between _____
(3)   (4)   (5)

_____

_____,

whose address(es) is/are: _____
(6)

_____

_____,

hereafter called "grantor", and _____
(7)

_____

_____,

whose address(es) is/are: _____
(8)

_____

_____,

hereafter referred to as "grantee". Even if there is more than one grantor or grantee, they will be referred to in the singular for the remainder of this deed.

2. Future tax statements. Future tax statements for the property transferred in this

deed should be sent to the following name(s) and address(es): _____
(9)

_____

_____.

3. Consideration, description, words of conveyance, and estate conveyed. In consideration of grantee paying grantor the sum of One Dollar ($1.00), receipt of which grantor hereby acknowledges, and in consideration of grantee paying or transferring

and delivering to the grantor the following: _____
(10)

_____

_____

_____

_____,

grantor hereby conveys, grants, gives, bargains, sells, releases, and transfers to grantee and grantee's heirs and assigns forever, a fee simple estate in the following described property, to be held in the following manner:

_____
(11)

_____

_____

_____

_____

_____

_____

_____

_____

_____.

To have and to hold the above property by grantee and grantee's heirs and assigns forever, along with all the tenements, hereditaments, and appurtenances belonging to the above property.

4. Covenants. Grantor, for himself, herself, or itself, and for his, her, or its heirs and successors forever, makes the following covenants with grantee and grantee's heirs and assigns forever:

a) Grantor is the lawful owner of a fee simple estate in the above property and has the right to convey the above property;

b) There are no encumbrances against the above property except those listed above;

c) Grantor and grantor's heirs and successors will warrant and defend forever the title to the above property against all lawful claims made against the property (made by anyone claiming by, through, or under grantor); [12]

d) At the expense of grantee or grantee's heirs or assigns, grantor and grantor's heirs and successors will do whatever is reasonably necessary to perfect or confirm the title of grantee or grantee's heirs or assigns to the above property;

e) The grantor makes the following covenant regarding the condition of the property:

_____
[13]

_____

_____

_____

_____

_____

_____.

5. Dower, curtesy, homestead, and community property rights.

_____,
[14]

the spouse of grantor, whose address is _____
[15]

_____,

for the consideration stated above, hereby gives up his or her right, title, interest, separate estate, dower, and right of dower or curtesy, as the case may be, in the above property, and hereby also gives up any homestead, community property, or other rights he/she/they may have in the above property.

Fig. 10-4. (Cont'd). *Page 3 of 6* **175**

6. Grantor's source of title. The name(s) of the grantor(s) at the time that the grantor(s) obtained title to the above property was/were: _____
                                                                    (16)

_____ .

Grantor(s) obtained title as follows: _____
                                                        (17)

_____

_____

_____ .

7. Uses of property. This deed will not allow use of the property it describes in violation of applicable land use laws and regulations. Before signing or accepting this deed the person acquiring fee title to the property should check with the appropriate city or county planning department to verify approved uses.

8. Declaration of value. The undersigned grantor hereby declares that the true value of the property transferred in this deed is $_____ .
                                                              (18)

9. Date, place, and signatures. IN WITNESS WHEREOF, I/we have signed this deed on _____ , at _____
                              (19)   (20)

_____

_____ .

_____ (SEAL)   _____ (SEAL)
          (21)   (21)
        Grantor   Grantor

_____   _____
          (21)   (21)
   Grantor's spouse   Grantor's spouse

We, _____

_____ ,
                              (22)

hereby acknowledge that we witnessed _____

_____
                              (23)

_____ ,

who is/are known to us personally, sign the above assignment on _____
                                                              (24)

in our presence and that _____

_____
                              (25)

_____

acknowledged to us and it appeared to us that he/she/they signed said assignment freely and voluntarily.

Dated this _____ day of _____, _____.
         (26)   (27)   (28)

_____   _____
              (29)   (29)
        Witness   Witness

_____   _____

_____   _____

_____   _____

Individual Notary:

STATE OF _____)
                  (30)
) ss.

COUNTY OF _____)
                  (31)

I, _____,
                              (32)

a resident of and notary public in and for the state and county named above, who am duly commissioned and sworn and legally authorized to administer oaths and affirmations, hereby certify that on _____,
                                                                (33)

_____,
                              (34)

who is/are known to me personally to be the signer(s) of the above deed, appeared before me and, after being first duly sworn by me under penalty of perjury, swore on his/her/their oath(s) to the truth of the facts in the above deed, and signed and acknowledged said deed in my presence, of his/her/their own free will and for the purposes explained in said deed.

Subscribed and sworn to before me this _____ day of _____,
                                              (35)   (36)
_____.

                    _____
                                                        (38)
                    Notary Public
(SEAL)   My Commission expires: _____
(40)   (39)

Corporate Notary:

Fig. 10-4. (Cont'd). *Page 5 of 6* **177**

STATE OF _____)
(41)

) ss.

COUNTY OF _____)
(42)

I, _____,
(43)

am a resident of and notary public in and for the state and county named above, who am duly commissioned and sworn and legally authorized to administer oaths and affirmations, and I hereby certify that on _____,
(44)

_____
(45)

_____,

who is/are known to me personally to be the person(s) who signed the above deed, appeared before me and, after being first duly sworn by me under penalty of perjury, swore on his/her/their oath(s) to the truth of the facts in the above deed, and signed and acknowledged said deed in my presence, of his/her/their own free will, and for the purposes explained in said deed, and further said that he/she/they hold(s) the following

office(s) in the following corporation: _____
(46)

_____

_____,

the corporation on whose behalf the above deed was signed, that he/she/they know(s) the seal of said corporation if there is any such seal, and if there is any such seal the seal affixed to the above deed is the corporate seal and was affixed by order of the board of directors of the corporation, and that he/she/they signed the above deed on behalf of the corporation by order of the board of directors of said corporation.

Subscribed and sworn to before me this _____ day of _____,
(47)   (48)

_____.
(49)

_____
(50)

Notary Public

(SEAL)   My Commission expires: _____
(52)   (51)

This instrument was prepared by _____
(53)

_____,

whose address is _____
(54)

_____.

STATE OF _____)

) ss.

COUNTY OF _____)

I certify that the above deed was recorded in my office on the following date:
_____, at _____ _____.M., and is duly recorded in Book _____, at Page _____ (or as Recorder's Fee No. _____), of the Deed Records of the above state and county.

_____

                                    Recorder

By: _____

                                  Deputy

Transfer Fee: $_____

Fig. 10-5. Quitclaim Deed (Blank). *Page 1 of 6* **179**

Quitclaim Deed

1. Parties and date. This quitclaim deed is made on the _____ day of
_____, _____, by and between _____
(3)   (4)   (5)

_____

_____,

whose address(es) is/are: _____
(6)

_____

_____,

hereafter called "grantor", and_____
(7)

_____

_____,

whose address(es) is/are: _____
(8)

_____

_____,

hereafter referred to as "grantee". Even if there is more than one grantor or grantee, they will be referred to in the singular for the remainder of this deed.

2. Future tax statements. Future tax statements for the property transferred in

this deed should be sent to the following name(s) and address: _____
(9)

_____

_____.

3. Consideration, description, words of conveyance, and estate conveyed. In consideration of grantee paying grantor the sum of One Dollar ($1.00), receipt of which grantor hereby acknowledges, and in consideration of grantee paying or transferring

and delivering to the grantor the following: _____
(10)

_____

_____

_____,

grantor hereby releases, transfers, and forever quitclaims to grantee the following interest in the following property, to be held in the following manner: _____
(11)

_____

_____

_____

_____

_____

_____

_____

_____

_____.

To have and to hold the above property by grantee and grantee's heirs and assigns forever, along with all the tenements, hereditaments, and appurtenances belonging to the above property.

4. Covenants. Grantor is not covenanting that grantor is the lawful owner of any estate in the above property, has the right to convey the above property, that there are no encumbrances against the above property, that grantor or grantor's heirs will warrant and defend the title to the above property against lawful claims made against the property, or that grantor or grantor's heirs will do anything to perfect grantee's title to the above property. The grantor makes the following covenant regarding the condition

of the property: _____
                                           (12)

_____

_____

_____

_____

_____.

Grantor and grantee intend this deed to convey to grantee whatever interest grantor may have in the property.

5. Dower, curtesy, homestead, and community property rights.

_____, the spouse of grantor, whose
                                    (13)

address is _____
                                           (14)

_____,

for the consideration stated above, hereby gives up his or her right, title, interest, separate estate, dower, and right of dower or curtesy, as the case may be, in the above property, and hereby also gives up any homestead, community property, or other rights he or she may have in the above property.

Fig. 10-5. (Cont'd). *Page 3 of 6* **181**

6. Grantor's source of title. The name(s) of the grantor(s) at the time that the grantor(s) obtained title to the above property was/were: _____
(15)

_____.

_____

Grantor(s) obtained title as follows: _____
(16)

_____

_____

_____.

7. Uses of property. This deed will not allow use of the property it describes in violation of applicable land use laws and regulations. Before signing or accepting this deed, the person acquiring fee title to the property should check with the appropriate city or county planning department to verify approved uses.

8. Declaration of value. The undersigned grantor hereby declares that the true value of the property transferred in this deed is $_____.
(17)

9. Date, place, and signatures. IN WITNESS WHEREOF, I/we have signed this deed on _____ at _____
(18)   (19)

_____

_____.

_____(SEAL)   _____(SEAL)
(20)   (20)
          Grantor   Grantor

_____   _____
(20)   (20)
     Grantor's spouse   Grantor's spouse

We, _____,
                                    (21)

hereby acknowledge that we witnessed _____
                                                    (22)

_____,

who is/are known to us personally, sign the above deed on _____,
                                                                        (23)

in our presence, and that _____
                                                (24)

_____

acknowledged to us and it appeared to us that he/she/it/they signed said deed freely and voluntarily.

Dated this _____ day of _____, _____.
                    (25)   (26)   (27)

_____   _____
                    (28)   (28)
            Witness   Witness

_____   _____

_____   _____

Individual Notary:

STATE OF _____)
                        (29)

) ss.

COUNTY OF _____)
                            (30)

I, _____, a resident of and notary
                        (31)

public in and for the state and county named above, who am duly commissioned and sworn and legally authorized to administer oaths and affirmations, hereby certify that

on _____,
                                    (32)

_____,
                                    (33)

who is/are known to me personally to be the signer(s) of the above deed, appeared before me and, after being first duly sworn by me under penalty of perjury, swore on his/her/their oath(s) to the truth of the facts in the above deed, and signed and

Fig. 10-5. (Cont'd). *Page 5 of 6* **183**

acknowledged said deed in my presence, of his/her/their own free will and for the purposes explained in said deed.

Subscribed and sworn to before me this _____ day of _____,
(34)   (35)

_____.
(36)

_____
(37)

Notary Public:

(SEAL)   My Commission Expires: _____
(38)

Corporate Notary:

STATE OF _____)
(39)

) ss.

COUNTY OF _____)
(40)

I, _____,
(41)

am a resident of and notary public in and for the state and county named above, who am duly commissioned and sworn and legally authorized to administer oaths and

affirmations, and I hereby certify that on _____,
(42)

_____
(43)

_____

who is/are known to me personally to be the person(s) who signed the above deed, appeared before me and, after being first duly sworn by me under penalty of perjury, swore on his/her/their oath(s) to the truth of the facts in the above deed, and signed and acknowledged said deed in my presence, of his/her/their own free will, and for the purposes explained in said deed, and further said that he/she/they hold(s) the following

office(s) in the following corporation: _____
(44)

_____,

the corporation on whose behalf the above deed was signed, that he/she/they know(s) the seal of said corporation if there is any such seal, and if there is any such seal the seal affixed to the above deed is the corporate seal and was affixed by order of the board of directors of the corporation, and that he/she/they signed the above deed on behalf of the corporation by order of the board of directors of said corporation.

Subscribed and sworn to before me on this _____ day of _____
(45)   (46)

_____.
(47)

_____
(48)

Notary Public

(SEAL)   My Commission expires: _____
(50)   (49)

This instrument was prepared by: _____,
(51)

whose address is _____
(52)

_____.

STATE OF _____)

) ss.

COUNTY OF _____)

I certify that the above deed was recorded in my office on the following date:

_____, at _____ _____.M.,

and is duly recorded in Book _____, at Page _____,

(or as Recorder's Fee No. _____), of the Deed Records of the above

state and county.

_____

Recorder

By: _____

Deputy

Transfer Fee: $_____

Chapter 11
Promissory Note

A promissory note is a promise by a signer of a note to pay a holder of a note a certain amount of money on certain terms.

A person who lends money to another person uses a promissory note to confirm, in writing, the terms of the loan. The promissory note may be the lender's only proof that he or she loaned money to another person. By itself, a promissory note is an unsecured promise to pay money. If the signer does not pay the note, the holder cannot foreclose upon specific property; the holder has to sue the signer. If the holder wins the lawsuit, the holder gets a judgment against the signer for a certain amount of money, plus interest, plus attorney's fees and costs if the promissory note says the holder can recover those fees and costs.

Once a holder has a judgment against a signer, the holder has to try to collect that judgment by attaching the signer's bank accounts, garnishing the signer's wages, or forcing the signer to sell real property. A holder may find it difficult to collect his or her judgment—the signer can discharge these types of judgments in bankruptcy.

This chapter discusses promissory notes and provides a blank promissory note for people who are not regularly in the business of lending money. Certain federal and state laws apply to people who are regularly in the business of lending money. These laws are beyond the scope of this chapter.

SECURING A PROMISSORY NOTE

To secure a promissory note, the signer of a note can sign a mortgage, trust deed, or a security agreement. These documents give the holder of a note specific property to foreclose upon if the signer does not pay the note. If the property securing a note is land, a holder uses a mortgage or trust deed. If personal property secures a note, a holder uses a security agreement.

Different states have different laws on the proper forms for mortgages, trust deeds, and security agreements. You should not try to prepare these documents yourself. You should use a simpler method of ensuring that you get paid: Have someone other than the signer of the note guaranty the note. The next section of this chapter explains how to do this.

GUARANTYING A PROMISSORY NOTE

The holder of a note can ask someone to guaranty a note signed by another person. The person guarantying the note promises to pay the holder if the signer does not pay the holder.

Because you may find it difficult to collect a judgment against someone, you should only lend money to people you are confident will pay you back. If you are not sure if the borrower will pay you back, have someone who you are confident will pay you back guaranty the promissory note. If you do not have confidence in the borrower and cannot find someone you have confidence in to guaranty the note, you probably should not lend money to that borrower. If you do lend money in those circumstances, have an attorney prepare an ironclad mortgage, trust deed, or security agreement to secure the note.

Usury Laws

Some states have laws which make it illegal to charge more than a certain percentage of interest each year. These laws are called *usury laws*. A promissory note violates these laws if it provides for interest greater than the amount these laws allow.

State usury laws differ widely. Figure 11-1 lists, for all 50 states and the District of Columbia, the sections of each state's laws that discuss the maximum rate of interest each state allows. You can find these laws by going to a law library in your state. A law library is located at your county courthouse. Ask the librarian to help you find the law referred to in FIG. 11-1. Or, contact your local consumer protection office.

Some states tie the maximum rate of interest to the Federal Reserve discount rate on 90-day commercial paper in effect in the Federal Reserve Bank in the district where the loan occurs. Your local banker will know the rate, or will be able to obtain the rate for you.

Figure 11-1 is based on 1987 and 1988 laws. The legislatures of the 50 states meet at different times. Some legislatures only meet once every two years. When a state legislature passes a law, the legislature or a publishing company publishes that law at a later time. Several months can pass before the legislature or publisher sends that law to the libraries around the country. As you read these words, months or years will have also passed from the time this book was edited, printed, and distributed. For these reasons, this book, like all legal books, cannot be absolutely current.

Figure 11-1 indicates whether the information for a particular state is based on the 1987 or 1988 laws of that state. If you want to confirm whether or not your state has changed its laws, go to a law library in your state and read the most current version of the law referred to in FIG. 11-1. Even if the law has changed, the new law will usually have the same number as the old law. Check what are known as the "pocket parts" of your state's laws. Pocket parts are supplements which contain the latest revisions of a state's laws. Or, again, call your local consumer protection agency.

The rates of interest in FIG. 11-1 apply to people who are not regularly in the business of lending money. Different rates apply to banks, credit card companies, and other companies that are in the business of lending money.

The rates of interest in FIG. 11-1 refer to simple interest, not compound interest. Compound interest is interest charged on interest. A holder compounds interest when he or she takes interest owed by a signer, adds it to the principal balance, and then charges the interest rate of the note on the new balance. Most states prohibit charging compound interest on loans.

All interest rates in FIG. 11-1 are annual interest rates unless otherwise stated. Some states allow different rates of interest for consumer and non-consumer loans. Most states define consumer loans as loans where the lender is regularly in the business of lending money. California, Arkansas, and Hawaii define consumer loans as loans where the borrower uses the loan primarily for personal, household, or family purposes. These states do not require that a lender be in the business of lending money in order for a loan to be classified as a consumer loan. Since this chapter does not cover loans made by lenders who are regularly in the business of lending money, consumer-loan rates of interest do not apply to the forms in this chapter, except in California, Arkansas, and Hawaii. Figure 11-1 describes the maximum rates of interest in California, Arkansas, and Hawaii for consumer and non-consumer loans.

The maximum rates of interest in FIG. 11-1 always refer to rates agreed to in writing. Most states have lower maximum interest rates if the parties do not put their agreement in writing.

Fig. 11-1. State Laws on Usury.

Alabama—8-8-1 (1987 Update). Six percent (6%) on an oral contract and eight percent (8%) on a written contract.

Alaska—45.45.010 (1987 Update). The maximum interest rate is five percentage points above the annual rate charged by member banks of the Twelfth Federal Reserve District on the day on which the parties sign the contract or the lender commits to lending the money. Usury laws do not apply to loans greater than $100,000.

Arizona—44-1201 (1988 Update). Parties may agree in writing to any rate of interest.

Arkansas—4-57-104 and Arkansas Constitution Article 19, Section 13 (1987 Update). Maximum interest rate for general loans cannot be more than five percentage points above the Federal Reserve discount rate on 90-day commercial paper in effect in the Federal Reserve Bank in the Federal Reserve District in which Arkansas is located. The applicable discount rate is the rate at the time that the lender makes the loan. For consumer loans, the maximum interest rate is seventeen percent (17%).

California—Constitution Article 15 Section 1 (1988 Update). The Constitution of California says the maximum interest rate is ten percent (10%) on loans where the proceeds are used for personal, family, or household purposes. The maximum interest rate on loans where the proceeds are used for other purposes is the higher of ten percent (10%) or not more than five percent (5%) above the rate prevailing on the 25th of the month preceding the earlier of the date the parties sign the contract or the date of making the loan as established by the Federal Reserve Bank of San Francisco on advances to member banks. Savings and loans, banks, credit unions, pawnbrokers, lenders of real estate-secured loans, and certain other lenders registered with the state or federal government are exempt from these limitations.

Colorado—5-12-103 (1987 Update). The maximum interest rate is forty-five percent (45%).

Connecticut—37-4 (1987 Update). The maximum interest rate is twelve percent (12%).

Delaware—6-2301 (1987 Update). The maximum interest rate is not more than five percent (5%) above the Federal Reserve discount rate for loans of $100,000 or less. For loans greater than $100,000, there is no maximum rate of interest if the loan is not secured by a mortgage on the debtor's principal residence.

District of Columbia—28-3301 (1988 Update). The maximum interest rate is twenty-four percent (24%).

Florida—687.02 and .03 (1988 Update). The maximum interest rate is eighteen percent (18%) simple interest for loans of $500,000 or less. For loans greater than $500,000, the maximum interest rate is twenty-five percent (25%).

Georgia—7-4-2 (also known as 57-101) (1988 Update). On loans of $3,000 or less, the maximum interest rate is sixteen percent (16%). On loans greater than $3,000, the parties may agree to any rate of interest, not to exceed 5% per month. (7-4-18).

Hawaii—478-4 (1987 Update). The maximum interest rate is 1% per month or 12% per year for consumer credit transactions and for home business loans. For other loans, no maximum interest rate was found.

Idaho—28-42-201 (1988 Update). The maximum interest rate is whatever amount the parties agree to.

Illinois—17-6404 (1988 Update). The maximum rate of interest is nine percent (9%).

Indiana—No maximum rate of interest was found for loans where the lender is not regularly in the business of lending money (1988 Update).

Iowa—535.2(3)(a) (1988 Update). The maximum rate of interest is two percent (2%) above the monthly average of the 10-year constant maturity interest rate of United States government notes and bonds, as published by the Board of Governors of the Federal Reserve System for the second calendar month preceding the month during which the maximum rate based thereon will be effective, rounded to the nearest one-quarter of one percent (0.25%) per year. Contact the Superintendent of Banking for Iowa, who is required to determine and publish in the Iowa Administrative Bulletin, or as a legal notice in a newspaper of general circulation in Polk County, the maximum rate of interest in effect in Iowa.

Kansas—16.207 (1987 Update). The maximum rate of interest is fifteen percent (15%).

Kentucky—360.010 (1987 Update). The maximum rate of interest is not more than four percentage points above the discount rate on 90-day commercial paper in effect at the Federal Reserve Bank in the Federal Reserve District where the transaction is consummated, or nineteen percent (19%), whichever is less, if the loan is for $15,000 or less. If the loan is for more than $15,000, Kentucky law sets no maximum rate of interest.

Louisiana—Civil Code Article 2924 (1988 Update). The maximum rate of interest is twelve percent (12%).

Maine—No statute was found which established a maximum rate of interest (1987 Update).

Maryland—Commercial Law 12-103 (1987 Update). The maximum rate of interest is eight percent (8%), but the interest rate can be higher under certain conditions. Those conditions are lengthy. Anyone who wants to charge more than 8% interest should read Section 12-103.

Massachusetts—Chapter 107, Section 3, Chapter 140, Section 90 (1987 Update). For loans under $1,000, the maximum rate of interest is eighteen percent (18%). For loans of $1,000 or more, the maximum rate of interest is twenty percent (20%). See Chapter 271, Section 49.

Michigan—19.15(1) (1988 Update). The maximum rate of interest is seven percent (7%).

Minnesota—334.01 (1988 Update). The maximum rate of interest is eight percent (8%) on loans under $100,000. On loans of $100,000 or more, there is no limit on the interest rate.

Mississippi—75-17-1(2) (1987 Update). The maximum rate of interest is the greater of ten percent (10%) or not more than five percent (5%) above the discount rate, excluding surcharges, on 90-day commercial paper in effect at the Federal Reserve Bank in the Federal Reserve District where the lender is located.

Missouri—408.030 (1988 Update). The maximum rate of interest is ten percent (10%) or the market rate, whichever is higher. The market rate is equal to the monthly index of long-term U.S. government bond yields for the second preceding calendar month before the beginning of the calendar quarter, plus three percent (3%) rounded to the nearest tenth of a percent. The calendar quarters begin on January 1, April 1, July 1, and October 1 of each year.

Montana—31-1-107 (1987 Update). The maximum rate of interest is not more than six percent (6%) above the prime rate of major New York banks as published in the *Wall Street Journal* edition dated three business days before execution of the loan agreement.

Nebraska—45-101.03(1) and .04(4) (1987 Update). The maximum rate of interest is sixteen percent (16%) on loans of less than $25,000. There is no maximum rate of interest on loans of $25,000 or more.

Nevada—99.050 (1987 Update). The parties may agree to any rate of interest.

New Hampshire—399-A-3 (1988 Update). The parties to a loan may agree in writing to any amount of interest for loans greater than $10,000. For loans of $10,000 or less, a lender must obtain a license from the State Banking Commission and cannot charge greater than two percent (2%) per month on loans up to $600, and not more than one and one-half percent (1½%) on amounts between $600 and $1,500.

New Jersey—31:1-1(a) (1988 Update). The maximum rate of interest is sixteen percent (16%).

New Mexico—56-8-11.1 (1987 Update). New Mexico law provides that any interest rate may be agreed to in writing.

New York—General Obligations Laws 5-501(1), Banking Law Section 14(a) (1988 Update). The maximum rate of interest is sixteen percent (16%).

North Carolina—24-1.1 (1987 Update). On loans greater than $25,000, there is no maximum rate of interest. On loans of $25,000 or less, the maximum rate of interest is the amount announced and published by the Commissioner of Banks on the 15th

Fig. 11-2. (Cont'd). 189

day of each month for the following calendar month on six-month U.S. Treasury Bills plus six percent (6%), or sixteen percent (16%), whichever is greater.

North Dakota—47-14-09 (1987 Update). The maximum interest rate is not more than five and one-half percent (5.5%) above the current cost of money as reflected by the average rate of interest payable on U.S. Treasury Bills maturing in six months in effect for North Dakota for six months immediately prior to the month in which the loan occurs, as computed and declared on the last day of each month by the State Banking Commissioner. These usury laws do not apply to loans in excess of $35,000.

Ohio—1343.01 (1988 Update). On loans of $100,000 or less, the maximum interest rate is eight percent (8%). On loans over $100,000, there is no maximum interest rate.

Oklahoma—14A-3-605 (1988 Update). The maximum rate of interest is forty-five percent (45%).

Oregon—82.010(3)(a) and (b) (1987 Update). There is no maximum rate of interest on loans over $50,000. On loans of $50,000 or less, for business or agricultural loans the maximum interest rate is the greater of twelve percent (12%), or five percent (5%) above the discount rate, including surcharges, on 90-day commercial paper in effect at the Federal Reserve Bank in the Federal Reserve District where the lender is located on the date of the loan. For loans other than business or agricultural loans, the rate is the same, except the rate does not include surcharges.

Pennsylvania—41-PS-201, 41-301, 41-302, 18-911(h)(1)(IV) (1988 Update). With certain exceptions, the maximum rate of interest is 6%. For the exceptions, the maximum rate of interest is 25%. The exceptions are loans in excess of $50,000, loans secured by real property other than residential real property, loans to corporations, business loans greater than $10,000, and unsecured, non-collateralized loans greater than $35,000.

Rhode Island—6-26-2 (1987 Update). The maximum rate of interest is the greater of twenty-one percent (21%), or nine percent (9%) above the Treasury Bill Index for the week preceding the date of the debtor's agreement. The Treasury Bill Index for any week shall be the highest rate for U.S. Treasury Bills with maturities of one year or less as established at the auction of such Treasury Bills during such week or, if no such auction is conducted during such week, at the auction next preceding such week. The Director of Business Regulations shall keep a record of the Treasury Bill Index and shall publish it not less than weekly in a newspaper of general circulation.

South Carolina—(1987 Update). The parties to a loan may agree in writing to any interest rate.

South Dakota—54-3-1.1 (1988 Update). There is no maximum rate of interest.

Tennessee—47-14-103 (1987 Update). The maximum rate of interest depends on a number of different circumstances, but is generally four percent (4%) above the prime loan rate published by the Federal Reserve System, or twenty-four percent (24%), whichever is less.

Texas—Civil Statutes Article 5069-1.01(d), -1.02, -1.04 (1988 Update). The maximum rate of interest that parties can agree to is the rate based on 26-week U.S. Treasury Bills for the week preceding the week in which the lender makes the loan, with a maximum rate of twenty-four percent (24%).

Utah—15-1-1(2) (1988 Update). The parties may agree in writing to any rate of interest.

Vermont—Title 9-41(a) (1988 Update). The maximum rate of interest is twelve percent (12%).

Virginia—Section 6.1-330.55 (1988 Update). The maximum rate of interest is twelve percent (12%).

Washington—19.52.020 (1988 Update). The maximum interest rate is the higher of twelve percent (12%), or four percent (4%) above the equivalent coupon issue yield (as published by the Federal Reserve Bank of San Francisco), of the average bill rate for 26-week Treasury Bills as determined at the first bull market auction conducted during the calendar month immediately preceding the establishing of the interest rate by written agreement of the parties.

West Virginia—47-6-5(b) (1988 Update). The parties may agree in writing to an interest rate not greater than eight percent (8%) per year.

Wisconsin—138.05(1)(a) (1988 Update). The maximum rate of interest is twelve percent (12%) on loans under $150,000. There is no limit on loans of $150,000 or more unless the loan is secured by the debtor's principal residence.

Wyoming—No law was found setting any maximum rate of interest (1987 Update).

Sample Promissory Note (FIG. 11-2)

Figure 11-2 is a sample promissory note. The following numbered paragraphs match the numbered paragraphs in the sample.

1. Date. Every promissory note should state the date when it becomes effective, which should be the same date that the note is signed.

2. Parties. Every promissory note should explain who is promising to pay the money described in the note and who is entitled to receive that money. If there is more than one signer or holder, a note should explain what happens if one of the parties dies before the signers pay the note in full. Most husbands and wives want the survivor to continue to make or receive payments under a note when one of them dies, without going through a probate court. A probate court manages a deceased person's affairs. The sample note contains wording to allow the survivor of the signers to continue to make payments without having to go through a probate court. That wording is, ". . . or the survivor, not as tenants in common". The parties do not want a *tenancy in common*. In a tenancy in common, when one joint owner dies, a probate court manages the deceased owner's interest in joint property.

A promissory note should list the addresses of the signer and holder. The residences of the signer and holder affect which state's laws govern the note.

3. Promise to pay. A promissory note must state that the signer of the note is promising to pay the holder a certain amount of money on certain terms. The note should describe the terms of payment in detail, including the amount of any monthly payments, the day of the month when payments are due, the first month that payments that are due, the interest rate, the date interest begins, and whether interest is included in, or is to be paid in addition to, the payments described in the note.

In the sample note, the signers will make monthly payments. In some notes, the signer does not make any payments until the date when the entire balance owed under the note is due. In those types of notes, the payment paragraph would read as follows:

The signers of this note jointly and severally promise to pay to the holders of this note the sum of $2,500.00, plus interest as described below, on or before May 6, 1991. All unpaid balances under this note shall bear interest at the rate of six percent (6%) per year, beginning May 6, 1989.

"Jointly and severally" means each signer is responsible for paying the entire amount promised under the note. The holder cannot recover double the amount of the note, but the holder can pursue either signer for the entire amount.

A promissory note should explain why the signers are promising to pay money to the holders. Usually, the holders have loaned money to the signers.

4. Usury statement. This paragraph protects the holder of the note against state usury laws. It explains that the parties do not intend to violate those laws. If they do so inadvertently, the holder gives the signer credit against the principal balance for any interest the signer paid in excess of the state usury law limit.

Including the usury paragraph in a promissory note will not guaranty that a court will not find that a note is usurious if the note charges interest greater than the legal rate, but it does support a lender's argument that if the lender did violate a state's usury law, the lender did so inadvertently.

5. Waiver—acceleration. In this paragraph of the sample, the signers waive certain rights. By having the signers waive these rights, the holder of the note does not have to demand that the signers make any required payment (demand and presentment), does not have to give notice that the signers have not made a required payment (notice of nonpayment), and does not have to obtain or give notice of a bank or other official certification of nonpayment of a required payment (protest and notice of protest).

The signers agree that if they fail to make any of the payments required by the note, the holder can *accelerate* the balance. Accelerating the balance means the entire unpaid balance of principal and interest, not just one or two monthly payments, is immediately due.

6. Expenses. A note should state that if the holder of the note pays expenses and attorney's fees to recover the sums promised in the note, the signers agree to repay those costs. If the note does not provide for this, the lender cannot recover those attorney's fees.

7. Date and place. A promissory note should state the date when and the address where the promissory note is signed.

8. Signatures. The signers of a note should sign their names exactly as they are written in Paragraph 2.

9. Guaranty. If the signers do not pay as required by the note, the guaranty makes the person who guarantees the note responsible to the holder for any sums due under the note. In the sample, the guarantor agrees that the holder does not have to exhaust his remedies against the signers before pursuing the guarantor under the guaranty. This agreement means that the holder does not have to sue the signers before demanding payment from the guarantor. As soon as the signers fail to make a payment, the holder can demand that payment from the guarantor. The guarantor waives the same rights to notice that the signers waived in the promissory note.

Promissory Note

1. Date. This note is effective on the 5th day of June, 1989.

2. Parties. The signers of this note are Ann Marie Jones and John Frederick Jones, or the survivor, not as tenants in common, whose address is 222 Third Street, Waynecastle, Pennsylvania, County of Burr, 17294. The holder of this note is John James Smith, whose address is 333 Fourth Street, Waynecastle, Pennsylvania, County of Burr, 17294.

3. Promise to pay. In consideration of the holder of this note loaning the signers the sum of TEN THOUSAND DOLLARS ($10,000.00), receipt of which is hereby acknowledged, the signers of this note jointly and severally promise to pay the holder the sum of TEN THOUSAND DOLLARS ($10,000.00), in monthly payments of not less than THREE HUNDRED DOLLARS ($300.00) each, payable on the first day of each month, beginning with the month of July, 1989, and continuing until the signers pay all money they owe under this note, including principal and interest. All unpaid balances shall bear interest at the rate of SIX PERCENT (6%) per year, beginning June 5, 1989. The monthly payments shall include interest.

4. Usury statement. The parties do not intend this note to obligate the signers of this note to pay any money in excess of the legal rate of interest allowed by the laws of the Commonwealth of Pennsylvania. If the signers do pay any money in excess of the legal rate of interest allowed by the laws of the Commonwealth of Pennsylvania, the holder shall apply such excess money to reduce the principal amount the signers owe the holder.

5. Waiver—acceleration. The signers of this note waive demand, presentment for payment, protest, notice of protest, and notice of nonpayment, and agree that since time is of the essence, if any payment under this note is not paid when due, the holder shall have the right to accelerate and make immediately due and payable the entire unpaid balance of principal and interest.

6. Expenses. If the holder of this note incurs any expenses to enforce any provision of this note, including reasonable attorney's fees, either before or after a lawsuit is begun to enforce this note, the signers of this note agree to pay the holder's expenses and reasonable attorney's fees, including any attorney's fees at trial and on any appeal of any suit or action.

7. Date and place. Signed this 5th day of June, 1989, at 333 Fourth Street, Waynecastle, Pennsylvania, County of Burr, 17294.

8. Signatures.

_____
Ann Marie Jones, Signer

_____
John Frederick Jones, Signer

Fig. 11-2. (Cont'd). *Page 2 of 2* **193**

9. Guaranty. For value received, the undersigned, Joseph Allen Robinson, hereafter called guarantor, unconditionally guarantees the payment of all payments required by the above promissory note as and when they are due. The undersigned also waives demand, presentment for payment, protest, notice of protest, and notice of nonpayment, and agrees that the holder of the note does not have to exhaust the holder's rights against the signers before pursuing the undersigned under this guaranty.

Signed this 5th day of June, 1989.

_____

Joseph Allen Robinson, Guarantor

How to Record Payments   If a promissory note provides for monthly or regular payments, and the note provides that interest shall be included in the monthly or regular payments, a holder should apply part of each monthly payment to interest and part to the principal balance. The following example and FIGS. 11-3, 11-4, and 11-5 explain how to record monthly payments.

Assume the beginning balance is $10,000.00 and the interest rate is ten percent (10%), beginning January 1, 1989. Also assume that the monthly payments are $500.00 each, and that the first payment is due February 1, 1989.

To determine how much of the February 1, 1989 payment is principal and how much is interest, multiply the balance ($10,000.00) times the yearly interest rate (10%), and divide the result by the number of days in a year (365), which gives you the daily amount of interest (see FIG. 11-3). Multiply the amount of daily interest times the number of days from when interest began (1-1-89), to the date of the first payment (2-1-89), which is 31 days. The result is the amount of the payment that you should apply to interest. Subtract the rest of the $500.00 payment from the original $10,000 principal balance, to give the new balance. Interest has then been paid to 2-1-89.

To determine how much of the March 1, 1989 payment is principal and how much is interest, multiply the new balance ($9,584.94) times the yearly interest rate (10%), and divide the result by the number of days in a year (365), which gives you the daily amount of interest (see FIG. 11-4). Multiply the amount of daily interest times the number of days from when the signer last paid interest (2-1-89) to the date of this new payment (3-1-89), which is 28 days. The result is the amount of the payment that you should apply to interest. Subtract the rest of the $500.00 payment from the last principal balance, to give the new balance. Interest is then paid to 3-1-89.

Figure 11-5 is an example of how to record installment payments.

Fig. 11-3. Calculating Principal and Interest—First Payment (Example).

```
$10,000.00    (Original principal balance)
  x  10%      (Yearly interest rate)
----------
$1,000.00     (Interest per year)
  ÷ 365       (Number of days per year)
----------
   $2.74      (Interest per day)
  x  31       (Number of days of interest—between beginning of note and first payment)
----------
  $84.94      (Amount of first payment to be applied to interest)


  $500.00     (First payment)
 −  84.94     (Amount of first payment to be applied to interest)
----------
  $415.06     (Amount of first payment to be applied to principal)


$10,000.00    (Original principal balance)
 −  415.06    (Amount of first payment to be applied to principal)
----------
$ 9,584.94    (New principal balance after first payment)
==========
```

(Numbers have been rounded to nearest $0.01)

Fig. 11-4. Calculating Principal and Interest—Second Payment (Example).

$ 9,584.94	(Original principal balance)
× 10%	(Yearly interest rate)
$958.49	(Interest per year)
÷ 365	(Number of days per year)
$2.63	(Interest per day)
× 28	(Number of days of interest—between first and second payments)
$73.64	(Amount of second payment to be applied to interest)
$500.00	(Second payment)
− 73.64	(Amount of second payment to be applied to interest)
$426.36	(Amount of second payment to be applied to principal)
$9,584.94	(Last principal balance—from FIG. 11-3)
− 426.36	(Amount of second payment to be applied to principal)
$ 9,158.58	(New principal balance after second payment)

(Numbers have been rounded to nearest $0.01)

Fig. 11-5. Recording Installment Payments (Example).

Date of Payment	Amount of Payment	Amount Applied to Interest	Amount Applied to Principal	Interest Paid To	Principal Balance
—	—	—	—	—	$10,000.00
2-1-89	$500.00	$84.94	$415.06	2-1-89	$9,584.94
3-1-89	$500.00	$73.64	$426.36	3-1-89	$9,158.58

Instructions for Blank Promissory Note (FIG. 11-6)

Figure 11-6 is a blank promissory note. The form has blank spaces with a number under each blank. Before filling in any of the blanks, make several photocopies of the form. Use one or more copies as work copies, one as an original, and the rest for future work copies or originals. Fill out a work copy first and be sure it is correct, then type or print in the blanks on your original form.

The following numbered instructions match the numbers under the blanks in the form:

(1,2,3) Enter the day, month, and year that the note is signed.

(4) Enter the full name(s) of the signer(s) of the note. If there is more than one signer, explain what happens to a signer's interest in the note if one of the signers dies before the signers pay the note in full. See the sample note and explanation of the sample for wording to create joint ownership with right of survivorship, which avoids probate.

(5) Enter the address(s) of the signer(s) of the note.

(6) Enter the full name(s) of the holder(s) of the note. If there is more than one holder, explain what happens to a holder's interest in the note if one of the holders dies before the note is paid in full. See the sample note and explanation of the sample for wording to create joint ownership with right of survivorship, which avoids probate.

(7) Enter the address(es) of the holder(s) of the note.

(8) Enter the consideration for the note. The consideration is the reason why the signer is promising to pay the holder the money described in the note, such as the fact that the holder loaned money to the signer.

(9) Enter the amount of money the signer is promising to pay to the holder, first in words, then in numbers in the parentheses.

(10) Enter the terms of payment, including the amount of any regular payments, the day of the month regular payments are due, the first month payments are due, if the note requires monthly payments, the interest rate, the date interest begins, whether interest is included in or the signer will pay interest in addition to any payments described in the note, the date the whole balance is due if there are no regular or monthly payments, and any other terms of payment.

(11) Enter the name of the state where the signer signs the promissory note, which should be the same state where the holder of the note resides. Enter the name of the state in both blanks with the number 11 under them.

(12,13,14) Enter the day, month, and year that the signer signs the note.

(15) Enter the address where the signer signs the note.

(16) The signer should sign his, her, or their full names on these lines.

(17) If no one is guarantying the note, leave the rest of the note blank and mark a large "X" through the guaranty paragraph. Ignore instructions 18 through 21. If someone is guarantying the note, enter the full name of the guarantor(s) in Blank 17, and follow instructions 18 through 21.

(18,19,20) Enter the date the guarantor(s) sign the guaranty.

(21) The guarantor(s) should sign his, her, or their full name(s) on these lines.

The signer and guarantor should keep copies of the signed note. The holder should keep the original note. Once the signer pays the note in full, the holder should write "Paid in Full" on the holder's copy of the note, date it, sign it, and return it to the signer. The signer should then give the guarantor a copy of the "Paid in Full" note.

Fig. 11-6. (Cont'd). *Page 2 of 2* **197**

Promissory Note

1. Date. This note is effective on the _____ day of _____,
(1)   (2)

_____.
(3)

2. Parties. The signer(s) of this note is/are _____
(4)

_____,

whose address(es) is/are _____
(5)

_____,

hereafter called signer. The holder(s) of this note is/are _____
(6)

_____,

whose address(es) is/are _____
(7)

_____,

hereafter called holder. Even if there is more than one signer or holder, the parties will be referred to in the singular for the rest of this note.

3. Promise to pay. In consideration of _____
(8)

_____,

receipt of which is hereby acknowledged, the signer of this note promises, jointly and severally if there is more than one signer, to pay to the holder the sum of

_____ ($_____),
(9)   (9)

on the following terms: _____
(10)

_____

_____

_____

_____

_____.

4. Usury statement. The parties do not intend this note to obligate the signer of this note to pay any money in excess of the legal rate of interest allowed by the laws of the State of _____. If the signer does pay any money in excess
(11)

of the legal rate of interest allowed by the laws of the State of _____,
(11)

the holder shall apply such excess money to reduce the principal amount the signer owes the holder.

5. Waiver—acceleration. The signer of this note waives demand, presentment for payment, protest, notice of protest, and notice of nonpayment, and agrees that since time is of the essence, if any payment under this note is not paid when due, the holder shall have the right to accelerate and make immediately due and payable the entire unpaid balance of principal and interest.

6. Expenses. If the holder of this note incurs any expenses to enforce any provision of this note, including reasonable attorney's fees, either before or after a lawsuit is begun to enforce this note, the signer of this note agrees to pay the holder's expenses and reasonable attorney's fees, including any attorney's fees at trial and on appeal of any suit or action.

7. Date and place. Signed this _____ day of _____,
(12)   (13)

_____, at _____
(14)   (15)

_____.

8. Signatures.

_____, Signer
(16)

_____, Signer
(16)

9. Guaranty. For value received, the undersigned, _____
(17)

_____,
hereafter called guarantor, unconditionally guarantees the payment of all payments required by the above promissory note as and when they are due. The undersigned also waives demand, presentment for payment, protest, notice of protest, and notice of nonpayment, and agrees that the holder of the note does not have to exhaust the holder's rights against the signer before pursuing the undersigned under this guaranty.

Signed this _____ day of _____, _____.
(18)   (19)   (20)

_____
(21)
Guarantor

_____
(21)
Guarantor

Chapter 12
Bill of Sale

A bill of sale is a written document in which the owner of personal property transfers ownership of the property to someone else.

Personal property includes money, goods, and movable objects. It does not include real property, such as land or buildings attached to land.

Someone who sells personal property gives a bill of sale to the buyer when the property does not have a certificate of title. If property has a certificate of title, the certificate has a section for the seller to complete when transferring the title to someone else. Filling out this transfer section and giving the title to the buyer will transfer ownership the same way that a bill of sale does.

A seller can give a bill of sale to a buyer even when property has a certificate of title. The bill of sale can include more information than the transfer section of a certificate of title. For instance, a bill of sale can include any warranties that the seller makes about the condition or quality of the property.

A seller gives a buyer a bill of sale when the buyer has fully paid the seller for the property being sold. If the buyer pays in full when the seller transfers the property to the buyer, the seller gives the buyer a bill of sale at that time. If the buyer only pays part of the price for the property as a down payment and the rest in payments in the future, the seller and buyer sign a contract for the sale of personal property over time (see Chapter 13 for a discussion of this type of contract). Under this type of contract, the seller gives the buyer a bill of sale when the buyer pays the final payment under the contract.

TYPES OF BILLS OF SALE

Bills of sale may or may not include warranties of title and warranties as to the condition of the property. There are four main warranties of title:

- Warranty that the seller is the owner of the property
- Warranty that the seller has the right to sell the property

- Warranty that the property is free and clear of all encumbrances (an encumbrance is any right in or to the property owned by someone other than the seller or buyer, such as a bank loan, mechanic's lien or easement)

- Warranty that the seller will defend the buyer's rights to the property against someone else's claims that he or she has a right or interest in the property

In a bill of sale without warranties of title, a seller transfers his or her interest in property to a buyer, but the seller does not guaranty that he or she is the owner of the property or has the right to sell the property. The buyer takes the risk that the seller might not have the right to sell the property. The seller says, in effect, "I do not know if I am the owner of this property, but if I do have any ownership rights in this property, I am giving those rights to this buyer."

In a bill of sale without warranties of title, the seller does not represent that there are no liens or encumbrances against the property or that the seller will defend the buyer's rights to the property against claims made by others. A bank loan or mechanic's lien could encumber the property. The seller could have given a bill of sale for the property to another person on the day before giving the bill of sale to the buyer.

In a bill of sale with warranties of title, a seller does represent that he or she is the owner of the property and has the right to transfer the property. The seller represents that he or she will defend the buyer's rights to the property against claims by anyone who says the seller is not the owner of the property. The seller also represents that the property is free of any liens or encumbrances at the time of the sale.

A bill of sale can transfer property with an encumbrance on it, such as a bank loan. The forms in this chapter do not include such a bill of sale because the terms of the bank loan or other encumbrance may make such a bill of sale invalid. If you are a buyer or a seller of property with an encumbrance that will remain on the property after the sale, have an attorney review the encumbrance documents to be sure you can sell the property subject to the encumbrance.

A bill of sale should describe whether or not the seller makes any warranties as to the quality or condition of the property. If a seller sells property "as is" ("as is" means that the seller makes no representations as to the condition or quality of the property), the buyer takes his or her chances as to defects in the property. On the other hand, if the seller warrants that the property is in good working condition at the time of the sale, and that the seller has told the buyer of any defects in the property that the seller is aware of, the buyer can sue the seller for any loss the buyer suffers if the property was not in the condition that the seller said it was.

The samples and forms in this chapter are for simple bills of sale. Bills of sale can be complex, such as a bill of sale involving many pieces of complicated equipment with detailed warranties about each piece of equipment. If you need a complex bill of sale prepared, contact an attorney.

You should use the forms and samples in this chapter only if you are not normally in the business of buying and selling the type of property described in the bill of sale. Certain federal and state laws apply to people who are normally in the business of buying and selling property. These laws are beyond the scope of this book.

Sample Bill of Sale—With Warranties (FIG. 12-1)

Figure 12-1 contains the following information that all bills of sale should contain:

- Name and address of the owner of the property.

- Name and address of the person receiving the property.

- Consideration paid for the property. In any bill of sale, the consideration is what each party gives to the other party in exchange for what each party receives from the other party. In this sample, the consideration the buyer gives to the seller is $200. The consideration the seller gives to the buyer is the chainsaw. If the seller is giving the property to the receiver as a gift, the consideration should be one dollar and "love and affection" or simply one dollar, depending on whether love and affection are the basis of the gift.

- Words of transfer. The words of transfer in the sample are "grant, transfer, sell, and deliver". These words transfer ownership of the property to the receiver. The seller must also physically deliver the property to the receiver. If the seller keeps the property, problems can occur if someone or something destroys the property, or if the seller or someone else claims that the seller did not intend to transfer the property to the buyer.

- Description of the property. A bill of sale should include a description of the property that is so clear there will be no confusion as to what property the bill of sale refers to. Include any model, serial, identification, license, title, or other identifying numbers. Include the manufacturer's name and the name of the "make" of the property, such as "Stihl" chainsaw or "Sears" lawnmower. Describe any attachments that accompany the property, such as the cutting chain in the sample.

- The date when, and the place where, the owner signed the bill of sale.

- Signature of the seller or owner.

- Notary section. An owner does not always have to sign a bill of sale in front of a notary public, but it is wise to do so. The blank bills of sale in this book include notary sections.

In addition to the above elements that all bills of sale should include, FIG. 12-1 includes warranties of title and warranties as to the condition of the property, as explained earlier in this chapter. The buyer can sue the seller if any of the warranties turn out to be false. For instance, if the seller's warranty that he is the owner of the chainsaw and has the right to sell the saw is false, and the true owner takes the saw away from the buyer, the buyer can sue the seller for all the money the buyer paid to the seller. As another example, if the seller's warranty that the saw was in good condition turns out to be false, and the buyer has to have the saw repaired for $40, the buyer can sue the seller for that expense.

If the bill of sale is for a vehicle with an odometer, such as an automobile, motorcycle, or boat, the seller should make a statement regarding the accuracy of the odometer reading on the vehicle. The seller could make any of the following statements, depending on which applies to the particular situation:

- "Seller represents that the odometer of the vehicle described in this bill of sale now reads 56,250 miles. Seller represents that, to the best of his or her knowledge, the odometer reading corresponds to the actual mileage of the vehicle. Seller also represents that, to seller's knowledge, the odometer has not been altered or disconnected in any way."

- "Seller represents that, to the best of his or her knowledge, the odometer reading for this vehicle equals the amount of miles the vehicle has been driven above 100,000 miles."

- "Seller represents that, to the best of his or her knowledge, the odometer reading for this vehicle is not accurate."

- "Seller represents that, even though the odometer was repaired or altered during repair, the mileage shown on the odometer is accurate."

The blank forms at the end of this chapter leave a blank for an odometer statement. If you are preparing a bill of sale for a vehicle with an odometer, use one of the above statements, or any appropriate combination of them, in that blank.

Bill of Sale
(with Warranties of Title)

I, John M. Jones, whose address is 222 Third Street, Waynecastle, Pennsylvania, 17294, as seller, in consideration of Two Hundred Dollars ($200.00), paid to me this day by Edward J. Harris, as buyer, whose address is 333 Fourth Street, Waynecastle, Pennsylvania, 17294, hereby grant, transfer, sell, and deliver to buyer, all seller's rights, title, and interest in a 1985 Model 031-AV Stihl chainsaw with a 20″ blade, Serial No. 0123456, Model No. 457821, including one cutting chain for said saw.

I warrant that I am the sole owner of the above property, that there are no liens or encumbrances on the property, and that I have the right to sell the property. I warrant that I will defend buyer against any claims made against buyer or the property which challenge these warranties made by me.

I represent that, at the time of the sale of this property, the property is in good working condition and, to my knowledge, there are no material defects in the property.

Signed at 222 Third Street, Waynecastle, Pennsylvania, 17294.

Dated: 2/02/89

_____

John M. Jones

COMMONWEALTH OF PENNSYLVANIA)
) ss.

COUNTY OF BURR)

I, Wanda C. Twobucks, a resident of and a notary public in and for the Commonwealth of Pennsylvania, who am duly commissioned and sworn and legally authorized to administer oaths and affirmations, hereby certify that on February 2, 1989, John M. Jones, who is known to me personally to be the person who is named as seller in the above bill of sale, appeared before me and, after being first duly sworn by me under penalty of perjury, swore on his oath to the truth of the facts in the above bill of sale, and signed and acknowledged said bill of sale in my presence, of his own free will, and for the purposes explained in said bill of sale.

Subscribed and sworn to before me this 2nd day of February, 1989.

_____

Notary Public

(SEAL)   My commission expires: 2/09/90

Sample Bill of Sale—Without Warranties (FIG. 12-2)

Figure 12-2 contains the information that all bills of sale should contain, but does not contain warranties that the seller owns the property, has the right to sell the property, will defend against claims anyone makes against the property, that there are no liens or encumbrances against the property, or warranties as to the condition of the property.

The words of transfer in FIG. 12-2 are different from FIG. 12-1. Here, the words of transfer are "quitclaims, releases, and delivers" because the seller is not claiming that he owns the property. He is simply releasing to the buyer whatever interest he may have in the property.

Figure 12-2 transfers property to two buyers. It uses wording which affects who owns the property if one of the buyers dies. Most husbands and wives want the survivor to own property automatically when one of them dies. The wording "as joint tenants, to be held jointly with right of survivorship, not as tenants in common" provides for that. The buyers do not want to own the property as "tenants in common". In a tenancy in common when one owner dies, that owner's interest in the property passes according to his or her will, or according to the laws of his or her state if there is no will. It may be necessary to probate the deceased person's estate to transfer ownership of his or her property. Probate is the process of going to court to manage the affairs of a deceased person. You can avoid probate by owning property as joint tenants with right of survivorship, not as tenants in common.

With a bill of sale such as FIG. 12-2, the buyer should investigate who owns the property and whether there are any liens or encumbrances against the property. In the case of a car, because the property has a certificate of title, the buyer can determine who owns the property by requesting that the Department of Motor Vehicles search the title to the property. The buyer can determine whether or not there are liens or encumbrances against the property by asking the Department of Motor Vehicles whether anyone is listed as a security interest holder on the title to the vehicle or whether anyone has filed a lien against the property.

If the property does not have a certificate of title, the buyer cannot do a search. If the buyer suspects that the property may be stolen, the buyer can give the police the serial, model, and identification numbers of the property and ask whether anyone has reported the property stolen.

If the property does not have a certificate of title, the buyer can investigate whether or not there are any liens or encumbrances against the property by contacting the secretary of state's office and the county clerk's office in the county and state where the property is located. The buyer should ask whether anyone has filed any claims against the property. These offices will need the name of the seller and a description of the property.

With a bill of sale such as FIG. 12-2, the buyer should examine the property thoroughly to be sure it is in good condition. If the buyer is not qualified to examine the property, he or she should consider hiring someone who is qualified to inspect the property. Such an inspection is often inexpensive. If the inspection uncovers a defect, the buyer can renegotiate the price downward to compensate for the cost of the inspection and repair of the defect.

This chapter includes two blank bills of sale. Figure 12-3 includes warranties of title. Figure 12-4 does not. Both forms provide space to describe whether the property is sold "as is", or whether the seller is representing that the property is in good working condition. Both forms provide space to describe the representations the seller makes regarding the odometer, if the bill of sale involves a vehicle that has an odometer.

The instructions for filling out FIG. 12-4 are the same as the instructions for filling out FIG. 12-3. The differences in the forms do not involve the blank spaces. The differences are in the wording that is preprinted on the forms. Choose the correct form for your situation and then follow the detailed instructions below.

Bill of Sale
(without Warranties of Title)

I, John M. Jones, whose address is 222 Third Street, Waynecastle, Pennsylvania, 17294, as seller, in consideration of Two Hundred Dollars ($200.00), paid to me this day by Edward J. Harris and June S. Harris, husband and wife, as buyers, whose address is 333 Fourth Street, Waynecastle, Pennsylvania, 17294, hereby quitclaim, release, and deliver to buyers, as joint tenants, to be held jointly with right of survivorship, not as tenants in common, all my right, title, and interest in a 1985 Model 031-AV Stihl chainsaw with a 20″ blade, Serial No. 0123456, Model No. 457821, including one cutting chain for said saw.

I make no warranties as to my ownership of this property, my right to sell this property, or as to whether or not there are any liens or encumbrances against this property. I make no warranties that I will defend buyer against claims made by other people against the property or against buyer.

I am selling my right, title, and interest in this property "as is", with no representations as to the condition or quality of the property.

Signed at 222 Third Street, Waynecastle, Pennsylvania, 17294.

Dated: 2/02/89

_____

John M. Jones

COMMONWEALTH OF PENNSYLVANIA)
) ss.
COUNTY OF BURR)

I, Wanda C. Twobucks, a resident of and a notary public in and for the Commonwealth of Pennsylvania, who am duly commissioned and sworn and legally authorized to administer oaths and affirmations, hereby certify that on February 2, 1989, John M. Jones, who is known to me personally to be the person who is named as seller in the above bill of sale, appeared before me and, after being first duly sworn by me under penalty of perjury, swore on his oath to the truth of the facts in the above bill of sale, and signed and acknowledged said bill of sale in my presence, of his own free will, and for the purposes explained in said bill of sale.

Subscribed and sworn to before me this 2nd day of February, 1989.

_____

Notary Public

(SEAL) My commission expires: 2/09/90

Bill of Sale
(with Warranties of Title)

I, _____
(1)

_____,

whose address is _____
(2)

_____

_____,

as Seller, in consideration of _____
(3)

_____ ($_____)

paid to me this day by _____
(4)

_____,

as Buyer, whose address is _____
(5)

_____

_____,

hereby grant, transfer, sell, and deliver to Buyer, (as joint tenants, to be held jointly
(6)
with right of survivorship, not as tenants in common,) all right, title, and interest in the
following property: _____
(7)

_____

_____

_____

_____

_____.

I warrant that I am the sole owner of the above described property and that there are no liens or encumbrances on the property. I warrant that I have the right to sell this property. I will warrant and defend my ownership of and right to sell this property, and my representation that there are no liens or encumbrances against the property, against any claims made by anyone challenging those rights.

I make the following representation(s) regarding the condition of this property and regarding any odometer on this property: _____
(8)

_____

_____

_____

_____

_____.

Signed at _____.
(9)

Dated: _____
(10)

_____   _____
Seller   (11)   Seller   (11)

STATE OF _____)
(12)

) ss.

COUNTY OF _____)
(13)

I, _____,
(14)

a resident of and notary public in and for the state and county named above, who am duly commissioned and sworn and legally authorized to administer oaths and

affirmations, hereby certify that on _____,
(15)

_____,
(16)

who is/are known to me personally to be the signer(s) in the above bill of sale, appeared before me and, after being first duly sworn by me under penalty of perjury, swore on his/her/their oath(s) to the truth of the facts in the above bill of sale, and signed and acknowledged said bill of sale in my presence, of his/her/their own free will, and for the purposes explained in said bill of sale.

Subscribed and sworn to before me this _____ day of _____,
(17)   (18)

_____.
(19)

_____
Notary Public   (20)

(SEAL)   My Commission expires:_____
(22)   (21)

Instructions for Blank Bills of Sale (FIG. 12-3 and 12-4)

Figures 12-3 and 12-4 have blank spaces with a number under each space. Before filling in any of the blanks, make several photocopies of the desired form. Use one copy as a work copy, one as an original, and the rest for future work copies or originals. Fill out the work copy first and be sure it is correct, then type or print in the blanks on your original bill of sale. The following numbered instructions match the numbers under the blanks in each form:

(1) Enter the name(s) of the seller(s).

(2) Enter the address(es) of the seller(s).

(3) Enter the consideration for the sale, that is, the amount of money or property the buyer paid or traded for the property. Enter the amount of money in words and in numbers. If the seller is giving the property to the buyer, put "one dollar and love and affection", or "one dollar," depending on whether love and affection are the basis of the gift.

(4) Enter the name(s) of the buyer(s)

(5) Enter the address(es) of the buyer(s).

(6) If there is more than one buyer, and they wish to own the property jointly with right of survivorship so that the survivor will own the property automatically when one of them dies, leave the language in the parentheses alone. If there is only one buyer, or if there is more than one buyer but they do not wish to own the property in this manner, cross out the language in the parentheses. The seller(s) should initial the cross-out.

(7) Enter a full description of the property sold. Include any model, title, and serial numbers, the year of manufacture, the brand name, any equipment or attachments sold with the property, and any other information necessary to make it clear beyond doubt what property the bill of sale is referring to.

(8) Enter any warranties regarding the condition of the property. If the property is sold "as is", use the language in FIG. 12-2 for "as is" sales. If the property is sold with representations regarding its working condition, use language similar to the language used in FIG. 12-1, or use language which describes exactly what representations the seller is making about the property. If the bill of sale is for a vehicle with an odometer, include the appropriate odometer statement for the vehicle. See the explanation of FIG. 12-1 for several different types of wording a seller can use regarding odometers. If the bill of sale is not for a vehicle with an odometer, print or type, "property does not have an odometer."

(9) Enter the city and state where the bill of sale is signed.

(10) Enter the date when the bill of sale is signed.

(11) The seller(s) should sign his/her/their full name(s) in front of a notary public for the county and state where the bill is signed.

The following items should be completed by a notary public:

(12) Enter the state where the notary public is authorized to notarize documents and where the bill of sale is signed.

(13) Enter the county where the bill of sale is signed.

(14) Enter the name of the notary public.

(15) Enter the date the seller(s) signed the bill of sale.

(16) Enter the name(s) of the seller(s).

(17,18,19) Enter the day, month, and year when the seller(s) signed the bill of sale.

(20) The notary public should sign here.

(21) The notary public should indicate when his or her commission expires.

(22) The notary public should affix his or her seal to the bill of sale.

After the bill of sale is signed, notarized, and sealed, the buyer should keep the original bill of sale.

Bill of Sale
(without Warranties of Title)

Even if there is more than one Seller or Buyer, all parties are referred to in the singular in this bill of sale.

I, _____
(1)

_____,

whose address is _____
(2)

_____

_____,

as Seller, in consideration of _____
(3)

_____

_____ ($ _____),

paid to me this day by _____
(4)

_____,

as Buyer, whose address is _____
(5)

_____

_____,

hereby quitclaim, release, and deliver to Buyer(s), (as joint tenants, to be held jointly
(6)
with right of survivorship, not as tenants in common,) all right, title, and interest in the

following property: _____
(7)

_____

_____

_____

_____

_____.

I make no warranties as to my ownership of this property, right to sell this property, whether there are any liens or encumbrances against this property, or as to my defending this property or the Buyer against claims made against the property or against Buyer.

I make the following representation(s) regarding the condition of this property and regarding any odometer on this property: _____
(8)

_____

_____

_____

_____

_____.

Signed at _____.
(9)

Dated: _____
(10)

_____   _____
(11)   (11)
Seller   Seller

STATE OF _____)
(12)

) ss.

COUNTY OF _____)
(13)

I, _____,
(14)

a resident of and notary public in and for the state and county named above, who am duly commissioned and sworn and legally authorized to administer oaths and

affirmations, hereby certify that on _____,
(15)

_____,
(16)

who is/are known to me personally to be the signer(s) in the above bill of sale, appeared before me and, after being first duly sworn by me under penalty of perjury, swore on his/her/their oath(s) to the truth of the facts in the above bill of sale, and signed and acknowledged said bill of sale in my presence, of his/her/their own free will, and for the purposes explained in said bill of sale.

Subscribed and sworn to before me this _____ day of _____,
(17)   (18)

_____.
(19)

_____
Notary Public   (20)

(SEAL)   My Commission expires:_____
(22)   (21)

Chapter 13

Personal Property
Sales Contract

A personal property sales contract is an agreement in which the seller of personal property finances the buyer's purchase of the property. A clear, written contract defines and protects the rights of the seller and buyer.

Personal property includes goods and movable objects, such as cars, boats, and lawn mowers. Personal property does not include real property, such as land or buildings attached to land.

You should read this chapter in conjunction with Chapter 12 on bills of sale. If a seller sells personal property that does not have a certificate of title, the seller gives the buyer a bill of sale for the property when the buyer pays the seller in full under the sales contract. If property has a certificate of title, the seller completes the transfer section of the certificate and gives the certificate to the buyer when the buyer pays the seller in full under the sales contract. Filling out the transfer section of a certificate of title, and giving the certificate to the buyer, transfers ownership the same way that a bill of sale does.

A seller can give a bill of sale to a buyer even when property has a certificate of title. A bill of sale can include more information than the transfer section of a certificate of title, such as warranties regarding the condition of the property.

A seller should not use the personal property sales contract in this chapter when a buyer pays the full price for property at the time the seller gives the property to the buyer. In that case, if the property has a certificate of title, the seller endorses and gives the buyer the certificate of title. If property does not have a certificate of title, the seller gives the buyer a bill of sale.

Only people who are not normally in the business of selling personal property can use the personal property sales contract in this chapter. Certain federal and state laws apply to people who are regularly in the business of selling personal property. Those laws are beyond the scope of this chapter.

The personal property sales contract in this chapter is a secured agreement. If the buyer does not pay according to the terms of the agreement, the seller can repossess or foreclose upon specific collateral. The collateral is the personal property being bought.

Although an oral sales contract is valid in some circumstances, you should assume that a personal property sales contract must be in writing. Both parties should sign and date two original contracts in the presence of a notary public for the state where the parties sign the contract. The seller should keep one original contract, and the buyer should keep the other.

Before signing a personal property sales contract for a vehicle, a seller and buyer should contact their local Department of Motor Vehicles. They should notify the Department of Motor Vehicles of the sale, and ask for any forms that the Department requires them to complete at the time of the sale. The seller and buyer should ask a representative of the Department of Motor Vehicles whether or not the seller has to turn in his or her license plates at the time of the sale.

If one of the parties to the contract is a minor, the other party should be aware that in most states a minor can refuse to live up to a contract, unless the contract is for a "necessity". Most states do not consider cars and boats necessities.

Usury Laws

Some states have laws which make it illegal to charge more than a certain percentage of interest each year. These laws are called *usury laws*. A personal property sales contract violates these laws if it provides for interest greater than the amount these laws allow.

State usury laws differ widely. Figure 13-1 lists, for all 50 states and the District of Columbia, the sections of each state's laws that discuss the maximum rate of interest each state allows. You can find these laws by going to a law library in your state. A law library is located at your county courthouse. Ask the librarian to help you find the law referred to in FIG. 13-1. Or, contact your local consumer protection office.

Some states tie the maximum rate of interest to the Federal Reserve discount rate on 90-day commercial paper in effect in the Federal Reserve Bank in the district where the loan occurs. Your local banker will know the rate, or will be able to obtain the rate for you.

Figure 13-1 is based on 1987 and 1988 laws. The state legislatures of the 50 states meet at different times. Some legislatures only meet once every two years. When a state legislature passes a law, the legislature or a publishing company publishes that law at a later time. Several months can pass before the legislature or publisher sends that law to the libraries around the country. As you read these words, months or years will have also passed from the time this book was edited, printed, and distributed. For these reasons, this book, like all legal books, cannot be absolutely current.

Figure 13-1 indicates whether the information for a particular state is based on the 1987 or 1988 laws of that state. If you want to confirm whether or not your state has changed its laws, go to a law library in your state and read the most current version of the law referred to in FIG. 13-1. Even if the law has changed, the new law will usually have the same number as the old law. Check what are known as the "pocket parts" of your state's laws. Pocket parts are supplements which contain the latest revisions of a state's laws. Or, again, call your local consumer protection agency.

The rates of interest in FIG. 13-1 apply only to people who are not regularly in the business of selling personal property. Different rates apply to others.

The rates of interest in FIG. 13-1 refer to simple interest, not compound interest. Compound interest is interest charged on interest. A seller compounds interest when he or she takes interest owed by a buyer, adds it to the principal balance, and then charges the interest rate of the contract on the new balance. Most states prohibit charging compound interest in sales contracts.

All interest rates in FIG. 13-1 are annual interest rates unless otherwise stated. Some states allow different rates of interest for consumer sales and non-consumer sales. Most states define consumer sales as sales where the seller is regularly in the business of selling the type of property that is being sold. California, Arkansas, and Hawaii define consumer sales as sales where the buyer uses the property primarily for personal, household, or family purposes. These states do not require that a seller be in the business of selling the property in order to have a consumer sale. Since this chapter does not cover sales made by sellers who are regularly in the business of selling property, consumer-sale rates of interest do not apply to the forms in this chapter, except in California, Arkansas, and Hawaii. Figure 13-1 describes the maximum rates of interest in California, Arkansas, and Hawaii for consumer and non-consumer sales.

The maximum rates of interest in FIG. 13-1 always refer to rates agreed to in writing. Most states have lower maximum interest rates if the parties do not put their agreement in writing.

References to "loans" in FIG. 13-1 apply to personal property sales contracts. A seller in a personal property sales contract is lending money to the buyer by selling property to the buyer over time.

Fig. 13-1. State Laws on Usury.

Alabama—8-8-1 (1987 Update). Six percent (6%) on an oral contract and eight percent (8%) on a written contract.

Alaska—45.45.010 (1987 Update). The maximum interest rate is five percentage points above the annual rate charged by member banks of the Twelfth Federal Reserve District on the day on which the parties sign the contract or the lender commits to lending the money. Usury laws do not apply to loans greater than $100,000.

Arizona—44-1201 (1988 Update). Parties may agree in writing to any rate of interest.

Arkansas—4-57-104 and Arkansas Constitution Article 19, Section 13 (1987 Update). Maximum interest rate for general loans cannot be more than five percentage points above the Federal Reserve discount rate on 90-day commercial paper in effect in the Federal Reserve Bank in the Federal Reserve District in which Arkansas is located. The applicable discount rate is the rate at the time that the lender makes the loan. For consumer loans, the maximum interest rate is seventeen percent (17%).

California—Constitution Article 15 Section 1 (1988 Update). The Constitution of California says the maximum interest rate is ten percent (10%) on loans where the proceeds are used for personal, family, or household purposes. The maximum interest rate on loans where the proceeds are used for other purposes is the higher of ten percent (10%) or not more than five percent (5%) above the rate prevailing on the 25th of the month preceding the earlier of the date the parties sign the contract or the date of making the loan as established by the Federal Reserve Bank of San Francisco on advances to member banks. Savings and loans, banks, credit unions, pawnbrokers, lenders of real estate-secured loans, and certain other lenders registered with the state or federal government are exempt from these limitations.

Colorado—5-12-103 (1987 Update). The maximum interest rate is forty-five percent (45%).

Connecticut—37-4 (1987 Update). The maximum interest rate is twelve percent (12%).

Delaware—6-2301 (1987 Update). The maximum interest rate is not more than five percent (5%) above the Federal Reserve discount rate for loans of $100,000 or less. For loans greater than $100,000, there is no maximum rate of interest if the loan is not secured by a mortgage on the debtor's principal residence.

District of Columbia—28-3301 (1988 Update). The maximum interest rate is twenty-four percent (24%).

Florida—687.02 and .03 (1988 Update). The maximum interest rate is eighteen percent (18%) simple interest for loans of $500,000 or less. For loans greater than $500,000, the maximum interest rate is twenty-five percent (25%).

Georgia—7-4-2 (also known as 57-101) (1988 Update). On loans of $3,000 or less, the maximum interest rate is sixteen percent (16%). On loans greater than $3,000, the parties may agree to any rate of interest, not to exceed 5% per month. (7-4-18).

Hawaii—478-4 (1987 Update). The maximum interest rate is 1% per month or 12% per year for consumer credit transactions and for home business loans. For other loans, no maximum interest rate was found.

Idaho—28-42-201 (1988 Update). The maximum interest rate is whatever amount the parties agree to.

Illinois—17-6404 (1988 Update). The maximum rate of interest is nine percent (9%).

Indiana—No maximum rate of interest was found for loans where the lender is not regularly in the business of lending money (1988 Update).

Iowa—535.2(3)(a) (1988 Update). The maximum rate of interest is two percent (2%) above the monthly average of the 10-year constant maturity interest rate of United States government notes and bonds, as published by the Board of Governors of the Federal Reserve System for the second calendar month preceding the month during which the maximum rate based thereon will be effective, rounded to the nearest one-quarter of one percent (0.25%) per year. Contact the Superintendent of Banking for Iowa, who is required to determine and publish in the Iowa Administrative Bulletin, or as a legal notice in a newspaper of general circulation in Polk County, the maximum rate of interest in effect in Iowa.

Kansas—16.207 (1987 Update). The maximum rate of interest is fifteen percent (15%).

Kentucky—360.010 (1987 Update). The maximum rate of interest is not more than four percentage points above the discount rate on 90-day commercial paper in effect at the Federal Reserve Bank in the Federal Reserve District where the transaction is consummated, or nineteen percent (19%), whichever is less, if the loan is for $15,000 or less. If the loan is for more than $15,000, Kentucky law sets no maximum rate of interest.

Louisiana—Civil Code Article 2924 (1988 Update). The maximum rate of interest is twelve percent (12%).

Maine—No statute was found which established a maximum rate of interest (1987 Update).

Maryland—Commercial Law 12-103 (1987 Update). The maximum rate of interest is eight percent (8%), but the interest rate can be higher under certain conditions. Those conditions are lengthy. Anyone who wants to charge more than 8% interest should read Section 12-103.

Massachusetts—Chapter 107, Section 3, Chapter 140, Section 90 (1987 Update). For loans under $1,000, the maximum rate of interest is eighteen percent (18%). For loans of $1,000 or more, the maximum rate of interest is twenty percent (20%). See Chapter 271, Section 49.

Michigan—19.15(1) (1988 Update). The maximum rate of interest is seven percent (7%).

Minnesota—334.01 (1988 Update). The maximum rate of interest is eight percent (8%) on loans under $100,000. On loans of $100,000 or more, there is no limit on the interest rate.

Mississippi—75-17-1(2) (1987 Update). The maximum rate of interest is the greater of ten percent (10%) or not more than five percent (5%) above the discount rate, excluding surcharges, on 90-day commercial paper in effect at the Federal Reserve Bank in the Federal Reserve District where the lender is located.

Missouri—408.030 (1988 Update). The maximum rate of interest is ten percent (10%) or the market rate, whichever is higher. The market rate is equal to the monthly index of long-term U.S. government bond yields for the second preceding calendar month before the beginning of the calendar quarter, plus three percent (3%) rounded to the nearest tenth of a percent. The calendar quarters begin on January 1, April 1, July 1, and October 1 of each year.

Montana—31-1-107 (1987 Update). The maximum rate of interest is not more than six percent (6%) above the prime rate of major New York banks as published in the *Wall Street Journal* edition dated three business days before execution of the loan agreement.

Nebraska—45-101.03(1) and .04(4) (1987 Update). The maximum rate of interest is sixteen percent (16%) on loans of less than $25,000. There is no maximum rate of interest on loans of $25,000 or more.

Nevada—99.050 (1987 Update). The parties may agree to any rate of interest.

New Hampshire—399-A-3 (1988 Update). The parties to a loan may agree in writing to any amount of interest for loans greater than $10,000. For loans of $10,000 or less, a lender must obtain a license from the State Banking Commission and cannot charge greater than two percent (2%) per month on loans up to $600, and not more than one and one-half percent (1½%) on amounts between $600 and $1,500.

New Jersey—31:1-1(a) (1988 Update). The maximum rate of interest is sixteen percent (16%).

New Mexico—56-8-11.1 (1987 Update). New Mexico law provides that any interest rate may be agreed to in writing.

New York—General Obligations Laws 5-501(1), Banking Law Section 14(a) (1988 Update). The maximum rate of interest is sixteen percent (16%).

North Carolina—24-1.1 (1987 Update). On loans greater than $25,000, there is no maximum rate of interest. On loans of $25,000 or less, the maximum rate of interest is the amount announced and published by the Commissioner of Banks on the 15th

Fig. 13-1. (Cont'd). 215

day of each month for the following calendar month on six-month U.S. Treasury Bills plus six percent (6%), or sixteen percent (16%), whichever is greater.

North Dakota—47-14-09 (1987 Update). The maximum interest rate is not more than five and one-half percent (5.5%) above the current cost of money as reflected by the average rate of interest payable on U.S. Treasury Bills maturing in six months in effect for North Dakota for six months immediately prior to the month in which the loan occurs, as computed and declared on the last day of each month by the State Banking Commissioner. These usury laws do not apply to loans in excess of $35,000.

Ohio—1343.01 (1988 Update). On loans of $100,000 or less, the maximum interest rate is eight percent (8%). On loans over $100,000, there is no maximum interest rate.

Oklahoma—14A-3-605 (1988 Update). The maximum rate of interest is forty-five percent (45%).

Oregon—82.010(3)(a) and (b) (1987 Update). There is no maximum rate of interest on loans over $50,000. On loans of $50,000 or less, for business or agricultural loans the maximum interest rate is the greater of twelve percent (12%), or five percent (5%) above the discount rate, including surcharges, on 90-day commercial paper in effect at the Federal Reserve Bank in the Federal Reserve District where the lender is located on the date of the loan. For loans other than business or agricultural loans, the rate is the same, except the rate does not include surcharges.

Pennsylvania—41-PS-201, 41-301, 41-302, 18-911(h)(1)(IV) (1988 Update). With certain exceptions, the maximum rate of interest is 6%. For the exceptions, the maximum rate of interest is 25%. The exceptions are loans in excess of $50,000, loans secured by real property other than residential real property, loans to corporations, business loans greater than $10,000, and unsecured, non-collateralized loans greater than $35,000.

Rhode Island—6-26-2 (1987 Update). The maximum rate of interest is the greater of twenty-one percent (21%), or nine percent (9%) above the Treasury Bill Index for the week preceding the date of the debtor's agreement. The Treasury Bill Index for any week shall be the highest rate for U.S. Treasury Bills with maturities of one year or less as established at the auction of such Treasury Bills during such week or, if no such auction is conducted during such week, at the auction next preceding such week. The Director of Business Regulations shall keep a record of the Treasury Bill Index and shall publish it not less than weekly in a newspaper of general circulation.

South Carolina—(1987 Update). The parties to a loan may agree in writing to any interest rate.

South Dakota—54-3-1.1 (1988 Update). There is no maximum rate of interest.

Tennessee—47-14-103 (1987 Update). The maximum rate of interest depends on a number of different circumstances, but is generally four percent (4%) above the prime loan rate published by the Federal Reserve System, or twenty-four percent (24%), whichever is less.

Texas—Civil Statutes Article 5069-1.01(d), -1.02, -1.04 (1988 Update). The maximum rate of interest that parties can agree to is the rate based on 26-week U.S. Treasury Bills for the week preceding the week in which the lender makes the loan, with a maximum rate of twenty-four percent (24%).

Utah—15-1-1(2) (1988 Update). The parties may agree in writing to any rate of interest.

Vermont—Title 9-41(a) (1988 Update). The maximum rate of interest is twelve percent (12%).

Virginia—Section 6.1-330.55 (1988 Update). The maximum rate of interest is twelve percent (12%).

Washington—19.52.020 (1988 Update). The maximum interest rate is the higher of twelve percent (12%), or four percent (4%) above the equivalent coupon issue yield (as published by the Federal Reserve Bank of San Francisco), of the average bill rate for 26-week Treasury Bills as determined at the first bull market auction conducted during the calendar month immediately preceding the establishing of the interest rate by written agreement of the parties.

West Virginia—47-6-5(b) (1988 Update). The parties may agree in writing to an interest rate not greater than eight percent (8%) per year.

Wisconsin—138.05(1)(a) (1988 Update). The maximum rate of interest is twelve percent (12%) on loans under $150,000. There is no limit on loans of $150,000 or more unless the loan is secured by the debtor's principal residence.

Wyoming—No law was found setting any maximum rate of interest (1987 Update).

Sample Personal Property Sales Contract (FIG. 13-2)

Figure 13-2 is a sample personal property sales contract. The numbered paragraphs of the explanation that follows correspond with the numbered paragraphs of the sample.

1. Date. Every personal property sales contract should state the date that it becomes effective, which should be the date the seller(s) and buyer(s) sign the contract.

2. Parties. Every personal property sales contract should list the accurate names of all parties to the agreement. It should state what happens if one of the parties dies before the buyers pay the contract in full. Most husbands and wives want the survivor to continue to make or receive payments under a sales agreement when one of them dies, without going through a probate court (a probate court manages a deceased person's affairs). The sample contract contains wording to allow the survivor(s) of the sellers and buyers to continue to make or receive payments without having to go through a probate court. That wording is, ". . . or the survivor, not as tenants in common". The parties do not want a *tenancy in common.* A tenancy in common is a form of joint ownership, in which, when one joint owner dies, a probate court manages the deceased person's interest in joint property.

A personal property sales contract should list the addresses of the seller(s) and buyer(s). The residences of the seller(s) and buyer(s) affect what state's laws govern the contract.

3. Property. A personal property sales contract should describe the property being sold. The description should include any model, serial, title, and other identification numbers. The description should include the make of the property, the year it was manufactured, and any other information that will make it clear beyond doubt what property is being sold.

4. Price. A personal property sales contract should describe the price the buyers are paying for the property. The contract should describe how the buyers will pay the price, including the amount of any down payment, the amounts and dates of monthly payments, the interest rate, the beginning date for interest, and whether interest is included in or will be paid in addition to the monthly payments. In the sample, the buyers will make monthly payments. In some agreements, the buyers do not make any payments until the date the entire price is due. In those types of agreements, the payment paragraph would read as follows:.

Buyers agree to pay sellers for the vehicle the sum of Two Thousand Five Hundred Dollars ($2,500.00), plus interest as described below, on or before the 6th day of May, 1991. All unpaid balances under this note shall bear interest at the rate of SIX PERCENT (6%) per year, beginning May 6, 1989.

The second paragraph in the price section protects the sellers against state usury laws. It states that the parties do not intend to violate those laws. If they do so inadvertently, the sellers will give the buyers credit against the principal balance for any interest the buyers paid in excess of the state usury law limit.

The usury paragraph will not guaranty that a court will not find a contract usurious if the interest charged is greater than the legal rate, but it does support a seller's argument that if the seller did violate a state's usury law, the seller did so inadvertently.

5. Possession. A contract should describe when the buyers obtain possession of the personal property, which should be the date they sign the contract.

6. Proration. A contract should describe the proration date for any proratable items, such as insurance. Proration means that the sellers pay expenses on the property before the proration date, and the buyers pay expenses after that date (usually the buyers also agree to pay the expenses for the proration date). The proration date should be the date the buyers sign the contract and obtain possession of the property.

7. Insurance. A personal property sales contract should require the buyers to keep the property being sold in good condition. A contract should require the buyers to maintain adequate insurance for the property, including comprehensive, liability, and collision insurance for any motor vehicle. If buyers have adequate collision insurance for a vehicle and the buyers damage the vehicle, the buyers will have insurance money to repair the vehicle or pay the sellers in full for the vehicle. If buyers receive any insurance proceeds as a result of damage to the property, making the sellers loss payees under the insurance policy ensures that the buyers will pay the sellers what they owe them. The insurance check will include the names of the sellers to prevent the buyers from cashing it without the signatures of the sellers.

A personal property sales contract should require the buyers to prove to the sellers that the buyers have the insurance the contract requires. The sample contract contains language to accomplish this. If the buyers do not prove that they have the required insurance, the sellers should obtain any necessary insurance and charge the buyers for the cost of that insurance.

8. Liens. A personal property sales contract should state that the buyers cannot allow any liens to attach to the property, such as mechanic's liens. A contract should state that the buyers cannot use the property as collateral for any loans until the buyers have paid the sellers in full under the contract.

9. Default. A personal property sales contract should explain what the sellers can do if the buyers do not live up to any of the provisions of the contract. In such a case, the sellers can accelerate the balance. Accelerating the balance means the entire unpaid balance of principal and interest, not just one or two monthly payments, is immediately due. This remedy provides a strong incentive to the buyers to perform all the obligations of the contract.

A contract should be a secured agreement. The property being sold secures the buyers' performance of the contract. The property is collateral for the amount of money the buyers owe the sellers. The sellers have the right to repossess or sue to repossess the property if the buyers fail to live up to the contract.

If buyers breach a contract, the contract should allow the sellers to repossess the property they sold to the buyers, sell the property, and pursue the buyers for a *deficiency judgment*. A deficiency judgment is the difference between what the sellers sell the property for after repossessing it, and the sum of what the buyers still owe the sellers under the sales contract, plus sellers' attorney's fees and costs in repossessing and selling the property.

Sellers can only repossess property if they do so without *breaching the peace*. Breaching the peace means the sellers cannot repossess property if the buyers are present and refuse to allow the sellers to take the property. Sellers also breach the peace if they break into a garage or other closed area to repossess property. No one should attempt to repossess property without the advice of an attorney. If sellers cannot repossess property without breaching the peace, they must obtain a court order and the assistance of a sheriff.

10. Attorney's fees. A personal property sales contract should state that if one party incurs expenses to enforce any provision of the contract, including reasonable attorney's fees, the other party should have to pay those expenses and attorney's fees. If a contract does not include this paragraph, a party who has to hire an attorney to force the other party to live up to the contract cannot make the other party pay the attorney's fees he or she incurs.

11. Complete agreement. A contract should be the complete and final agreement of the parties regarding the sale. It should state that if the parties had any oral or written agreements before signing the contract, those agreements have no effect after signing the contract.

12. Condition of the property—warranties. Most sellers want to sell property "as is". "As is" means that once a buyer takes possession of property, any problems with the property are the buyer's problems, not the seller's. Selling the property "as is" does not mean that a seller does not have to live up to any *express warranties* the seller makes about the property. An express warranty is any statement of fact or promise about the property, or any description of the property.

The sample contains several warranties of title. The sellers represent that they own the property and have the right to sell it. They represent that they will defend the buyers against claims made against the property by anyone challenging any of the representations the sellers make in this paragraph. These warranties protect a buyer from a seller who sells the buyer something that the seller does not own, and from a seller who does not tell the buyer about a lien or encumbrance on the property.

The sample contains a warranty that the property is free of any liens or encumbrances at the time of the sale. An encumbrance is any right or interest someone other than the seller or buyer has in the property, such as a bank loan to finance the property, or a mechanic's lien for work done on the property.

A contract can transfer property with an encumbrance on it, but sellers and buyers should not try to prepare their own sales agreements if property is sold with an encumbrance on it. Have an attorney review the encumbrance document to be sure you can buy or sell the property subject to the encumbrance. The terms of a bank loan or other encumbrance may make such a contract invalid.

The warranties paragraph in the sample ends by saying that the warranties of title will survive the contract and continue after the buyers pay the sellers in full. The sellers must live up to the warranties of title even after the buyers pay the sellers all the money they owe them. When the contract is paid in full should not affect the sellers' defense of their ownership of and right to sell the property and their statement that there were no encumbrances on the property at the time of the sale.

13. Title. In the sample contract, the sellers and buyers changed the title to show the buyers as the owners and the sellers as security interest holders. The sellers hold the title until buyers pay the sellers in full, at which time the sellers sign off the title and deliver it to the buyers. The buyers then change the title into their own names, without the sellers showing as security interest holders.

By changing the title into the names of the buyers, the sellers protect themselves if the buyers are involved in an accident with the vehicle. If the title listed the sellers as owners of the vehicle at the time of the accident, someone involved in the accident might sue the sellers in a lawsuit arising from the accident.

By listing the sellers as security interest holders on the title, the buyers cannot transfer the title without the signatures of the sellers. Listing the sellers as security interest holders gives notice to the world that the sellers still have an interest in the property.

In the sample contract, the personal property has a certificate of title. For property with a certificate of title, the seller endorses and delivers the title to the buyer when the buyer pays the contract in full. The seller can also sign and deliver to the buyer a bill of sale for the property, which can include more information than the transfer section of a certificate of title, such as any warranties that the seller makes about the property.

If a buyer wants to receive a bill of sale when he pays the seller in full, that should be explained in the contract. The forms in Chapter 12 can be used to prepare a bill of sale.

For property that does not have a certificate of title, the seller should give the buyer a bill of sale when the buyer pays the seller in full. The contract should explain that. The forms in Chapter 12 can, again, be used to prepare the bill of sale.

For property with a registration, such as an automobile, the seller and buyer should change the registration to the name of the buyer at the time the parties sign the sales agreement. The buyer should keep the registration with the property.

14. Assignment. The sample contract prevents the buyers from selling or transferring the vehicle before paying the sellers in full. If the contract does not restrict the buyers' right to sell or assign the property before they pay the sellers in full, the buyers can do so.

15. Heirs and assigns. A contract should bind the heirs and successors of one of the parties, if one of them dies. A contract should also bind the *assigns* of the parties. An assign is anyone to whom a seller or buyer assigns his or her interest in a contract.

16. Odometer statement. If a sales contract involves a vehicle with an odometer, the seller should make a statement regarding the accuracy of the odometer reading on the vehicle. In the sample contract, the sellers represent that the reading is accurate and that, to their knowledge, no one altered the odometer.

If a seller cannot represent that an odometer is accurate and unaltered, the seller could make one or more of the following statements:

Seller represents that, to the best of his/her knowledge, the odometer reading for this vehicle equals the amount of miles the vehicle has been driven above 100,000 miles.

Seller represents that, to the best of his/her knowledge, the odometer reading for this vehicle is not accurate.

Seller represents that even though the odometer was repaired and altered during repair, the mileage shown on the odometer is accurate.

17. Address change. A personal property sales contract should require a buyer to inform a seller of the buyer's current address.

18. Use of property. A contract should prohibit a buyer from using the property for hire, or for any other improper or illegal purpose.

19. Waiver. In the sample contract, the buyers waive certain rights. When the buyers waive the rights listed in this provision, the sellers do not have to demand that the buyers make any required payment (demand and presentment), do not have to notify the buyers that they have not made a required payment (notice of nonpayment), and do not have to obtain or give notice of a bank or other official certification of nonpayment (protest and notice of protest).

20. Additional provisions. In this paragraph are any additional provisions to the agreement.

21. Financing statement. This paragraph of the sample explains that the agreement is a *financing statement*. A financing statement is a document which a *secured party* files with the county court and/or the secretary of state's office in the state where the secured party lives and in the county where the property is located. A secured party is anyone who has a security interest in collateral. A person holds a security interest in collateral if he or she can repossess or sue to repossess the collateral if the buyer of the property breaches the sales agreement in any way.

Secured parties do not have to file financing statements for the sale of property that has a certificate of title. A secured party sends the title to the Department of Motor Vehicles and changes it so that the buyer is shown as owner and the seller is shown as a security interest holder. Secured parties only need to file financing statements for property that does not have a certificate of title.

The purpose of filing a financing statement is to give notice to other creditors that a secured party has an interest in certain property a debtor has in his or her possession. If someone obtains a judgment usually against a debtor after a secured party files a financing statement against property in the debtor's possession, the person who obtained the judgment usually cannot sell the property without paying the secured party what the debtor owes the secured party.

The secretary of state's office in every state will have forms for financing statements. The forms are short, and are called *UCC-1 financing statements*. UCC stands for *Uniform Commercial Code*, which is a set of laws governing commercial transactions. A secured party can use these forms, instead of using the contract as a financing statement—as is done in the sample.

A financing statement should contain the names and addresses of the secured party and the debtor, a statement describing the collateral, and the signatures of both the debtor and secured party. If the collateral is crops or fixtures attached to real estate, the financing statement must describe the real estate affected. Some states require that financing statements include the social security or federal identification numbers of the debtor and secured party, the maturity date of the debt being secured, the original amount of the debt being secured, a statement as to whether or not the debtor is a transmitting utility, the name and address of the preparer of the financing statement, and an address where the secretary of state or county clerk should send the financing statement after recording it.

The Uniform Commercial Code provides that a secured party must file a financing statement in the county court and/or in the secretary of state's office, and/or in the county real estate recorder's office, in order to have priority over other creditors of the debtor in regard to certain collateral. Again, this only applies to collateral that does not have a certificate of title.

Where a secured party files a financing statement depends on a confusing set of rules. The safe thing to do is to file a copy of the financing statement in the following places:

- The office of the county clerk in the county of the debtor's residence, or where the debtor keeps the goods if the debtor is not a resident of the state
- The secretary of state's office
- The office of the county clerk in the county where the land is located, if the collateral is crops growing or to be grown on land
- The office where someone would record a mortgage on the real estate concerned, if the collateral is fixtures or will become fixtures, or if the collateral is timber or minerals (in this case, the financing statement must contain a description of the real estate concerned)
- The office of the county clerk of the county where the debtor has his or her place of business, if the debtor has a place of business in only one county in the state

A financing statement is valid for five years. If a sales contract will last longer than five years, the secured party should file a continuation financing statement in all the places where the original financing statement was filed. You can obtain continuation financing statements from the secretary of state's office in your state.

When a debtor pays a contract in full, the secured party should file a termination of a financing statement in all the offices where the original financing statement was filed. The purpose of a termination statement is to show that the property is no longer subject to the security interest of a secured party. You can obtain a termination statement from the secretary of state's office in your state.

22. Date and place. Every contract should describe the date when, and the address where, the parties signed the contract.

23. Signatures, guaranty, and notary. The parties should sign two original contracts in the presence of a notary public for the state in which the parties sign the contract. The seller should keep one original contract and the buyer should keep the other.

A seller should sell property to people he or she is confident will make the payments the contract requires. If a seller is not sure whether or not a buyer will make the payments, the seller should have someone that the seller is confident will make the payments guaranty the contract. The sample contract provides such a guaranty. If the buyers do not perform any of the obligations of the contract, the sellers can pursue the buyers and/or the guarantor to perform the contract. In the sample, the guarantor agrees that the sellers do not have to exhaust their remedies against the buyers before pursuing the guarantor under the guaranty. The sellers do not have to sue the buyers before demanding payment from the guarantor. As soon as the buyers fail to make a payment, the sellers can demand that payment from the guarantor.

How to record payments If a personal property sales contract provides for monthly or regular payments and provides that regular payments shall include interest, a seller should apply part of each monthly payment to interest and part to the principal balance. The method for recording payments is the same as for promissory notes (see Chapter 11).

Personal Property Sales Contract

1. Date. This contract is effective the 3rd day of May, 1989.

2. Parties. This contract is between John Joseph Smith and Mary Ellen Smith, husband and wife, or the survivor, not as tenants in common, whose address is 222 Third Street, Waynecastle, Pennsylvania, County of Burr, 17294, referred to as "sellers", and Edward Allen Johnson and Mary Elizabeth Johnson, husband and wife, or the survivor, not as tenants in common, whose address is 333 Fourth Street, Waynecastle, Pennsylvania, County of Burr, 17294, referred to as "buyers".

3. Property. Sellers agree to sell to buyers, and buyers agree to buy from sellers, a 1968 Ford Mustang automobile, Serial No. 25667892, Title No. 14167824, Vehicle Identification No. 666-443231.

4. Price. Buyers agree to pay sellers for the vehicle the sum of TWO THOUSAND FIVE HUNDRED DOLLARS ($2,500.00), as follows: Five Hundred Dollars ($500.00) upon signing this contract, receipt of which sellers hereby acknowledge. The remaining balance of Two Thousand Dollars ($2,000.00) shall be payable in monthly payments of not less than Two Hundred Dollars ($200.00) each, payable on the first day of each month, beginning with the month of June, 1989, and continuing until the buyers pay the entire unpaid balance, including principal and interest. All unpaid balances shall bear interest at the rate of SIX PERCENT (6%) per year from May 3, 1989, until paid. Monthly payments shall include the interest described above.

The parties do not intend to obligate buyers to pay any money in excess of the legal rate of interest allowed by the laws of the Commonwealth of Pennsylvania. If buyers do pay any money in excess of the legal rate of interest allowed by the laws of the Commonwealth of Pennsylvania, the sellers shall apply such excess money to reduce the principal amount the buyers owe the sellers.

5. Possession. Buyers shall be entitled to possession of the vehicle on May 3, 1989.

6. Proration. The parties shall prorate any proratable items regarding this vehicle as of May 3, 1989.

7. Insurance. Buyers agree at all times to keep the vehicle in good condition and fully covered by comprehensive, liability, and collision insurance with an insurance company acceptable to sellers. Collision insurance shall be equal to the full insurable value of the vehicle. Liability insurance shall be not less than required by the Commonwealth of Pennsylvania. The insurance policy must contain a loss payee clause naming the sellers as loss payees, and must require at least ten (10) days written notice to sellers before it can be cancelled. Upon request by sellers, buyers shall promptly deliver to sellers an original policy evidencing that buyer is maintaining all insurance required by this contract. If buyers do not show such evidence to sellers at sellers' request, sellers shall be entitled to declare

Fig. 13-2. (Cont'd). *Page 2 of 4* **223**

a default of this contract and/or obtain insurance required by this contract, and add the cost of such insurance to the balance owed by buyers to sellers under this contract.

8. Liens. Buyers agree to keep this vehicle free of all liens and encumbrances until buyers pay sellers in full under the terms of this contract.

9. Default. If buyers fail to perform any of the terms of this contract, sellers shall be entitled to pursue any and all of their legal remedies against buyers, including repossession of the vehicle, sale of the vehicle, and obtaining a deficiency judgment against buyers. Since time is of the essence in this contract, if buyers fail to perform any obligation of this contract exactly when required by this contract, sellers may make the entire unpaid balance under this contract, including principal and interest, immediately due and payable. This contract shall act as a security agreement to secure buyers' performance of all obligations under this contract. Buyers grant sellers a security interest in the vehicle sold and in the proceeds of any sale of the vehicle.

10. Attorney's fees. If either party incurs any expenses to enforce any provision of this contract, including reasonable attorney's fees, either before or after either party begins a lawsuit or other action under this contract, the losing party in such suit or action, or the party causing the other party to incur such expenses if there is no suit or action, agrees to pay the other party's expenses and reasonable attorney's fees, including attorney's fees at trial and on any appeal of any suit or action.

11. Complete agreement. This contract is the complete and final agreement of the parties regarding this sale. This contract replaces any prior written or oral agreements.

12. Condition of property—representations. Sellers represent that sellers are the owners of, and have the right to sell, the property being sold in this contract. Sellers will defend the buyers' rights to the property against claims made against the property by anyone challenging the representations in this paragraph. Sellers also represent that the property is free of any liens or encumbrances at the time of this sale. These representations will survive this contract and continue after the buyers pay this contract in full. Sellers are selling the vehicle to buyers "as is". Buyers understand that sellers are making no representations regarding the condition of the vehicle.

13. Title. Sellers will transfer the title to the vehicle into the names of buyers, with sellers shown on the title as security interest holders. Sellers will hold the title until buyers pay this contract in full. At the time the contract price is paid in full, sellers will endorse the title and deliver it to buyers.

14. Assignment. Any attempt by buyers to sell, assign, or in any way transfer their interest in this vehicle or this contract without paying sellers in full for all sums the buyers owe under this contract shall be void.

15. Heirs and assigns. This contract is binding upon the heirs, successors, and assigns of the parties.

16. Odometer statement. The sellers state that the odometer of the vehicle described in this contract now reads 56,250 miles. Sellers represent that, to the best of their knowledge, the odometer reading corresponds to the actual mileage of the vehicle. Sellers also represent that, to their knowledge, the odometer has not been altered or disconnected in any way.

17. Address change. Buyers agree to notify sellers of any change of buyers' address within ten (10) days of such change of address. Buyers' present address is 333 Fifth Street, Waynecastle, Pennsylvania, 17294.

18. Use of property. Buyers agree not to use the vehicle sold under this contract for hire, or for any improper or illegal use.

19. Waiver. The buyers waive demand, presentment for payment, protest, notice of protest, and notice of nonpayment, and agree that if buyers fail to perform any obligation under this contract, the sellers shall have the right to pursue all sellers' legal remedies under this contract and under applicable law, without any prior notice to buyers.

20. Additional provisions. None.

21. Financing statement. This security agreement shall also be a financing statement under Article 9 of the Uniform Commercial Code of the Commonwealth of Pennsylvania. The names, addresses, and social security numbers of the debtors are Edward Allen Johnson and Mary Elizabeth Johnson, 333 Fourth Street, Waynecastle, Pennsylvania,County of Burr, 17294, 123-45-6789 and 987-65-4321, respectively. The names, addresses, and social security numbers of the secured parties are John Joseph Smith and Mary Ellen Smith, 222 Third Street, Waynecastle, Pennsylvania, County of Burr, 17294, 012-34-5678 and 876-54-3210, respectively. This financing statement covers a 1968 Ford Mustang automobile, Serial No. 25667892, Title No. 14167824, Vehicle I.D. No. 666-443231. This financing statement also covers proceeds and products of the collateral. Since the collateral does not consist of goods which are or will become fixtures, this financing statement does not describe any real estate. The initial indebtedness secured by this financing statement, and the maturity date of this contract, are listed above in Paragraph Four. This financing statement was prepared by Max M. Mumfee, Attorney at Law, 666 Fifth Street, Waynecastle, Pennsylvania. Debtor is not a transmitting utility. Return a copy of this financing statement to the secured parties at the address listed in this paragraph.

22. Date and place of signing. This contract is signed in duplicate by all parties on May 3, 1989, at 222 Third Street, Waynecastle, Pennsylvania, County of Burr, 17294.

23. Signatures, guaranty, and notary.

_____ _____
Seller Buyer

_____ _____
Seller Buyer

Fig. 13-2. (Cont'd). *Page 4 of 4* **225**

For value received, the undersigned, Betty Sue Smith, unconditionally guarantees buyers' performance of all their obligations under the above contract. The undersigned also waives demand, presentment for payment, protest, notice of protest, and notice of nonpayment, and agrees that the sellers do not have to exhaust their rights against the buyers before being entitled to pursue the undersigned under this guaranty.

Signed this 3rd day of May, 1989.

Betty Sue Smith
Guarantor

COMMONWEALTH OF PENNSYLVANIA   )
) ss.
COUNTY OF BURR   )

I, Wanda C. Twobucks, a resident of and notary public in and for the Commonwealth of Pennsylvania, who am duly commissioned and sworn and legally authorized to administer oaths and affirmations, hereby certify that on May 3, 1989, John Joseph Smith, Mary Ellen Smith, Edward Allen Johnson, Mary Elizabeth Johnson, and Betty Sue Smith, who are known to me personally to be the sellers, buyers, and guarantor in the above contract, appeared before me and, after being first duly sworn by me under penalty of perjury, swore on their oaths to the truth of the facts in the above contract, and signed and acknowledged said contract in my presence, of their own free will and for the purposes explained in said contract.

Subscribed and sworn to before me this 3rd day of May, 1989.

Notary Public
(SEAL)   My Commission Expires: 2/09/90

Instructions for Blank Personal Property Sales Contract (FIG. 13-3)

Figure 13-3 is a blank personal property sales contract. The form has blank spaces with a number under each blank. Before filling in any of the blanks, make several photocopies of the form. Use one or more copies as work copies, two as original contracts, and the rest for future work copies or originals. Fill out a work copy first and be sure it is correct, then type or print in the blanks on your two original contracts.

The following numbered instructions match the numbers under the blanks in the form:

(1,2,3) Enter the day, month, and year that the contract takes effect, which should be the same date the parties sign it.

(4) Enter the name(s) of the seller(s). If there is more than one seller, explain what happens if one of the sellers dies before the buyer pays the contract in full. See the sample and explanation of the sample for wording to create joint ownership with right of survivorship, which avoids probate.

(5) Enter the address(es) of the seller(s).

(6) Enter the name(s) of the buyer(s). If there is more than one buyer, explain what happens if one of the buyers dies before the buyers pay the contract in full.

(7) Enter the address(es) of the buyer(s).

(8) Enter a description of the property being sold, including the year the property was manufactured, the name of the company that manufactured the property, the make of the property, and any serial, model, title, and identification numbers.

(9) Enter the total sales price for the property. Include a description of the price in words, and then in numbers in the parentheses.

(10) Describe the terms of payment, including any down payment, the amount of any regular payment, the day of the month regular payments are due, the month that payments begin, the interest rate, the date interest begins, whether interest is included in or is to be paid in addition to any installment payments, the date the entire balance is due if there are no regular or monthly payments, and any other terms of payment.

(11,12) Enter the name of the state where the parties are signing the contract, which should be the same state where the seller lives.

(13) Enter the date the buyer is entitled to possession of the property.

(14) Enter the date for proration of any proratable items.

(15) Enter any warranties that the seller is making regarding the property. If the property is sold "as is", enter "Property sold as is. Seller makes no representations regarding the condition or quality of the property."

(16) Enter any representations that any bill of sale the seller delivers to the buyer will include. If a bill of sale will not have any representations, put "none" in this blank. If the seller will give the buyer a certificate of title instead of a bill of sale, put in this blank, "The seller will not give buyer a bill of sale because seller will endorse and deliver a certificate of title to buyer instead of giving buyer a bill of sale." If the property has no certificate of title, put "not applicable" in this blank.

(17) If the property has a certificate of title, put "not applicable". If the property does not have a certificate of title, enter any representations that the seller will include in the bill of sale the seller delivers to buyer when the buyer pays the contract in full. If the bill of sale will not have any representations, put "none" in this blank.

(18) If the sale involves a motor vehicle with an odometer, the seller should describe the accuracy or inaccuracy of the odometer reading on the vehicle in this blank.

Several possible wordings for odometer statements were included earlier in this chapter. If the sale does not involve a motor vehicle with an odometer, put "not applicable" in this blank.

(19) Enter the buyer's current address.

(20) Enter any additional provisions in this space. If there are none, put "none".

(21) If the sale involves a vehicle with a certificate of title, do not complete Blanks 21 through 26. Put "not applicable" in each of these blanks and go on to Blank 27. If the collateral is not a vehicle with a certificate of title, enter in Blank 21 the name of the state where the seller and buyer sign the contract, which should be the same state where the seller lives. After completing Blank 21 follow instructions for Blanks 22 through 26.

(22) Enter the name(s), address(es), and social security number(s) of the debtor(s). The buyer(s) is/are the debtor(s).

(23) Enter the name(s), address(es), and social security number(s) or federal employment identification number(s) of the secured party(ies). The seller(s) is/are the secured party(ies).

(24) Enter a description of the property that is being sold to the buyer, including any serial, model, title, and identification numbers. State whether the collateral is goods, such as a lawn mower, or crops, minerals, timber, equipment, or fixtures. An example of a fixture is a heating or cooling unit attached to a building.

(25) Enter a description of the real estate to which the collateral is attached, if the collateral is crops, minerals, timber, equipment, or fixtures. If the collateral is none of these, put "not applicable" in this blank. If Blank 25 does not contain enough space for the legal description, put "See Exhibit A" in Blank 25 and attach a copy of the legal description of the property to the sales contract. Label that attachment "Exhibit A" by writing that at the top or bottom of the page.

(26) Enter the name and address of the person who prepared the financing statement, which would be whoever prepared the sales contract.

(27) Enter the date the seller and buyer sign the contract.

(28) Enter the address where the seller and buyer sign the contract.

(29) The seller(s) should sign two original contracts in the presence of a notary public for the state where the seller(s) signs the contract. This form assumes that the seller, buyer, and any guarantor will sign at the same time in the presence of the same notary public.

(30) The buyer(s) should sign two original contracts in the presence of a notary public for the state where the buyer(s) signs the contract.

(31) If someone is guarantying the contract, enter the name(s) of the guarantor(s), and follow instructions 32 through 35. If no one is guarantying the contract, put a large "X" through the entire guaranty portion of this form, and ignore instructions 32 through 35.

(32,33,34) Enter the day, month, and year that the guarantor signs the guaranty.

(35) The guarantor(s) should sign on these lines in the presence of a notary public for the state where the parties signed the contract.

The following items should be completed by a notary public:

(36) Enter the state where the parties signed the contract.

(37) Enter the county where the parties signed the contract.

(38) Enter the name of the notary public.

(39) Enter the date the parties signed the contract.

(40) Enter the names of the seller(s), buyer(s) and any guarantor(s).

(41,42,43) Enter the day, month, and year thats the parties signed the contract.

(44) The notary public should sign here.

(45) Enter the date the notary public's commission expires.

(46) The notary public should affix his or her seal to the contract.

After completing two original contracts, the seller should keep one original contract and the buyer should keep the other.

If the sale involves a vehicle, seller and buyer should go to the state Department of Motor Vehicles to transfer title to the vehicle into the name of the buyer, showing seller as a security interest holder. Seller should keep the title until the buyer pays all sums the buyer owes under the contract, at which time the seller should sign off as security interest holder on the title, date his or her signature, deliver the title to the buyer, and deliver a copy of the endorsed title to any guarantor of the sales agreement. The seller should also sign and deliver a bill of sale to the buyer if the contract requires that. Seller and buyer should read Chapter 12 to prepare such a bill of sale. The buyer should take the title to the Department of Motor Vehicles to transfer it into the buyer's name, free of the security interest of the seller.

If the sale does not involve a vehicle with a certificate of title, the seller and buyer should make five (5) copies of the contract, and should sign and date all the copies. The seller should file the signed copies with all the offices described in the explanation of Paragraph 21 of the sample contract. If the seller does not want to use signed copies of the contract as financing statements, the seller can obtain financing statement forms from the secretary of state's office in the state where the seller sells the property. After obtaining those forms from the secretary of state's office, the seller should fill them out, sign them, have the buyer sign them, and file them with the offices described in the explanation of Paragraph 21 of the sample contract. When the buyer pays the contract in full, the seller should obtain, fill out, and file a termination of the financing statement in all the offices where the seller filed the original financing statement. At the same time, the seller should sign and deliver a bill of sale to the buyer. Seller and buyer should read Chapter 12 to prepare such a bill of sale.

Fig. 13-3. Personal Property Sales Contract (Blank). *Page 1 of 7*   **229**

Personal Property Sales Contract

1. Date. This contract is effective on the _____ day of _____,
(1)   (2)

_____.
(3)

2. Parties. This contract is between _____
(4)

_____

_____

_____,

whose address(es) is/are _____
(5)

_____

_____

_____,

referred to as "seller(s)", and _____
(6)

_____

_____,

whose address(es) is/are _____
(7)

_____

_____,

referred to as "buyer(s)". Even if there is more than one seller or buyer, the parties
will be referred to in the singular for the rest of this contract.

3. Property. Seller agrees to sell to buyer, and buyer agrees to buy from seller, the

following personal property: _____
(8)

_____

_____

_____

_____

_____

_____.

4. Price. Buyer agrees to pay seller for the property the sum of _____
(9)

_____ ($_____),

as follows: _____
                                    (10)

_____

_____

_____

_____

_____

_____.

The parties do not intend to obligate the buyer to pay any money in excess of the legal rate of interest allowed by the laws of the State of _____.
                                                                                    (11)
If the buyer does pay any money in excess of the legal rate of interest allowed by the State of _____, the seller shall apply such excess money
                           (12)
to the principal amount that the buyer owes the seller.

5. Possession. Buyer shall be entitled to possession of the property on

_____.
                (13)

6. Proration. The parties shall prorate any proratable items regarding this property as of _____.
                                            (14)

7. Insurance. Buyer agrees at all times to keep the property fully covered by comprehensive, liability, and collision or property damage insurance with an insurance company acceptable to seller. Collision or property damage insurance shall be equal to the full insurable value of the property. Liability insurance shall be not less than required by the State listed in Blank 21 of this contract. On all insurance policies, there shall be a loss payee clause naming the seller as a security interest holder. All insurance olicies must require at least ten (10) days written notice to seller before they can be cancelled. Upon request by seller, buyer shall promptly deliver to seller an original policy evidencing that buyer is maintaining all insurance required by this contract. If buyer does not show such evidence, seller shall be entitled to declare a default under this contract and/or obtain insurance required by this contract, and add the cost of such insurance to the balance owed by buyer to seller under this contract.

8. Liens. Buyer agrees to keep this property free of all liens and encumbrances until buyer pays seller in full under the terms of this contract.

9. Default. If buyer fails to perform any of the terms of this contract, seller shall be entitled to pursue any and all of seller's legal remedies against buyer, including repossession of the property, sale of the property, and obtaining a deficiency judgment against buyer. Since time is of the essence in this contract, if buyer fails to perform any of the terms of this contract exactly when required by this contract, seller may make the entire unpaid balance under this contract, including principal and interest, immediately due and payable. This contract shall act as a security agreement to secure buyer's performance of all obligations under this contract. Buyer grants seller a security interest in the property sold and in the proceeds of any sale of the property.

Fig. 13-3. (Cont'd). *Page 3 of 7* **231**

10. Attorney's fees. If either party incurs expenses to enforce any provision of this contract, including reasonable attorney's fees, either before or after either party begins a lawsuit or other action under this contract, the losing party in such suit or action, or the party causing the other party to incur such expenses if there is no suit or action, agrees to pay the other party's expenses and reasonable attorney's fees, including attorney's fees at trial and on any appeal of any suit or action.

11. Complete agreement. This contract is the complete and final agreement of the parties regarding this sale. This contract replaces any prior written or oral agreements.

12. Condition of property—representations. Seller represents that seller is the owner of, and has the right to sell, the property being sold in this contract. Seller will defend the buyer's rights to the property against claims made against the property by anyone challenging the representations in the paragraph. Seller also represents that the property is free of any liens or encumbrances at the time of this sale. These representations will survive this contract and continue after buyer pays this contract in full. Seller makes the following representation(s) regarding the condition of the property: _____

_____

_____.

13. Title. If this sale involves property with a certificate of title, seller will transfer the title to the property into the name of buyer, with seller shown on the title as a security interest holder. Seller will hold the title until buyer pays this contract in full. At the time this contract is paid in full, seller will endorse the title and deliver it to buyer. Seller will also deliver a bill of sale to buyer which will include the following representations:

_____
(16)

_____

_____

_____

_____

_____

_____.

If this sale involves property without a certificate of title, seller shall give buyer a bill of sale when buyer pays the contract price in full. The bill of sale shall include the following representations: _____
(17)

_____

_____

_____

_____

_____.

14. Assignment. Any attempt by buyer to sell, assign, or in any way transfer buyer's interest in this property or this contract without paying seller in full for all sums the buyer owes under this contract shall be void.

15. Heirs and assigns. This contract is binding upon the heirs, successors, and assigns of the parties.

16. Odometer statement. If this sale involves a motor vehicle with an odometer, seller makes the following representation regarding the odometer on this vehicle:

_____
(18)

_____

_____

_____

_____

_____.

17. Address change. Buyer agrees to notify seller of any change of buyer's address within ten (10) days of such change of address. Buyer's current address is

_____
(19)

_____

_____.

18. Use of property. Buyer agrees not to use this property for hire, or for any improper or illegal purpose.

19. Waiver. Buyer waives demand, presentment for payment, protest, notice of protest, and notice of nonpayment, and agrees that if buyer fails to perform any obligation under this contract, the seller shall have the right to pursue all seller's legal remedies under this contract and under applicable law, without any prior notice to buyer.

20. Additional provisions. _____
(20)

_____

_____

_____

_____

_____.

Fig. 13-3. (Cont'd). *Page 5 of 7* **233**

21. **Financing statement.** This security agreement shall also be a financing statement under Article 9 of the Uniform Commercial Code of the State of

_____ . The name(s), address(es), and social security
(21)

number(s) of the debtor(s) is/are _____
(22)

_____

_____

_____ .

The name(s), address(es) and social security or federal employment identification

number(s) of the secured party(ies) is/are: _____
(23)

_____

_____

_____ .

This financing statement covers the following property: _____
(24)

_____

_____

_____

_____ .

This financing statement also covers proceeds and products of the collateral. If the collateral consists of crops, minerals, timber, or fixtures or equipment attached to real

estate, the following is a description of the real estate: _____
(25)

_____

_____

_____

_____

_____ .

The initial indebtedness secured by this financing statement and the maturity date of this contract are listed above in Paragraph Four. This financing statement was prepared

by _____
(26)

_____

_____ .

Debtor is not a transmitting utility. Return a copy of this financing statement to the secured party at the address listed in this paragraph.

22. Date and place of signing. This contract is signed in duplicate on

_____ , at _____
                                                                (28)
            (27)

_____

_____.

23. Signatures, guaranty, and notary.

_____   _____
                            (29)   (30)
            Seller   Buyer

_____   _____
                            (29)   (30)
            Seller   Buyer

For value received, the undersigned, _____
                                                              (31)

_____,

unconditionally guarantees buyer's performance of all buyer's obligations under the
above contract. The undersigned also waives demand, presentment for payment,
protest, notice of protest, and notice of nonpayment, and agrees that the seller does
not have to exhaust seller's rights against the buyer before being entitled to pursue the
undersigned under this guaranty.

Signed this _____ day of _____, _____.
                       (32)   (33)   (34)

                        _____
                                                    (35)
                                Guarantor

                        _____
                                                    (35)
                                Guarantor

Fig. 13-3. (Cont'd). *Page 7 of 7*   **235**

STATE OF _____)
                  (36)
) ss.

COUNTY OF _____)
                  (37)

I, _____ ,
                  (38)

a resident of and notary public in and for the state and county named above, who am duly commissioned and sworn and legally authorized to administer oaths and affirmations, hereby certify that on _____ ,
                                                      (39)

_____
                                  (40)

_____

_____

_____ ,

who are known to me personally to be the seller(s), buyer(s), and guarantor(s), if any, in the above contract, appeared before me and, after being first duly sworn by me under penalty of perjury, swore on their oaths to the truth of the facts in the above contract, and signed and acknowledged said contract in my presence, of their own free will and for the purposes explained in said contract.

Subscribed and sworn to before me this_____ day of _____ ,
                                           (41)   (42)

_____ .
   (43)

_____
                                           (44)
Notary Public

(SEAL)   My Commission expires: _____
  (46)   (45)

Chapter 14
Contracts with Independent Contractors

This chapter explains contracts with independent contractors, such as contracts for home improvement or landscaping work. An *independent contractor* is someone who is in business for himself or herself—not an "employee" of someone else. Whether a worker is an independent contractor or an employee depends on the particular circumstances of the job. The important factors are the method of payment of the worker and who has the right to direct what work is done, how it is done, and when it is done.

An independent contractor has independence in choosing what work he or she will perform, and in choosing the methods to accomplish the work. An independent contractor is not subject to the control of the person that he or she is working for, except as to the final result of the work. An independent contractor is usually paid on a per-job basis. The independent contractor decides the number of hours to spend on the job and when he or she will do the work, except for completion dates when all or part of the work must be finished.

An employee usually does not control the details of his or her work, such as the place where work is performed, the time when work is performed, or how and when the employee is paid. An employee is usually paid a set salary or an hourly wage.

An employer can be held liable to someone who is hurt by an employee while the employee was doing work for the employer. This is usually not true if the worker was an independent contractor. The injured person can sue the contractor, but usually cannot sue the person who hired the independent contractor.

An employer is responsible for providing workers' compensation, unemployment insurance, and social security coverage for employees. Someone who hires an independent contractor does not have to provide any of these coverages. The independent contractor is responsible for his or her own workers' compensation, unemployment insurance, and social security coverage.

Certain wage and working condition laws apply to employer/employee relationships, but not to employer/independent-contractor relationships. These laws involve overtime pay, working conditions, hiring and firing, and other matters.

For the above reasons, it is usually advantageous to hire an independent contractor as opposed to an employee, but the disadvantage of doing so is loss of control. An employer has the right to tell an employee exactly what, when, where, and how he or she wants the work done. The essence of an employer/independent-contractor relationship is that the employer does not have that control over the independent contractor.

SIMPLE VS. COMPLEX CONTRACTS

Contracts with independent contractors range from hiring a landscaper to perform a one-day job on your land for a cost of several hundred dollars, to hiring an accountant to manage the records of a multimillion-dollar company for a cost of many thousands of dollars. When you hire a builder to build a new home for you, the builder is usually an independent contractor.

The contracts with the accounting firm and the house contractor will be much longer and more complex than the landscaping contract. Hiring an attorney to prepare or review the contract with the accountant or builder makes more sense than hiring an attorney to prepare or review the contract with the landscaper.

You can use the forms in this chapter to define the terms of your agreement with an independent contractor and to protect yourself against the independent contractor's breaking his or her agreement with you. You should use the samples and forms in this chapter in situations where the work an independent contractor will do is simple enough and the cost of the work is small enough, that preparing your own contract makes more sense than hiring an attorney to do so.

PREPARATION AND BIDS

Before you hire an independent contractor to perform landscaping, home improvement, or other work for you, decide as best you can exactly what you want the contractor to do. Research what materials you might want used and the costs of materials.

For landscaping and home improvement jobs, draw a diagram of what you want the property, house, or room to look like after the work is completed. Make movable, cut-out parts, such as trees, shrubs, doors, windows, electrical outlets, and lights. Experiment with different combinations of these objects on a general diagram of the property, house, or room. Always know where North, South, East, and West are located so you can consider sunlight in making decisions. Make the distances on the diagram as close to scale as possible.

After you have drawn a diagram of what you want, go to your local city and county zoning agencies. Your telephone book will list their addresses under the name of your city or county government. Show them your diagram or describe what you plan to do, and ask them whether zoning and building laws allow you to do what you plan to do. Ask what permits and licenses they require in order to do what you plan to do. Make sure you or your contractor complies with whatever instructions the zoning agencies give you.

Decide how much you can afford to spend for the work you have in mind. Call several contractors to inspect the location where they will do the work, to review your drawings, and to give you a written bid for the work. Before you agree to have a contractor come out to give you a bid for the job, confirm whether or not the contractor will charge a fee for the inspection.

Bids are important. They allow you to compare prices between contractors, to compare what materials each contractor proposes to use, and to compare how quickly each contractor proposes to complete the work.

You can tell a great deal about a contractor by his or her bid. You are looking for a contractor who knows his or her work well enough that he or she can tell you in advance what materials he or she will use, how many people will work on the job, how quickly the contractor can finish the job, and how much the whole and each part of the job will cost, including labor, materials, insurance, permits, and licenses.

Contractors often propose a low bid to get a job, and then increase the cost of the work as the work progresses, after it is inconvenient for you to change contractors. To avoid this, insist that a bid be a *firm bid*. A firm bid states that the contractor will not increase the cost of the job after the bid is accepted. Some contractors will object to this.

They may work on a *cost-plus* basis, which means you pay them for the costs of materials, plus 10 percent or some other percentage of the total costs.

A cost-plus arrangement is risky for the employer. The independent contractor is not telling the employer what the total price of the project will be, and therefore has a blank check on materials and labor. On the other hand, the risk of a firm bid is that, once you accept it, the contractor may use inferior materials or labor to complete the job for the quoted price. The solution is to require a firm bid that describes exactly what materials the contractor will use, and that states that the workmanship involved will be competent.

A sample bid, an explanation of the sample, and a blank bid are provided in this chapter, along with step-by-step instructions on how to complete the blank bid.

LIENS AND INSURANCE

A *lien* is a claim someone makes against a car, building, land, or other property, for work performed on (or materials supplied to) the property. For example, a *construction lien* is a claim filed by a contractor, subcontractor, or supplier of materials filed against a building or land, for work done or materials supplied to that building or land. A *subcontractor* is someone a contractor hires to perform part of a job. A property owner could pay a contractor the full price for a job, but if the contractor does not pay the subcontractors or suppliers, they can force the owner to pay again—this time, directly to them—by filing a lien against the owner's property.

You can avoid problems with liens by investigating the contractor before you hire him or her. Call the Better Business Bureau to find out how long the contractor has been in business and whether anyone has filed complaints against them. Call the licensing bureaus at city hall or the county courthouse, and find out if the contractor has all the licenses required by the city, county, or state. Your telephone book will list the telephone numbers of those bureaus under the name of your city, county, or state government.

If the independent contractor is a corporation, obtain the name of the owner of the business or the officer with the highest authority in the business. Obtain the street address of the contractor, not just a post office box number. Ask for several references from people for whom the contractor has worked. Contact those people. Ask your bank, or a friend who owns a business, to obtain a credit report to see whether the contractor has a good or bad credit rating.

You can also avoid problems with liens by requiring that the contractor have a *surety bond*. A surety bond is a contract between a contractor and an insurance company, in which the insurance company agrees to be responsible for the contractor's performance. In return, the contractor pays a premium to the insurance company.

If a contractor objects to a surety bond, think twice before you hire them. A surety bond is insurance for you. If the contractor has a surety bond, you can file a claim against that bond if the contractor fails to perform the work in any way.

If a contractor has a surety bond, confirm that fact by obtaining the name of the insurance company. Call the insurance company to verify that the contractor's bond will cover your situation. Ask the insurance company the amount of the surety bond, to be sure it is enough to cover any damage or loss you may suffer as a result of the contractor's work. Ask the contractor or the contractor's insurance company to give you a copy of the surety bond, or some written proof of coverage.

Before you hire workers to come to your property, contact your homeowner's insurance agent. Explain the work to be done. Ask your agent whether he or she recommends any additional precautions. Ask whether your homeowner's insurance policy will cover any injuries to workers or others on your property, and any damage to your property or other people's property caused by the workers. Ask the amount of coverage that you have for injuries to workers or others and for damage to property. Make sure you have enough coverage to protect your property and to protect yourself against lawsuits for injuries. I recommend insuring your property for replacement value—the cost of replacing any property that is completely destroyed. I recommend liability coverage of at least $100,000 per person and $300,000 per accident to cover injuries to workers or other people.

Sample Bid (FIG. 14-1)

You can obtain a bid for any type of job, but bids are more useful in home improvement and landscape work. Figure 14-1 illustrates a bid for such work. The following numbered paragraphs match the numbered paragraphs of the sample.

1. Parties. Every bid should identify the contractor, the person employing the contractor (who is usually the owner of the property), and the addresses of each. The contractor's address should be a street address, not a post office box.

2. Job description and diagram. This paragraph describes what the contractor proposes to do for the owner and refers to a diagram of the work to be done. In the sample, the contractor proposes to build a carport. The bid should describe where the contractor will construct the carport, who will supply materials and labor, and who will pay for any permit fees and other expenses.

With landscaping and home improvement bids, a picture is worth a thousand words. Exhibit "A", attached to the sample bid, describes the materials the contractor will use in the carport, and the dimensions of the carport. The diagram should indicate the dimensions of the materials that will be used. For instance, it makes a big difference whether the contractor uses 4-×-4-inch or 6-×-6-inch posts to support the carport. The owner wants 6-×-6-inch posts because they will provide better support than 4-×-4-inch posts. One contractor could submit a low bid using 4-×-4-inch posts. Unless the owner knew that the bid was low because of the undersized posts, the owner might be tempted to choose the low bid over a higher bid that proposed using 6-×-6-inch posts.

3. Warranties. No contractor should object to including warranties that the workmanship will be competent and that the completed structure will be fit for the purposes for which it is normally used. If a contractor will not make these warranties, the contractor is not showing much confidence in his or her work and workers.

As to warrantying against defects, the amount of time for this warranty is negotiable. If the owner could negotiate a 10- or 20-year warranty, the owner should do so. The owner should insist on some warranty against defects, so he or she will have an opportunity to observe the work over a period of time. If the carport falls down two days after the contractor builds it, the owner should be able to demand that the contractor rebuild the carport.

4. Materials. This paragraph describes what materials the contractor will use on the job. It states that the owner does not authorize the contractor to use old materials in building the carport. This provision is important in comparing bids. A contractor may submit a lower bid based on his assumption that he can use cheaper, older materials.

5. Supervision of workers. This paragraph explains that the contractor's authorized representative must supervise all the workers performing work on this job. The owner wants the contractor to properly supervise the workers. Also, having one person in charge of all the workers is convenient for the owner. The owner can talk to that person if the owner has any questions. This paragraph also provides that the contractor will use only competent and skilled workers for the job. The owner has no control over this other than to make the contractor state in the bid that the workers will be competent and skilled.

If they are not, this statement forces the contractor to repair or redo any unskilled or incompetent work.

6. Completion date. Every bid should describe when the contractor must complete the work. Anyone who has ever waited for a builder or other worker to complete a job knows that home improvement work can take longer than anyone expected. The solution is to set a specific date for completion of the work. A bid should also state that time is of the essence. This statement prevents the contractor from claiming that the time for completion of the work was not important in the bid.

7. Price, payment, and costs. This paragraph describes the amount of money that the owner will pay to the contractor for the work, and describes the terms of payment. An owner can pay a contractor in many different ways. The contractor would like the owner to pay the entire price before any work is begun. The owner would like to see the work completed before he or she pays any money to the contractor. The parties have to negotiate these terms. The owner should hold out for paying the largest portion of the price at the end of the work. It is not unreasonable for a contractor to want some type of a down payment to help the contractor cover the cost of materials and labor, but the purchase price is the contractor's motivation to do the work. Holding that motivation until the contractor completes the work increases the chances that the contractor will complete the job as and when he or she promised.

If the parties agree on a down payment and a later payment at the end of the contract, they can use the following wording:

For performing the work described above, owner shall pay contractor the total sum of One Thousand Dollars ($1,000.00), to be paid as follows: $300.00 upon signing this contract, and $700.00 when contractor has completed all the work under this contract.

If the parties agree on a down payment and monthly payments until completion of the contract, they can use the following wording:

For performing the work described above, owner shall pay contractor the total sum of $1,000.00, to be paid as follows: $300.00 upon signing this contract, and the remaining $700.00 in monthly installments of $100.00 each, payable on the first day of each month hereafter, beginning with the month of June, 1989, provided that whatever unpaid balance owner owes upon completion of the work will be due and payable when contractor completes the work.

This paragraph states that the bid is a firm bid (discussed earlier in this chapter). The owner wants the contractor to give a firm bid to prevent the contractor from raising the cost of the project after work begins.

This paragraph requires copies of receipts from all suppliers from whom the contractor purchased materials. This provision ensures that the contractor will use new materials for the carport, and that the contractor did not overstate the cost of materials in the bid.

This paragraph also helps the owner compare bids by asking the contractor to detail what the contractor's expenses will be for the job, including materials, licenses, permits, and labor. This itemization gives the owner an idea of whether the profit that the contractor proposes to make on the job is reasonable or unreasonable.

8. Changes in work. This paragraph explains that the contract cannot be changed without the written consent of both the contractor and the owner. After home improvement work begins, the contractor or the owner sometimes decides there should be changes in the project. Such changes are fine as long as both parties agree on those changes in writing, including any changes in the price for the job.

9. Time for accepting bid. This paragraph explains that the owner can only accept the bid for a certain period of time. Every bid should explain how long it will remain open. Because the prices of materials and labor increase, a contractor has to put a time limit on bids.

10. Costs and attorney's fees. This paragraph should be in every bid and in every contract of any kind. It explains that if either party incurs expenses to enforce any of the provisions of the bid, the other party will pay those expenses. It is only fair to make someone who breaches an agreement pay the other person's expenses incurred in forcing the breaching party to live up to the agreement. If this clause is not in a contract, the non-breaching party usually cannot force the breaching party to pay the non-breaching party's attorney's fees, even if the non-breaching party wins a lawsuit against the breaching party.

11. Date, place and signatures. Every bid should be dated and signed by the contractor. The bid should state where the contractor signed the bid because that will affect which state's laws govern the bid. If the contractor is a corporation, the bid should be signed by an authorized representative. The signature of the authorized representative should indicate what office the representative holds in the corporation. If there is a corporate seal, it should be affixed to the bid.

A bid should have a place at the end of it where the owner can accept the bid in writing. The owner should sign and date the acceptance. The owner's acceptance is what changes a proposal by the contractor into a binding contract between the owner and contractor.

Exhibits. Exhibit "A" is a diagram of the carport. A diagram is one of the best ways to show what the contractor proposes to do. It helps the contractor and the owner get a better idea of what the owner wants. It helps the contractor determine the type and dimensions of the materials he or she will use. In most cases, the contractor makes the final diagram for the job. Most contractors are experienced in making drawings of their projects. If a contractor is incapable of making such a drawing, you should reconsider whether or not the contractor is competent enough to perform the work.

Fig. 14-1. Bid by Independent Contractor (Sample). *Page 1 of 3*   **243**

Bid

1. Parties. The undersigned, ACME CONSTRUCTION COMPANY, whose business street address is 222 Third Street, Waynecastle, Pennsylvania, 17294, hereafter referred to as "contractor", hereby submits the following bid for work to John J. Jones, whose address is 333 Fourth Street, Waynecastle, Pennsylvania, 17294, hereafter referred to as "owner".

2. Job description and diagram. Contractor proposes to owner that contractor will supply all the materials and labor, and pay all license and other fees and expenses for the construction of an outdoor carport on owner's property, located at 333 Fourth Street, Waynecastle, Pennsylvania, 17294. The dimensions and materials for the carport will conform to the diagram made of the carport by the contractor, which the contractor has attached to this bid, marked Exhibit "A", and incorporated into this bid by this reference.

3. Warranties. The contractor will complete the construction of the carport in a substantial and workmanlike manner according to standard practices in the building trade and the carport shall conform with all applicable building codes and regulations. Contractor warrants that the carport will be fit for the normal purposes for which it is constructed, namely, the housing of a vehicle. Contractor will warrant against defects in materials and labor for one (1) year from the date of completion of the work.

4. Materials. All materials will be as specified on the attached Exhibit "A", and will be of good quality. All materials will be new.

5. Supervision of work. Contractor's authorized representative shall supervise all workers performing this work. All workers will be competent and skilled in their work.

6. Completion date. Contractor will complete all work on or before August 10, 1989. Contractor understands that time is of the essence in this project.

7. Price, payment, and costs. For performing the work described above, owner shall pay contractor the total sum of One Thousand Dollars ($1,000.00), to be paid upon contractor's completion of the work. This bid is a firm bid. Contractor shall perform all its obligations under this bid for the amount of this bid, and no more. Contractor will provide owner with copies of receipts for all material which contractor purchases from other suppliers. The contractor estimates the following costs of materials, licenses, permits, and labor:

Materials:	Six hundred ninety dollars	($690.00)
Licenses:	Ten dollars	($10.00)
Permits:	Twenty dollars	($20.00)
Labor:	Two hundred eighty dollars	($280.00)

8. Changes in work. No changes shall be made in the work proposed unless those changes are agreed to in writing, by both contractor and owner, and unless any necessary adjustment of the price for this work is also agreed to in writing by both contractor and owner.

9. Time for accepting bid. This bid may be accepted by owner until June 10, 1989, at which time it will automatically expire and become void if not accepted by owner in writing.

10. Costs and attorney's fees. If either party incurs any costs or expenses, including reasonable attorney's fees, to enforce any provision of this bid, whether incurred before or after either party files a lawsuit, the losing party in any such lawsuit, or the defaulting party if there is no such lawsuit, agrees to pay the other party's costs and expenses, including reasonable attorney's fees at trial and on any appeal of any lawsuit.

11. Date, place, and signatures. Dated this 10th day of May, 1989, at 333 Fourth Street, Waynecastle, Pennsylvania, 17294.

_____

ACME CONSTRUCTION COMPANY

(CORPORATE SEAL)   By: _____

Robert L. Smith, President

The above bid is hereby accepted, this 15th day of May, 1989.

_____

John J. Jones

Fig. 14-1. (Cont'd). *Page 3 of 3* **245**

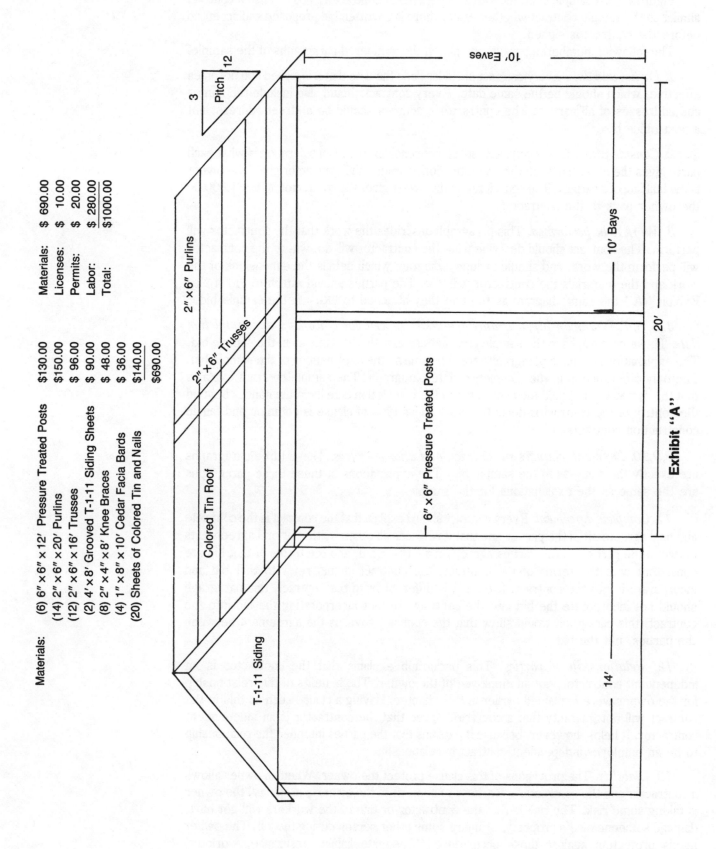

Materials:

(6) 6″ × 6″ × 12′ Pressure Treated Posts	$130.00
(14) 2″ × 6″ × 20′ Purlins	$150.00
(12) 2″ × 6″ × 16′ Trusses	$ 96.00
(2) 4′ × 8′ Grooved T-1-11 Siding Sheets	$ 90.00
(8) 2″ × 4″ × 8′ Knee Braces	$ 48.00
(4) 1″ × 8″ × 10′ Cedar Facia Bards	$ 36.00
(20) Sheets of Colored Tin and Nails	$140.00
	$690.00

Materials:	$ 690.00
Licenses:	$ 10.00
Permits:	$ 20.00
Labor:	$ 280.00
Total:	$1000.00

Pitch 12
3

2″ × 6″ Purlins

2″ × 6″ Trusses

Colored Tin Roof

6″ × 6″ Pressure Treated Posts

T-1-11 Siding

10′ Eaves

10′ Bays

20′

14′

Exhibit "A"

Sample Contract with an Independent Contractor (FIG. 4-2)

Figure 4-2 is a sample contract with an independent contractor. You can use a contract similar to the sample contract whether or not there is a written bid proposed and accepted before the contract is signed.

The following numbered paragraphs match the numbered paragraphs of the sample.

1. Parties and date. Every contract should include the date that it is signed and becomes effective, which should be the same date. Every contract should also include the names and addresses of all parties. The contractor's address should be a street address, not a post office box.

2. Consideration. Every contract must have consideration. Consideration is what each party gives the other party. In this case, the consideration the contractor gives the owner is the building of a carport. The consideration the owner gives the contractor is the $1,000.00 the owner pays to the contractor.

3. Work to be performed. This paragraph describes the work that the contractor will perform. The contract should describe what the contractor will do, where the contractor will perform the work, and should include a diagram which details the dimensions of the work and the materials the contractor will use. The parties should attach to FIG. 4-2 as Exhibit "A" the same diagram as the one they attached to FIG. 4-1, the sample bid.

4, 5, 6, 7. Workmanship, warranty, materials, supervision of workers, and completion date. These paragraphs in the sample contract are exactly the same as in the sample bid. The explanations of those paragraphs are the same as the explanations of the sample bid. The only difference is in the completion date paragraph. The sample contract explains that the owner will not hold the contractor to the completion date if circumstances beyond the control of the contractor delay the work. This type of clause is common and fair in construction contracts.

8,9,10. Payment, changes in contract, and attorney's fees. These three paragraphs are exactly the same as in the sample bid. The explanations of these three paragraphs are the same as the explanations for the sample.

11. Complete agreement. Every contract should explain that the contract is the complete and final agreement of the parties and that it replaces all other written or oral agreements between the parties. If the parties agreed on a written bid, and the terms of that bid are consistent with the terms of the contract, the contract should refer to that bid and incorporate it into the contract. If the bid is different from the contract, this paragraph should not incorporate the bid into the contract. By not incorporating the bid into the contract, this paragraph would show that the contract governs the agreement between the parties, not the bid.

12. Relationship of parties. This paragraph explains that the contractor is an independent contractor, not an employee of the owner. The benefits of this relationship for the owner were explained earlier in this chapter. Having a clause such as this in the contract will not guaranty that a court will agree that the contractor is an independent contractor. It helps, however, because it explains that the parties intended the relationship to be an employer/independent-contractor relationship.

13. Liability. The provisions of this clause protect the owner. When an owner allows a contractor and the contractor's workers to come onto the owner's property, the owner is taking some risk. The risk is that the contractor or one of the workers will get hurt, damage someone else's property, or injure some other person during the job. The owner needs protection against those occurrences. Adequate liability insurance, workers' compensation, unemployment insurance, and social security coverage are the best protection. Also, an adequate surety bond will ensure that if the contractor does not complete the job as agreed, the owner can file a claim against the contractor's insurance company for the owner's losses.

The owner wants to confirm that the contractor has the insurance required by the contract. The owner can do this by obtaining copies of the insurance policies. The owner should contact the insurance company of the contractor to be sure that the contractor's coverage will cover the work the contractor performs on the owner's property.

Besides requiring that the contractor have proper insurance, the liability paragraph protects the owner by making the contractor agree to indemnify the owner for any losses that the owner suffers as a result of the contractor's work. *Indemnify* means that the contractor will pay the owner back for any losses that the owner suffers. For instance, if one of the contractor's workers breaks one of the owner's windows, the contractor will pay for that damage.

14. Assignment. If a contract does not restrict the contractor from assigning the contractor's rights under the contract, the contractor usually can assign those rights. Most owners do not want that; they want the contractor that they made the deal with to be the contractor who performs the work. In the sample, this paragraph restricts the contractor's right to assign the contract. This clause ensures that the contractor will not assign the contract to someone without the owner's approval.

15. Cleanup. A contractor cannot avoid creating some debris in a construction or landscaping job, but some contractors and workers are overly sloppy. Nails and other construction debris can be dangerous. With a little attention to where debris is placed during construction, workers can keep a construction site reasonably clean. A contract should include a clause which requires the contractor to leave the property in a safe, clean, and sanitary condition.

16. Date, place, and signatures. The parties should sign and date two original contracts. The contractor and owner should each keep an original contract. Every contract should indicate where the parties signed the contract, because that will affect which state's laws govern the contract. If the contractor is a company, the person signing for the company should be a representative that the company authorizes to sign the contract. If the company has a corporate seal, the representative should affix the corporate seal to the contract.

Exhibits.   Exhibit ''A'' is attached to the contract, as discussed above.

Contract With Independent Contractor

1. Parties and date. This contract is made and entered into on June 5, 1989, by John J. Jones, whose address is 333 Fourth Street, Waynecastle, Pennsylvania, 17294, hereafter referred to as "owner", and ACME CONSTRUCTION COMPANY, whose address is 222 Third Street, Waynecastle, Pennsylvania, 17294, hereafter referred to as "contractor".

2. Consideration. In consideration of the mutual promises and covenants contained in this contract the parties agree to abide by all the terms of this contract.

3. Work to be performed. Contractor agrees to supply all the materials and labor and pay all license, permit, and other fees and expenses for the construction of an outdoor carport on owner's property located at 333 Fourth Street, Waynecastle, Pennsylvania, 17294. The dimensions, location, and materials for the carport will conform to the diagram of the carport made by the contractor, which contractor has attached to this contract, marked Exhibit "A", and incorporated into this contract by this reference.

4. Workmanship—warranty. The contractor will complete construction of the carport in a substantial and workmanlike manner according to standard practices in the building trade, and the carport shall conform with all applicable building codes and regulations. Contractor warrants that the carport will be fit for the normal purposes for which it is constructed, namely, the housing of a vehicle. Contractor will warrant against defects in materials and labor for one (1) year from the date of completion of the work.

5. Materials. All materials will be as specified on the attached Exhibit "A", and will be of good quality. All materials will be new.

6. Supervision of workers. Contractor's authorized representative shall supervise all workers performing the work. All workers will be competent and skilled in their work.

7. Completion date. Contractor will complete all work on or before August 10, 1989. Contractor understands that time is of the essence in this contract. The owner shall extend this completion date if there are delays caused by acts of God, unavoidable circumstances, or the negligence of owner or owner's agents or employees other than contractor. The extension shall equal the length of the delay caused by any of the above factors.

8. Payment. For performing the work described above, owner shall pay contractor the total sum of One Thousand Dollars ($1,000.00), to be paid upon contractor's completion of the work. This bid is a firm bid. Contractor shall perform all its obligations under this bid for the amount of this bid, and no more. Contractor will provide owner with copies of receipts for all materials which contractor purchases from other suppliers.

The contractor estimates the following costs of materials, licenses, permits and labor:

Materials:	Six hundred ninety dollars	($690.00)
Licenses:	Ten dollars	($10.00)
Permits:	Twenty dollars	($20.00)
Labor:	Two hundred eighty dollars	($280.00)

Fig. 14-2. (Cont'd). *Page 2 of 4* **249**

9. Changes in contract. No changes shall be made in the work proposed unless those changes are agreed to in writing by both contractor and owner, and unless any necessary adjustment of the price for this work is also agreed to in writing by both contractor and owner.

10. Attorney's fees. If either party incurs any costs or expenses, including reasonable attorney's fees, to enforce any provision of this contract, whether incurred before or after either party files a lawsuit to enforce this contract, the losing party in any such lawsuit, or the defaulting party if there is no such lawsuit, agrees to pay the other party's reasonable costs and expenses, including reasonable attorney's fees at trial and on any appeal of any lawsuit.

11. Complete agreement. With the exception of the bid proposed by contractor to owner, dated May 10, 1989, which bid is incorporated into this contract by reference, this contract is the complete and final agreement of the parties. It replaces any other prior written or oral agreements between the parties.

12. Relationship of parties. Both owner and contractor agree that contractor is an independent contractor, not an employee of owner. Contractor will have control over the details and methods of the work. Owner's control is limited to satisfaction or dissatisfaction with the final work product. Contractor, not owner, is responsible for providing workers' compensation, unemployment insurance, social security, and other coverages and benefits for contractor and any workers contractor employs to work on this job.

13. Liability. Contractor, not owner, assumes all the risk involved in performing this contract, such as any injuries to contractor, workers, or members of the public from the use or condition of tools and equipment the contractor uses, or from any other causes. During the term of this contract, contractor agrees to carry public liability, workers' compensation, and employers' liability insurance in amounts acceptable to owner and in amounts required by all applicable laws. At owner's request, contractor will give owner certificates of insurance proving that contractor has this insurance and other coverage before contractor begins the work described in this contract. Contractor will also carry and, at owner's request, give owner proof of a surety bond in an amount acceptable to owner to cover owner for contractor's nonperformance of any of the terms of this contract. Contractor shall hold harmless and indemnify owner for any loss to or claims against owner arising from the performance or nonperformance of this contract by contractor, or contractor's agents, employees, or officers. This indemnity includes losses or claims resulting from injury to persons or property, and includes losses or claims resulting from violation of any applicable laws, including laws regarding payment of federal, state, or other taxes, or contributions required by employment insurance, social security, or income tax laws.

14. Assignment. Any attempt by contractor to sell, assign, or in any way transfer contractor's rights or obligations in this contract without owner's prior written consent shall be void.

15. Cleanup. After completing the work described herein, contractor will clean all debris from the work area and leave owner's property in a safe, clean, and sanitary condition.

16. Date, place, and signatures. IN WITNESS WHEREOF, the parties have signed this contract in duplicate this 5th day of June, 1989, at 333 Fourth Street, Waynecastle, Pennsylvania, 17294.

ACME CONSTRUCTION COMPANY

BY: _____

_____

John J. Jones, Owner   Robert L. Smith, President

CORPORATE SEAL

Fig. 14-2. (Cont'd). *Page 4 of 4* **251**

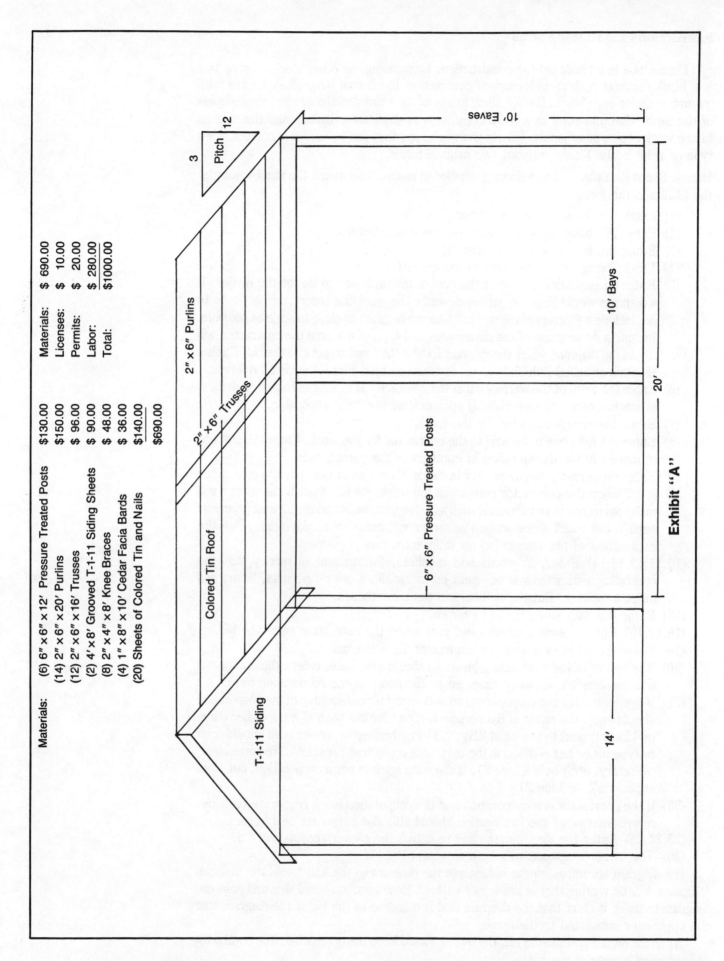

Materials:

(6) 6" × 6" × 12' Pressure Treated Posts	$130.00
(14) 2" × 6" × 20' Purlins	$150.00
(12) 2" × 6" × 16' Trusses	$96.00
(2) 4' × 8' Grooved T-1-11 Siding Sheets	$90.00
(8) 2" × 4" × 8' Knee Braces	$48.00
(4) 1" × 8" × 10' Cedar Facia Bards	$36.00
(20) Sheets of Colored Tin and Nails	$140.00
	$690.00

Materials:	$ 690.00
Licenses:	$ 10.00
Permits:	$ 20.00
Labor:	$ 280.00
Total:	$1000.00

Pitch 3/12

10' Eaves

10' Bays

20'

14'

2" × 6" Purlins

2" × 6" Trusses

Colored Tin Roof

6" × 6" Pressure Treated Posts

T-1-11 Siding

Exhibit "A"

Instructions for Blank Forms

Figure 14-3 is a blank bid for construction, landscaping, or other work. Figure 14-4 is a blank contract with an independent contractor. The forms have blank spaces with a number under each blank. Before filling in any of the blanks, make several photocopies of the form. Use one copy as a work copy, two as duplicate originals, and the rest as future work copies or originals. Fill out the work copy first and be sure it is correct, then type or print in the blanks on your two original forms.

Blank Bid (FIG. 14-3)   The following numbered instructions match the numbers under the blanks in the form:

(1) Enter the name of the contractor.

(2) Enter the business street address of the contractor.

(3) Enter the full name of the owner(s).

(4) Enter the street address(es) of the owner(s).

(5) Enter an explanation of what the contractor proposes to do for the owner. If a diagram would help the parties describe the work the contractor proposes to do, include a diagram of the work. Make the diagram as close to scale as possible. Include a description of the dimensions and type of material the contractor will use in the diagram. Mark the diagram Exhibit "A" and staple it to the bid. Explain that you attached Exhibit "A" to, and incorporated it into, the bid by reference.

(6) Enter the term of the warranty that the contractor is making in regard to defects in workmanship or materials. If appropriate, use "not applicable."

(7) Enter the completion date for the work.

(8) Enter the full price to be paid to the contractor for the work. Enter the amount of money in words, and then in numbers in the parentheses.

(9) Enter the terms of payment. For instance, if the owner is to pay the contractor in full when the contractor completes the work, explain that. If the owner will make payments in installments, such as a down payment and then a final payment, explain the exact dates when the owner will make those payments. See the explanation of the sample bid for different terms of payment.

(10,11,12,13,14) Enter, in words and numbers, the amount of money that the contractor estimates will be spent on materials, licenses, permits, labor, and other expenses. Put the numbers in the parentheses.

(15) Enter the date when the bid expires.

(16,17,18) Enter the day, month, and year when the contractor signs the bid.

(19) Enter the address where the contractor signs the bid.

(20) The owner of the contracting business should sign here, unless the contractor is a corporation, in which case, enter the name of the corporation here.

(21) If the contractor is a corporation, an authorized representative of the corporation should enter the name of the corporation on Line 20, then sign his or her name on Line 21, next to the word "By:". The authorized representative should print or type his or her position in the corporation (such as president, vice president, secretary, etc.) below Line 21. If the contractor is not a corporation, put "not applicable" on Line 21.

(22) If the contractor is a corporation and the corporation has a corporate seal, the representative of the corporation should affix the corporate seal here.

(23,24,25) Enter the day, month, and year that the owner accepts the bid.

(26) The owner(s) should sign here to accept the bid.

If a diagram accompanies the bid, staple the diagram to the bid. Label the diagram "Exhibit A", by writing that at the top or bottom. Both parties should sign and date the diagram to make it clear that the diagram that is attached to the bid is the diagram that the contractor submitted to the owner.

After the owner accepts the bid, the owner should keep the original bid. The contractor should keep a copy of the bid.

Fig. 14-3. Bid by Independent Contractor (Blank). *Page 1 of 3* **253**

Bid

1. Parties. The undersigned, _____
(1)

_____,

whose business street address is _____
(2)

_____,

hereafter referred to as "contractor", hereby submits the following bid for work to

_____
(3)

_____,

whose address(es) is/are _____
(4)

_____

_____,

hereafter referred to as "owner". Even if there is more than one owner, they will be referred to in the singular for the remainder of this bid.

2. Job description and diagram. Contractor proposes to owner that contractor

will do the following: _____
(5)

_____

_____

_____

_____

_____

_____

_____.

3. Warranties. The contractor will complete all work in a substantial and workmanlike manner according to standard practices in the contractor's trade, and the work shall conform to all applicable building codes or other codes and regulations. Contractor warrants that the final product of the work will be fit for the normal purposes for which it is intended. Contractor will warrant against defects in materials and labor

for a period of _____
(6)

from the date of completion of the work.

4. Materials. If there is a diagram attached as an exhibit, all materials will be as specified on the attached exhibit. Whether or not there is an exhibit attached hereto, all materials will be of good quality. All materials will be new.

5. Supervision of work. Contractor's authorized representative shall supervise all workers performing this work. All workers will be competent and skilled in their work.

6. Completion date. Contractor will complete all work on or before

_____. Contractor understands that time is
(7)

of the essence in this project.

7. Price, payment, and costs. For performing the work described above, owner

shall pay contractor the total sum of _____
(8)

_____ ($ _____),

to be paid as follows: _____
(9)

_____

_____

_____

_____ .

This bid is a firm bid. Contractor shall perform all its obligations under this bid for the amount of this bid, and no more. Contractor will provide owner with copies of receipts for all material which contractor purchases from other suppliers. The contractor estimates the following costs of materials, licenses, permits, labor, and other expenses:

Materials: _____ ($ _____)
(10)

Licenses: _____ ($ _____)
(11)

Permits: _____ ($ _____)
(12)

Labor: _____ ($ _____)
(13)

Other Exp: _____ ($ _____)
(14)

8. Changes in work. No changes shall be made in the work proposed unless those changes are agreed to in writing by both contractor and owner and unless any necessary adjustment of the price for this work is also agreed to in writing by both contractor and owner.

9. Time for accepting bid. This bid may be accepted by owner until

_____, at which time it will automatically
(15)

expire and become void if not accepted by owner in writing.

10. Costs and attorney's fees. If either party incurs any costs or expenses, including reasonable attorney's fees, to enforce any provision of this bid, whether incurred before or after either party files a lawsuit, the losing party in any such lawsuit, or the defaulting party if there is no such lawsuit, agrees to pay the other party's costs and expenses, including reasonable attorney's fees at trial and upon appeal of any trial.

Fig. 14-3. (Cont'd). *Page 3 of 3* **255**

11. Date, place, and signatures. Dated this _____ day of _____,
(16)   (17)

_____, at _____
(18)   (19)

_____.

_____
(20)

(CORPORATE SEAL)   By: _____
(22)   (21)

The above bid is hereby accepted, this _____ day of _____,
(23)   (24)

_____.
(25)

_____
(26)

_____
(26)

Blank Contract With an Independent Contractor (FIG. 14-4)   The following numbered instructions match the numbers under the blanks in the form:

(1) Enter the date the contract is signed and effective, which should be the same date.

(2) Enter the name(s) of the owner(s) (the person(s) for whom the work is being performed).

(3) Enter the address(es) of the owner(s).

(4) Enter the name of the contractor.

(5) Enter the street address of the contractor.

(6) Enter an explanation of what the contractor agrees to do. For instance, a contractor can agree to ''supply all labor and materials, and pay all the license, permit, and other fees and expenses for the construction of a carport on owner's property located at . . .'', etc. See the sample bid and sample contract for an example of the type of wording you can use here.

  If the contractor prepared a diagram of the work, attach the diagram to the contract as an exhibit. The diagram should be as close to scale as possible. The diagram should explain what materials the contractor will use in the project. A full discussion of these diagrams was presented earlier in this chapter.

(7) Enter the terms of any warranty against defects in materials and workmanship. If the contractor is not making any such warranties, put ''not applicable'' here.

(8) Enter the date for completion of the project.

(9) Enter, in words and numbers, the amount of money that the owner is paying the contractor for the work the contractor will perform. Put the numbers in the parentheses.

(10) Enter the terms of payment, such as payment in full upon completion of the work, payment in full before work begins, or a down payment of part of the price and the payment of the remainder upon completion of the work. See the sample bid, sample contract, and the explanation of the sample bid for a full discussion of this.

(11,12,13,14,15) Enter, in words and numbers, an estimate of the amount of money that the contractor will spend on materials, licenses, permits, labor, and other expenses. Put the numbers in the parentheses.

(16) If there was a written bid proposed by the contractor and accepted by the owner and the terms of that bid are the same as the terms of this contract, refer to the bid in this space. Give the date of the bid and say that the contract incorporates the bid by reference. If the contractor proposed a written bid with terms different from this contract or if the contractor did not propose any written bid, put ''not applicable'' here.

(17,18,19) Enter the day, month, and year the parties sign the contract.

(20) Enter the address where the parties sign the contract.

(21) The owner(s) should sign his/her/their name(s) here.

(22) The contractor should sign his or her name here, unless the contractor is a corporation, in which case, enter the name of the corporation here.

(23) If the signer for the contractor signs on behalf of a corporation, the signer should enter the name of the corporation on Line 22, then sign his or her name next to the word ''By:'' on Line 23, and indicate his or her position in the corporation (such as president, vice president, secretary, etc.) below Line 23. If the contractor is not a corporation, put ''not applicable'' on Line 23.

(24) If the signer for the contractor is signing on behalf of a corporation and the corporation has a corporate seal, affix the corporate seal in this place.

If a diagram accompanies the contract, staple the diagram to the contract. Label the diagram ''Exhibit A'', by writing that at the top or bottom. Both parties should sign and date the diagram.

After the parties sign two originals of the contract, each party should keep one original contract.

Contract With Independent Contractor

1. Parties and date. This contract is made and entered into on

_____, by _____
(1)   (2)

_____

_____,

whose address(es) is/are _____
(3)

_____,

hereafter referred to as "owner", and _____
(4)

whose business street address is _____
(5)

_____,

hereafter referred to as "contractor". Even if there is more than one owner, they are referred to in the singular for the remainder of this contract.

2. Consideration. In consideration of the mutual promises and covenants contained in this contract, the parties agree to abide by all the terms of this contract.

3. Work to be performed. Contractor agrees to do the following:

_____
(6)

_____

_____

_____

_____

_____

_____

_____

_____

_____.

4. Workmanship—warranty. The contractor will complete all work in a substantial and workmanlike manner according to standard practices in the contractor's trade, and the work shall conform to all applicable building or other codes and regulations. Contractor warrants that the final product of contractor's work will be fit for the normal purposes for which it is intended. Contractor will warrant against defects in materials and labor for a period of _____ from the date of completion of the work.
(7)

5. Materials. If a diagram of the work is attached as an exhibit, all materials will be as specified on the attached exhibit. Whether or not there is an exhibit attached hereto, all materials will be of good quality. All materials will be new.

6. Supervision of workers. Contractor's authorized representative shall supervise all workers performing this work. All workers will be competent and skilled in their work.

7. Completion date. Contractor will complete all work on or before _____ (8)

_____. Contractor understands that time is of the essence in this contract. The owner shall extend this completion date if there are delays caused by acts of God, unavoidable circumstances, or the negligence of owner or owner's agents or employees other than contractor. The extension shall equal the length of the delay caused by any of the above factors.

8. Payment. For performing the work described above, owner shall pay contractor

the total sum of _____ (9)

_____ ($ _____),

to be paid as follows: _____ (10)

_____

_____

_____

_____

_____.

This bid is a firm bid. Contractor shall perform all his, her, or its obligations under this bid for the amount of this bid, and no more. Contractor will provide owner with copies of receipts for all materials which contractor purchases from other suppliers. Contractor estimates the following costs of materials, licenses, permits, labor, and other expenses:

Materials: _____ ($ _____)
(11)

Licenses: _____ ($ _____)
(12)

Permits: _____ ($ _____)
(13)

Labor: _____ ($ _____)
(14)

Other Exp: _____ ($ _____)
(15)

9. Changes in contract. No changes shall be made in the work proposed unless those changes are agreed to in writing by both contractor and owner, and unless any necessary adjustment of the price for this work is also agreed to in writing by both contractor and owner.

10. Attorney's fees. If either party incurs any costs or expenses, including reasonable attorney's fees, to enforce any provision of this contract, either before or after either party files a lawsuit, the losing party in any lawsuit, and the defaulting party if there is no lawsuit, agrees to pay the other party's costs and expenses, including reasonable attorney's fees at trial and on any appeal of any lawsuit.

Fig. 14-4. (Cont'd). *Page 3 of 4* **259**

11. Complete agreement. This contract is the complete and final agreement of the parties regarding the above work. It replaces all other prior written or oral agreements between the parties, except: _____
(16)

_____

_____.

12. Relationship of parties. Both owner and contractor agree that contractor is an independent contractor, not an employee of owner. Contractor will have control over the details and methods of the work. Owner's control is limited to satisfaction or dissatisfaction with the final work product. Contractor, not owner, is responsible for providing workers' compensation, unemployment insurance, social security, and other coverages and benefits for contractor and any workers contractor employs to work on this project.

13. Liability. Contractor, not owner, assumes all the risk involved in performing this contract, such as any injuries to contractor, workers, or members of the public from the use or condition of tools and equipment the contractor uses, or from any other causes. During the term of this contract, contractor agrees to carry public liability, workers' compensation, and employers' liability insurance in amounts acceptable to owner and in amounts required by all applicable laws. At owner's request, contractor will give owner certificates of insurance proving that contractor has this insurance and other coverage before contractor begins the work described in this contract. Contractor will also carry and, at owner's request, give owner proof of a surety bond in an amount acceptable to owner to cover owner for contractor's nonperformance of any of the terms of this contract. Contractor shall hold harmless and indemnify owner for any loss to, or claims against, owner arising from the performance or nonperformance of this contract by contractor, or contractor's agents, employees, or officers. This indemnity includes losses or claims resulting from injury to persons or property, and includes losses or claims resulting from violation of any applicable laws, including laws regarding payment of federal, state, or other taxes, or contributions required by employment insurance, social security, or income tax laws.

14. Assignment. Any attempt by contractor to sell, assign, or in any way transfer contractor's rights or obligations in this contract without owner's prior written consent shall be void.

15. Cleanup. After completing the work described herein, contractor will clean all debris from the work area and leave owner's property in a clean, safe, and sanitary condition.

16. Date, place, and signatures. IN WITNESS WHEREOF, the parties have signed this contract in duplicate, this _____ day of _____, _____.
(17)   (18)   (19)

at _____
(20)

_____.

_____
(21)
Owner

_____
(22)
Contractor

_____
(21)
Owner

By: _____
(23)

(CORPORATE SEAL)
(24)

Chapter 15
Power of Attorney

A power of attorney is a document in which one person gives another person the power to perform certain acts for the person who signs the power of attorney.

A person who signs a power of attorney is called a *principal*. A person who receives a power of attorney is called an *agent*, or an *attorney-in-fact*.

A *general* power of attorney gives an agent the power to perform a broad range of acts.

A *special*, or *limited*, power of attorney gives an agent the power to perform a particular act or acts.

A *durable* power of attorney is a power of attorney that remains effective after a principal becomes mentally or physically disabled.

The word *attorney* in *power of attorney* means that the principal is appointing someone to act for him or her. It does not mean that the agent has to be an attorney.

USES FOR A POWER OF ATTORNEY

A power of attorney can authorize an agent to buy, sell or deal in other ways with a principal's property. The following are some examples of the kinds of things a power of attorney allows an agent to do for a principal:

- If you live in one state and are selling real estate in another state, you can give a friend or real estate agent a special power of attorney to sign whatever documents are necessary to close the sale. This saves you the time and expense of traveling to the closing. You would give a special power of attorney because you are authorizing the agent to do one specific thing, that is, sign documents to close the sale of specific real estate.

- If you have a medical condition which will eventually make you incapable of handling your own affairs, such as Alzheimer's disease, you can give a general power of attorney to your spouse or another person before you become completely incapacitated. With a power of attorney, your agent can manage your property and make other decisions for you after you become incapacitated.

- If you are going on a trip and know that decisions have to be made regarding some of your property, such as buying or selling stock or exercising stock options, you can give a spouse or another person a power of attorney to make those decisions.

If one specific action needs to be taken while you are gone, you can give a special power of attorney limited to doing that one specific action. If you are not sure what may need to be done while you are gone, you can give a general power of attorney to your agent to enable the agent to do whatever needs to be done in your absence.

- If you and your spouse are going on a trip and are leaving your minor children with someone else, you can give that person a power of attorney to make medical or other decisions regarding your children. You can give the agent a special or general power of attorney depending on how much power you want to give the agent. If you only want to give the agent the power to make medical decisions, give the agent a special power of attorney. If you want to give the agent broad powers to make medical, school, and other types of decisions regarding the children, give the agent a general power of attorney. A general power of attorney gives an agent a great deal of power over the principal and the principal's property. You should only give it to someone you trust completely.

HEALTH CARE DECISIONS

Traditionally, people used powers of attorney to give agents the power to deal with a principal's property, not to give agents the power to make health care decisions for a principal. The laws of many states are unclear as to what health care decisions an agent can make using a power of attorney. Figure 15-1 includes specific state requirements for health care powers of attorney. Things you can do to help convince medical personnel to honor a power of attorney are discussed later in this chapter.

State Laws on Powers of Attorney (FIG. 15-1)

Different states have different laws regarding how to sign a power of attorney, whether you must record a power of attorney, whether a power of attorney must describe real estate affected by the power, whether a principal's spouse must sign the power, whether a judge must approve the power, whether a state recognizes durable powers of attorney, and other matters. Figure 15-1 lists the sections of each state's laws that discuss powers of attorney. You can find these laws by going to a law library in your state. A law library is located at your county courthouse. Ask the librarian to help you find the law referred to in FIG. 15-1.

Figure 15-1 is based on 1987 and 1988 laws. The state legislatures of the 50 states meet at different times. Some legislatures only meet once every two years. When a state legislature passes a law, the legislature or a publishing company publishes that law at a later time. Several months can pass before the legislature or publisher sends that law to the libraries around the country. As you read these words, months or years will have also passed from the time this book was edited, printed, and distributed. For these reasons, this book, like all legal books, cannot be absolutely current.

Figure 15-1 indicates whether the information for a particular state is based on the 1987 or 1988 laws of that state. If you want to confirm whether or not your state has changed its laws, go to a law library in your state and read the most current version of the law referred to in FIG. 15-1. Even if the law has changed, the new law will usually have the same number as the old law. Check what are known as the "pocket parts" of your state's laws. Pocket parts are supplements which contain the latest revisions of a state's laws.

Some states limit the duration of powers of attorney that allow an agent to care for a principal's minor children. You should re-sign powers of attorney to care for minor children at least every three months.

Unless FIG. 15-1 indicates otherwise, a principal can sign a power of attorney if he or she is 18 years of age or older. When FIG. 15-1 says that a state recognizes durable powers of attorney, that means the state recognizes general and special durable powers of attorney.

Fig. 15-1. State Laws on Powers of Attorney.

Alabama—26-1-2 (1987 Update). Recognizes durable powers of attorney. A person must be 19 years old in order to sign a power of attorney.

Alaska—13.26.325, .330 (1987 Update). Recognizes durable powers of attorney.

Arizona—14-5501, -5502 (1988 Update). Recognizes durable powers of attorney.

Arkansas—28-68-101, -201, -202 (1987 Update). Recognizes durable powers of attorney. Sections 28-68-304 and -305 discuss signing a power of attorney in front of a judge, but these sections do not apply to *common law powers of attorney*, the type of power of attorney in this chapter. The form at the end of this chapter does not need to be signed in front of a judge.

California—Civil Code 2400 and the sections that follow it, and Civil Code 2430 and the sections that follow it (1988 Update). The general and special power of attorney forms at the end of the chapter can be used for non-health-care decisions. A person must use a special form provided by California law in order to have a valid power of attorney for health care decisions. The special form is found in the Civil Code of California, Section 2430 and the sections that follow it.

Colorado—15-14-501, -502 (1987 Update). Recognizes durable powers of attorney.

Connecticut—45-69o (1987 Update). Recognizes durable powers of attorney.

Delaware—12-4901 through -4905 (1987 Update). Recognizes durable powers of attorney.

District of Columbia—21-2081 through -2085 (1988 Update). Recognizes durable powers of attorney.

Florida—709.01, .015, .08 (1988 Update). Recognizes durable family powers of attorney. Florida law says a principal may appoint a spouse, parent, child, brother, sister, niece, or nephew as an agent in a durable family power of attorney. Florida law does not recognize general durable powers of attorney to non-family members.

Georgia—10-6-36 (also known as 4-214.1) (1988 Update). Recognizes durable powers of attorney.

Hawaii—560:5-501, -502 (1987 Update). Recognizes durable powers of attorney.

Idaho—15-5-501 through -507 (1988 Update). Recognizes durable powers of attorney.

Illinois—110½-11a-23 as amended by P.A. 85-701, Art. V, Section 5-2 (1988 update). Recognizes durable powers of attorney.

Indiana—30-2-11-1 through -7 (1988 Update). Recognizes durable powers of attorney.

Iowa—633.705, .706 (1988 Update). Recognizes durable powers of attorney.

Kansas—58-601, -602, -610 through -617 (1987 Update). Recognizes durable powers of attorney.

Kentucky—386.093 (1987 Update). Recognizes durable powers of attorney.

Louisiana—Civil Code Article 3027(A) and (B), 2985, 2987, 2992, 2994, and 2997 (1988 Update). Recognizes durable powers of attorney. Requires specification of powers for certain acts.

Maine—18-A-5-501 (1987 Update). Recognizes durable powers of attorney.

Maryland—Estates and Trusts 13-601, -602 (1987 Update). Recognizes durable powers of attorney.

Massachusetts—201B-1-7 (1987 Update). Recognizes durable powers of attorney.

Michigan—27.5495 (1988 Update). Recognizes durable powers of attorney.

Minnesota—523.01 through .25 (1988 Update). Recognizes durable powers of attorney. Minnesota law provides a form for durable powers of attorney.

Mississippi—87-3-1 through -17 (1987 Update). Recognizes durable powers of attorney.

Missouri—486.550 through .595 (1988 Update). Recognizes durable powers of attorney. 486.575 requires that a durable power of attorney be recorded.

Montana—72-5-501, -502 (1987 Update). Recognizes durable powers of attorney.

Nebraska—30-2664 through -2672 (1987 Update). Recognizes durable powers of attorney.

Nevada—111.450, .460, .470; 449.800 through .860 (1987 Update). Nevada recognizes durable powers of attorney. In order for a general durable power of attorney for health care to be valid, a person must use a form substantially similar to the form provided in 449.800. That form is different from the form at the end of this chapter.

New Hampshire—506:6 (1988 Update). Recognizes durable powers of attorney.

New Jersey—46:2B-8, -9 (1988 Update). Recognizes durable powers of attorney.

New Mexico—45-5-501, -502 (1987 Update). Recognizes durable powers of attorney.

New York—General Obligations Law 5-1501 through -1601 (1988 Update). Recognizes durable powers of attorney. New York law includes forms for durable powers of attorney and rules of construction for those forms.

North Carolina—32A-1-3; 32A-8, -9 (1987 Update). North Carolina recognizes durable powers of attorney, but requires that they be registered in the office of the register of deeds of the county in the state designated in the power of attorney, or if no place of registration is designated in the power of attorney, in the office of the register of deeds of the county in which the principal has his or her legal residence at the time of registration. Section 32A-11 requires that within thirty days after registering a power of attorney, an attorney-in-fact must file a copy of the power of attorney with the clerk of the supreme court in the county of registration. North Carolina law also requires that the attorney-in-fact keep full records of all transactions and of all property governed by the power of attorney. A power of attorney can waive the filing of any inventories and any accountings, in which case, an attorney-in-fact does not have to keep such records. Consult an attorney before preparing a power of attorney in North Carolina, and read the sections of North Carolina's laws referred to in this paragraph.

North Dakota—30.1-30-01 through -05 (1987 Update). Recognizes durable powers of attorney.

Ohio—1337.01 through .10 (1988 Update). Recognizes durable powers of attorney.

Oklahoma—58-1051 (1988 Update). Oklahoma law requires that a power of attorney be signed before a judge. Do not use the forms in this book for Oklahoma powers of attorney, unless you sign the form in the presence of a judge who approves the form before you sign it.

Oregon—126.407, .413 (1987 Update). Recognizes durable powers of attorney.

Pennsylvania—20 Pa CSA 5601 through 5607 (1988 Update). Recognizes durable powers of attorney.

Rhode Island—23-4.10-1, -2; 34-22-6.1 (1987 Update). Recognizes durable powers of attorney. If a person wishes to sign a durable power of attorney for health care decisions, he or she must use the form included in Sections 23-4.10-1 and -2. That form differs from the form at the end of this chapter.

South Carolina—62-5-501 (1987 Update). Recognizes durable powers of attorney. South Carolina law requires that a general durable power of attorney be executed and attested like a will and probated and recorded like a deed in the county where the principal resides when the instrument is recorded. Consult an attorney before preparing a power of attorney in South Carolina, and read the sections of South Carolina's laws referred to in this paragraph.

South Dakota—59-7-2.1 (1988 Update). Recognizes durable powers of attorney.

Tennessee—34-6-101 through -107 (1987 Update). Recognizes durable powers of attorney.

Texas—Probate Section 36A (1988 Update). Recognizes durable powers of attorney.

Utah—75-5-501, -502 (1988 Update). Recognizes durable powers of attorney.

Vermont—14-3051, -3052 (1988 Update). Recognizes durable powers of attorney.

Virginia—11-9.1, -9.2 (1988 Update). Recognizes durable powers of attorney.

Washington—11.94.010, .020 (1988 Update). Recognizes durable powers of attorney.

West Virginia—39-4-1 through -7 (1988 Update). Recognizes durable powers of attorney.

Wisconsin—243.07 (1988 Update). Recognizes durable powers of attorney.

Wyoming—3-5-101 (1987 Update). Recognizes durable powers of attorney.

USING A POWER OF ATTORNEY

Even though a power of attorney is valid, some banks, medical personnel, or others may refuse to honor it for a variety of reasons. Some insurance companies will not honor a power of attorney that is older than six months, one year, or some other time limit.

To convince people and institutions to honor a power of attorney, keep the power of attorney as current as possible. Talk with any medical personnel, bank officers, insurance representatives, or other persons who work where you might use the power of attorney. Ask them what their policies are regarding honoring powers of attorney.

To help convince a bank or other institution to honor a power of attorney, an agent can sign an affidavit relieving the bank, institution, or person from any liability for honoring it. This chapter includes a sample affidavit, an explanation of the sample, and a blank affidavit.

Another way to help convince a person or institution to honor a power of attorney is to include in the power of attorney a detailed description of the powers that the principal is giving the agent. Someone is more likely to allow an agent to do something for a principal using a power of attorney if the power of attorney specifically authorizes the agent to perform the act. The form for a general power of attorney at the end of this chapter includes a detailed description of the powers given to the agent.

Most states require that a principal or agent record a power of attorney before an agent can use it to buy or sell real estate. A principal or agent records a power of attorney by taking it to the recorder's office in each county where real estate affected by the power is located. A recorder will take the original power of attorney, make a copy of it, and keep the copy on file. The recorder will note on the original and the copy the exact time and date that he or she recorded the power of attorney, and will return the original to you within a week or so.

See the state laws section of Chapter 10 for further guidance on recording documents.

REVOKING A POWER OF ATTORNEY

If you want to revoke a power of attorney so that your agent cannot use it anymore, prepare and sign a revocation of a power of attorney. This chapter includes a sample revocation, an explanation of the sample, and a blank revocation.

Sample General Durable and Special Durable Powers of Attorney
(FIGS. 15-2 and 15-3)

Figure 15-2 is a sample general durable power of attorney. Figure 15-3 is a sample special durable power of attorney. The samples contain the following information that all powers of attorney should include:

Name of the principal.

Name of the agent.

Words giving the agent power to perform acts for the principal, and a description of the powers the principal gives the agent. The sample general durable power of attorney states that the principal empowers the agent to do anything that the principal could do. A power of attorney does not have to itemize all the different things an agent can do for a principal.

The blank general durable power of attorney in this chapter includes broad language empowering the agent to do anything the principal could do. It also itemizes specific powers that the principal gives the agent. The form includes these powers because including them may help persuade someone to honor the power of attorney.

The words empowering the agent, and the powers the principal gives the agent, in the sample special power of attorney are different from the words and powers in the sample general power of attorney. The special power of attorney only gives the agent limited powers. If you are giving an agent a special power of attorney, you might find the language you need for your description of limited powers among the powers listed in the blank general durable power of attorney in this chapter.

Release from liability for honoring the power of attorney. Releasing whoever honors the power of attorney from liability helps persuade them to honor the power of attorney.

A statement that the power of attorney is not affected by the subsequent disability of the principal. This statement is what makes a power of attorney "durable." Many principals want their powers of attorney to be effective after they become disabled. This clause accomplishes that goal.

A statement that if part of the power of attorney is invalid, the rest of the power of attorney will still be valid.

A statement as to what state law controls the power of attorney. This statement avoids disputes as to what state's laws govern the power of attorney. The laws of the state of residence of the principal should govern the power of attorney.

The date the principal signs the power of attorney, and the signature of the principal.

The agent's acceptance of the power of attorney. A principal cannot force an agent to become the principal's agent. An agent should accept this appointment in writing.

Statements and signatures of two witnesses. Some states require that two witnesses watch a principal sign a power of attorney, and that the witnesses sign a statement describing what they witnessed.

Notarization. A principal should sign a power of attorney in the presence of a notary public for the state in which the power of attorney is signed. The notary public should know the principal personally and should ask the principal to acknowledge signing the power of attorney and to swear under oath to the truth of the statements made in the paragraph above the notary's signature.

Waiver by the principal's spouse of the spouse's dower, curtesy, homestead, community property, and other rights. Some states give a husband or wife certain rights in real estate owned by his or her spouse, even if the real estate is in the name of only one spouse. These rights are called *dower rights* on behalf of women, and *curtesy rights* on behalf of men.

Many states have abolished dower and curtesy rights, but in states that still have these rights, a final divorce that dissolves the marriage of the parties forever will eliminate dower and curtesy rights. The present spouse of the principal should give up the spouse's dower or curtesy rights in property affected by a power of attorney so that the spouse cannot make a claim against an agent for disposing of the principal's property without the spouse's consent.

In some states, a husband or a wife has homestead or community property rights in his or her spouse's property. *Homestead rights* are the rights of a spouse to live in the family home until death. *Community property rights* exist in nine states: Arizona, California, Idaho, Louisiana, Nevada, New Mexico, Texas, Washington, and Wisconsin. Under community property laws, a spouse may have an interest in property owned by his or her spouse, even if title to the property is in the name of only one spouse. The present spouse of the principal should release homestead and community property rights so that the spouse cannot make a claim against the agent for disposing of the principal's property without the spouse's consent.

Name and address of the person who prepared the power of attorney. In order for a power of attorney to be recorded, some states require that the power of attorney state who prepared it.

Name and address where the recorder should send the power of attorney after recording it. The agent should instruct the recorder to return the power of attorney to the agent after recording because the agent must keep the power of attorney in his or her possession.

General Durable Power of Attorney

I, John M. Jones, as principal, hereby appoint Mary L. Jones as my agent, to be my attorney-in-fact, and give my agent the power to do anything I would be entitled to do, including but not limited to the power to do the following:

To sell any of the real, personal, intangible, or other property that I own now or in the future on any terms, and to use the proceeds of sale in any way.

To buy any real, personal, intangible, or other property on any terms, and to use, care for, or insure my present or future property in any way.

To borrow money, use credit cards, mortgage, or allow other encumbrances against property I own now or in the future on any terms.

To invest any of my real, personal, intangible, or other property in any real, personal, intangible, or other property.

To demand, release, receive, deposit, settle for, sue for, or do anything else with any real, personal, intangible, or other property which I am entitled to now or in the future. My agent is hereby named my representative payee to receive social security benefits.

To do anything that I could do with respect to retirement and employment benefits such as IRAs, employee benefit plans, self-employment benefit plans, or other retirement plans.

To do anything that I could do with respect to bank accounts of all kinds and accounts at other institutions, including opening, changing, and closing said accounts, and including writing and endorsing checks of all kinds.

To do anything that I could do with respect to any safe deposit box I have now or in the future, including opening, changing, and closing said boxes.

To do anything that I could do with respect to any legal action or claim.

To do anything that I could do with respect to trusts created by me or created for my benefit.

To do anything that I could do with respect to insurance policies on my life or the life of anyone in whom I have an insurable interest.

To do anything that I could do with respect to tax matters and tax returns for the years between 1980 and 2100, including the power to sign any power of attorney form required by the Internal Revenue Service or other taxing authority.

To make gifts of any of my property to anyone for any reason.

To lend money or other property of mine on any terms.

For any real, personal, or other property I own now or in the future, the power to lease, sublease, release, manage in any way, protect, insure, maintain, destroy, alter, grant easements upon, subdivide, develop, dedicate to the public, change boundaries or plats, collect rents and profits, and the power to do all acts that I could do regarding said property.

For any business in which I have an interest now or in the future, the power to operate said business and do anything regarding said business that I would be able to do.

With respect to my physical care, the power to do anything that I could do, including providing for my food, shelter, medical care, hospitalization, clothing, transportation, nursing home or similar institutional care, travel and recreational activities, religious needs, funeral and burial arrangements, making anatomical gifts, having access to medical records and other personal information, having the power to admit me to medical facilities, to hire and fire medical personnel, to give or withhold consent to medical and psychiatric treatment, including surgical procedures, and to grant releases to medical personnel.

I hereby authorize all persons or entities to release any medical or other information my agent requests regarding me to my agent, and I release said persons or entities from any liability for doing so.

If I revoke or amend this power of attorney, I release from any liability and will hold harmless from any loss any person or institution acting under instructions from my agent before such person or institution receives actual notice of the revocation or amendment.

This power of attorney shall not be affected by the subsequent disability or incapacity of the principal.

If any part of this power of attorney is invalid under any law, such invalidity shall not affect the remainder of this instrument.

This power of attorney shall be governed under the laws of the Commonwealth of Pennsylvania.

If this power of attorney is governed by a community property state, and the agent appointed under this power of attorney is the spouse of the principal, the agent's authority under this power of attorney only applies to the principal's separate property and the principal's one-half of community property, and is to be exercised only for the principal's benefit.

Additional provisions: None.

THIS POWER OF ATTORNEY IS A LEGAL DOCUMENT. IT PROVIDES THE PERSON DESIGNATED AS ATTORNEY-IN-FACT WITH BROAD POWERS OVER THE PRINCIPAL'S PROPERTY. THE POWERS EXIST FOR AN INDEFINITE PERIOD UNLESS OTHERWISE LIMITED, AND THE PRINCIPAL MAY REVOKE OR TERMINATE THE POWER OF ATTORNEY AT ANY TIME.

IN WITNESS WHEREOF, I have executed this power of attorney on January 5, 1989.

_____

John M. Jones, Principal

Fig. 15-2. (Cont'd). *Page 3 of 4* **269**

I, the undersigned agent, hereby accept the duties and obligations of the above appointment as attorney-in-fact for the above principal.

_____

Mary L. Jones, Agent

We hereby declare that on January 5, 1989, we witnessed John M. Jones, as principal, sign the above power of attorney in our presence, that he declared and published it to us as his power of attorney, that we know the principal personally and believe he is of sound mind and that he signed said power of attorney freely and voluntarily, and that we witnessed John M. Jones sign said power of attorney at his request and signed this statement at his request.

Dated this 5th day of January, 1989.

_____   _____

Allen M. Johnson, Witness   Frederick L. Roth, Witness
555 Sixth Street   777 Eighth Street
Waynecastle, Pennsylvania 17294   Waynecastle, Pennsylvania 17294

COMMONWEALTH OF
PENNSYLVANIA   )
) ss.
COUNTY OF BURR   )

I, Wanda C. Twobucks, a resident of and notary public in and for the commonwealth and county named above, who am duly commissioned and sworn and legally authorized to administer oaths and affirmations, hereby certify that on January 5, 1989, John M. Jones, who is known to me personally to be the principal in the above power of attorney, appeared before me, acknowledged signing the above power of attorney, and, after being first duly sworn by me under penalty of perjury, swore on his oath to the truth of the facts in the above power of attorney, declared said document to be a power of attorney that he gave to the above agent, signed it freely and voluntarily, and signed it in my presence and for the purposes explained in said power of attorney.

Subscribed and sworn to before me this 5th day of January, 1989.

_____

Wanda C. Twobucks

Notary Public
My Commission expires: 2/09/91.

(SEAL)   My   Commission_____

I, the spouse of John M. Jones, hereby approve the above power of attorney, and waive any dower, curtesy, homestead, community property, and other rights I have in property affected by the above power of attorney.
Dated this 5th day of January, 1989.

_____

Mary L. Jones

This instrument was prepared by John M. Jones, whose address is 222 Third Street, Waynecastle, Pennsylvania, 17294.

After Recording Return To:
Mary L. Jones
222 Third Street
Waynecastle, Pennsylvania 17294

Special Durable Power of Attorney

I, John M. Jones, as principal, hereby appoint Mary L. Jones as my agent, to be my attorney-in-fact, and give my agent the power to do the following only:

To sign any and all documents necessary to sell and transfer the title to my 1985 Ford Esquire Station Wagon automobile, Serial No. 12345, License No. 678954, Title No. 321578, and Vehicle Identification No. 987654321.

If I revoke or amend this power of attorney, I release from liability and will hold harmless from any loss any person or institution acting under instructions from my agent before such person or institution receives actual notice of the revocation or amendment.

This power of attorney shall not be affected by the subsequent disability or incapacity of the principal.

If any part of this power of attorney is invalid under any law, such invalidity shall not affect the remainder of this instrument.

This power of attorney shall be governed under the laws of the Commonwealth of Pennsylvania.

If this power of attorney is governed by a community property state, and the agent appointed under this power of attorney is the spouse of the principal, the agent's authority under this power of attorney only applies to the principal's separate property and the principal's one-half of community property, and is to be exercised only for the principal's benefit.

THIS POWER OF ATTORNEY IS A LEGAL DOCUMENT. IT MAY PROVIDE THE PERSON DESIGNATED AS ATTORNEY-IN-FACT WITH BROAD POWERS OVER THE PRINCIPAL'S PROPERTY. THE POWERS EXIST FOR AN INDEFINITE PERIOD UNLESS OTHERWISE LIMITED, AND THE PRINCIPAL MAY REVOKE OR TERMINATE THE POWER OF ATTORNEY AT ANY TIME.

IN WITNESS WHEREOF, I have executed this power of attorney on January 5, 1989.

_____

John M. Jones, Principal

I, the undersigned agent, hereby accept the duties and obligations of the above appointment as attorney-in-fact for the above principal.

_____

Mary L. Jones, Agent

We hereby declare that on January 5, 1989, we witnessed John M. Jones as principal, sign the above power of attorney in our presence, that he declared and published it to us as his power of attorney, that we know the principal personally and believe he is of sound mind and that he signed said power of attorney freely and voluntarily, and that we witnessed John M. Jones sign said power of attorney at his request and signed this statement at his request.

Dated on this 5th day of January, 1989.

Allen M. Johnson, Witness
555 Sixth Street
Waynecastle, Pennsylvania 17294

Frederick L. Roth, Witness
777 Eighth Street
Waynecastle, Pennsylvania 17294

COMMONWEALTH OF PENNSYLVANIA)

) ss.

COUNTY OF BURR   )

I, Wanda C. Twobucks, a resident of and notary public in and for the state and county named above, who am duly commissioned and sworn and legally authorized to administer oaths and affirmations, hereby certify that on January 5, 1989, John M. Jones, who is known to me personally to be the principal in the above power of attorney, appeared before me, acknowledged signing the above power of attorney, and, after being first duly sworn by me under penalty of perjury, swore on his oath to the truth of the facts in the above power of attorney, declared said document to be a power of attorney that he gave to the above agent, signed it freely and voluntarily, and signed it in my presence and for the purposes explained in said power of attorney.

Subscribed and sworn to before me this 5th day of January, 1989.

Wanda C. Twobucks
Notary Public
My Commission expires: 2/09/91.

(SEAL)

I, the spouse of John M. Jones, hereby approve the above power of attorney, and waive any dower, curtesy, homestead, community property, and other rights I have in property affected by the above power of attorney.

Dated this 5th day of January, 1989.

Mary L. Jones

Fig. 15-3. (Cont'd). *Page 3 of 3* **273**

This instrument was prepared by John M. Jones, whose address is 222 Third Street, Waynecastle, Pennsylvania, 17294.

After Recording Return To:
Mary L. Jones
222 Third Street
Waynecastle, Pennsylvania 17294

Sample Affidavit of Agent (FIG. 15-4)

Figure 15-4 is a sample affidavit of agent. An agent can use this type of affidavit to persuade someone to honor a power of attorney. Some states *require* that a person honor a power of attorney if an agent signs an affidavit similar to FIG. 15-4.

The sample affidavit includes the following information that all such affidavits should include:

Name of the agent.

Name of the principal.

A reference to and a copy of the original power of attorney. The agent should staple a copy of the power of attorney to the affidavit.

A statement that the principal is alive and that the power of attorney is still in effect. A person honoring a power of attorney must know whether or not the principal has died or has revoked the power of attorney. When a principal dies, powers of attorney that the principal signed while alive become void. If an agent states that a principal is alive and has not revoked the power of attorney, the law allows the person honoring the power of attorney to rely on that statement.

Explanation of the reasons for preparing the affidavit. Every affidavit should state the reason why the agent is making the affidavit. In the sample, the agent is using a power of attorney to withdraw funds from and to close the principal's bank account.

A statement that the agent understands that someone will rely on the affidavit, and the power of attorney attached to it. This statement helps persuade someone to honor a power of attorney because it makes an agent liable for losses suffered by the person honoring a power of attorney.

The date that the agent signed the affidavit and the signature of the agent.

Notarization. An agent should sign an affidavit in the presence of a notary public for the state in which the affidavit is signed. The notary public should know the agent personally, and should ask the agent to acknowledge signing the affidavit and to swear under oath to the truth of the statements in the affidavit.

After an agent signs an affidavit, the person honoring the power of attorney should keep the original affidavit, and the agent should keep a copy.

Name and address of the person who prepared the affidavit. Some states require that an affidavit must state the name and address of whoever prepared it. A person preparing an affidavit of an agent can record the affidavit, but does not have to do so and usually has no reason to do so.

Affidavit of Agent

COMMONWEALTH OF PENNSYLVANIA)

      ss.)

   COUNTY OF BURR)

I, Mary L. Jones, being first duly sworn, upon my oath and under penalty of perjury declare that:

John M. Jones appointed me as his attorney-in-fact by signing a power of attorney, a true copy of which I have attached to this affidavit and incorporate herein by this reference.

John M. Jones is still alive and has not revoked or amended the attached power of attorney, and said power of attorney is still in effect.

I make this affidavit for the purpose of withdrawing John M. Jones' funds from, and closing, the account of John M. Jones at First State Bank, 363 1st Street, Waynecastle, Pennsylvania, 17294, Account No. 2345678.

I understand that First State Bank is relying on this affidavit and the attached power of attorney in honoring the power of attorney and my actions under it.

IN WITNESS WHEREOF, I have signed this affidavit on January 5, 1989.

————————————————— Mary L. Jones, Agent

I, Wanda C. Twobucks, a resident of and notary public for the commonwealth and county named above, who am duly commissioned and sworn and legally authorized to administer oaths and affirmations, hereby certify that on January 5, 1989, Mary L. Jones, who is known to me personally to be the signer of the above affidavit, appeared before me and, after being first duly sworn by me under penalty of perjury, swore on her oath to the truth of the facts in the above affidavit, and signed and acknowledged said affidavit in my presence, of her own free will and for the purposes explained in said affidavit.

Subscribed and sworn to before me this 5th day of January, 1989.

———————————————————————

Wanda C. Twobucks
Notary Public
My commission expires: 2/09/91
  (SEAL)

This instrument was prepared by Mary L. Jones, whose address is 222 Third Street, Waynecastle, Pennsylvania, 17294.

Sample Revocation of Power of Attorney (FIG. 15-5)

Figure 15-5 is a sample revocation of a power of attorney. The sample contains the following information that all such revocations should include:

Name of the principal in the original power of attorney.

Name of the agent in the original power of attorney.

A reference to the original power of attorney, including the date that the principal signed the power of attorney. The principal should attach a copy of the power of attorney to the revocation and incorporate it into the revocation by reference. The principal should mark the copy "Exhibit A", and mark "REVOKED" in large letters on the power of attorney.

The dates when, and the places where, the principal or agent recorded the original power of attorney, if it was recorded.

A statement revoking the power of attorney and declaring that it is null and void.

The date that the principal signed the revocation, and the signature of the principal.

Statements and signatures of two witnesses who witnessed the principal sign the revocation. A principal should sign a revocation the same way he or she signed the original power of attorney.

Notarization. A principal should sign a revocation in the presence of a notary public for the state in which the revocation is signed. The notary public should know the principal personally, and should ask the principal to acknowledge signing the revocation and to swear under oath to the truth of the statements in the paragraph above the notary's signature.

Name and address of the person who prepared the revocation. Some states require that a revocation include the name and address of the person who prepared it.

Name and address where the recorder should return the revocation after recording it. The principal should instruct the recorder to return the revocation to the principal after recording.

Revocation of Power of Attorney

I, John M. Jones, a resident of the Commonwealth of Pennsylvania, appointed Mary L. Jones as my agent by a written power of attorney dated January 5, 1989, a copy of which power of attorney I have attached hereto, marked Exhibit "A", marked "REVOKED", and incorporate herein by this reference, which power of attorney was recorded on the following date in the following county in the following book and page:

Date Recorded	County Where Recorded	Book/Page No.
1/05/89	Burr Co., Pennsylvania	222/333

I hereby revoke the above power of attorney given to Mary L. Jones, and said power of attorney is hereby null and void.

Dated this 5th day of January, 1990.

_____

John M. Jones, Principal

We hereby declare that on January 5, 1990, we witnessed John M. Jones, as principal, sign the above revocation of a power of attorney in our presence, that he declared and published it as his revocation of a power of attorney, that we know the principal personally and believe he is of sound mind and that he signed said revocation freely and voluntarily, and that we witnessed John M. Jones sign said revocation at his request and signed this statement at his request.

Dated this 5th day of January, 1990.

_____   _____

Allen M. Johnson, Witness   Frederick L. Roth, Witness
555 Sixth Street   777 Eighth Street
Waynecastle, Pennsylvania 17294   Waynecastle, Pennsylvania 17294

Fig. 15-5. (Cont'd). *Page 2 of 2* **277**

COMMONWEALTH OF PENNSYLVANIA   )
) ss.
            COUNTY OF BURR   )

I, Wanda C. Twobucks, a resident of and notary public in and for the commonwealth and county named above, who am duly commissioned and sworn and legally authorized to administer oaths and affirmations, hereby certify that on January 5, 1990, John M. Jones, who is known to me personally to be the principal in the above revocation of a power of attorney, appeared before me, acknowledged signing the above revocation, and, after being first duly sworn by me under penalty of perjury, swore on his oath to the truth of the facts in the above revocation of a power of attorney, declared said document to be a revocation of a power of attorney that he gave to the above agent, signed it freely and voluntarily, and signed it in my presence and for the purposes explained in said revocation.

Subscribed and sworn to before me this 5th day of January, 1990.

_____ Wanda C. Twobucks
Notary Public
My Commission Expires: 02/09/91
(SEAL)

This instrument was prepared by John M. Jones, whose address is 222 Third Street, Waynecastle, Pennsylvania, 17294.

After Recording Return to:
John M. Jones
222 Third Street
Waynecastle, Pennsylvania 17294

Instructions for Blank Forms

This chapter includes four forms:

- Figure 15-6 is a general durable power of attorney.
- Figure 15-7 is a special durable power of attorney.
- Figure 15-8 is an affidavit for an agent to use with a power of attorney.
- Figure 15-9 is a revocation of power of attorney.

Each form has blank spaces with numbers under them. Before filling in any of the blanks, make several photocopies of the form. Use one or more copies as work copies, one as an original, and the rest for future work copies or originals. Fill out a work copy first and be sure it is correct, then type or print in the blanks on your original.

Blank General Durable Power of Attorney (FIG. 15-6) The following numbered instructions match the numbers under the blanks in FIG. 15-6:

(1) Enter the full name of the principal.

(2) Enter the full name of the agent.

(3) Enter the principal's state of residence, which should be the same as the state where the principal signs the power of attorney.

(4) Enter any additional provisions that you want to add to the power of attorney. If you do not want to add any additional provisions, enter "none" in this space.

(5) Enter the date that the principal signs the power of attorney.

(6) The principal, agent, witnesses, and notary should go through the following ritual when signing the power of attorney:

    a. The principal, agent, witnesses, and notary should assemble.

    b. The principal should sign the power of attorney with his or her full name on Line 6. Under the principal's signature, print or type his or her name.

    c. The principal should tell the agent, the witnesses, and the notary that the document he or she signed is a power of attorney that he or she is giving to the agent, and that he or she signed it voluntarily. The principal should then ask the witnesses to witness the power of attorney and to sign their names as witnesses.

    d. The witnesses should sign the power of attorney as witnesses on Lines 13 and 14 as described below.

    e. The notary public should administer an oath to the principal, asking whether the principal solemnly swears upon his or her oath and under penalty of perjury to tell the truth regarding the power of attorney. The principal should raise his or her right hand and declare under oath to the notary that he or she swears to tell the truth regarding the power of attorney, that he or she is the person named as principal in the power of attorney, that the document he or she signed is a power of attorney that he or she gave to the agent, that he or she signed it voluntarily in the presence of the witnesses, and that he or she asked the witnesses to witness the power of attorney and to sign their names to the power of attorney as witnesses.

    f. The notary should complete the remainder of the notary section as the following instructions describe.

(7) The agent should sign his or her full name on this line. Under the agent's signature, print or type his or her name.

(8) Enter the date the principal signed the power of attorney.

(9) Enter the name of the principal.

(10,11,12) Enter the day, month, and year that the witnesses sign the power of attorney.

(13) The first witness should sign his or her name on this line. Under the signature of the first witness, print or type the first witness's name. Put the witness's address on the lines below.

(14) Do the same for the second witness.

Items 15-28 should be completed by a notary public:

(15) Enter the name of the state where the notary public is authorized to notarize documents.

(16) Enter the name of the county where the notary public is authorized to notarize documents.

(17) Enter the name of the notary public.

(18) Enter the date the principal signs the power of attorney.

(19) Enter the name of the principal.

(20,21,22) Enter the day, month, and year that the notary public notarized the power of attorney.

(23) The notary public should sign on this line and print or type his or her name below it.

(24) Enter the date that the notary public's commission expires.

(25) The notary public should affix his or her seal next to his or her signature.

(26,27,28) Enter the day, month, and year that the principal's spouse signs the power of attorney. If the principal does not have a spouse, put "not applicable" in this blank.

(29) The principal's spouse should sign on this line. If the principal does not have a spouse, put "not applicable" in this blank. Under the spouse's signature, print or type his or her name.

(30) Enter the name of the person who prepared the power of attorney.

(31) Enter the address of the person who prepared the power of attorney.

(32) Enter the name and address of the agent. The agent wants the recorder to return the original power of attorney to the agent after recording.

After completing the form, make several copies of it. The principal and agent should each keep several copies. The agent should record the original power of attorney at the recorder's office in the county where the principal lives, in any county where the principal owns real property, and in any county where the agent will use the power. The principal should make and keep a list of all counties where the agent records the power of attorney. After recording the original power of attorney, the agent should keep the original power of attorney.

The agent may want to give copies of the power of attorney to any bank, medical institution, or other institution where the agent will use the power. The agent should talk with someone from these institutions about the policies of the institutions regarding powers of attorney.

When the agent needs to sign a document for the principal, the agent should sign as follows: "John James Smith, by Robert Allen Jones, his attorney-in-fact". (Smith is the principal. Jones is the agent.)

Blank Special Durable Power of Attorney (FIG. 15-7)   Follow the instructions for FIG. 15-6, above, except for the following:

(3) Describe exactly what power(s) the principal is giving the agent, and the length of time that the agent will have the power(s). If the power(s) affect particular property, describe the property so there is no doubt what property you are referring to. If Blank 3 does not have enough room to describe the property or the powers being given to the agent, put "See Exhibit A" in Blank 3, and attach

a page (or pages) which includes a description of the property or power. Label the page "Exhibit A" at the top, and staple the exhibit to the power of attorney.

(4) Enter the name of the principal's state of residence, which should be the same as the state where the principal signs the power of attorney.

Fig. 15-6. General Durable Power of Attorney (Blank). *Page 1 of 4* **281**

General Durable Power of Attorney

I, _____,
(1)

as principal, hereby appoint _____
(2)

as my agent, to be my attorney-in-fact, and give my agent the power to do anything I would be entitled to do, including but not limited to the power to do the following:

To sell any of the real, personal, intangible, or other property that I own now or in the future on any terms, and to use the proceeds of sale in any way.

To buy any real, personal, intangible, or other property on any terms, and to use, care for, or insure my present or future property in any way.

To borrow money, use credit cards, mortgage, or allow other encumbrances against property I own now or in the future on any terms.

To invest any of my real, personal, intangible, or other property in any real, personal, intangible, or other property.

To demand, release, receive, deposit, settle for, sue for, or do anything else with any real, personal, intangible, or other property which I am entitled to now or in the future. My agent is hereby named my representative payee to receive social security benefits.

To do anything that I could do with respect to retirement and employment benefits such as IRAs, employee benefit plans, self-employment benefit plans, or other retirement plans.

To do anything that I could do with respect to bank accounts of all kinds and accounts at other institutions, including opening, changing, and closing said accounts, and including writing and endorsing checks of all kinds.

To do anything that I could do with respect to any safe deposit box I have now or in the future, including opening, changing, and closing said boxes.

To do anything that I could do with respect to any legal action or claim.

To do anything that I could do with respect to trusts created by me or created for my benefit.

To do anything that I could do with respect to insurance policies on my life or the life of anyone in whom I have an insurable interest.

To do anything that I could do with respect to tax matters and tax returns for the years between 1980 and 2100, including the power to sign any power of attorney form required by the Internal Revenue Service or other taxing authority.

To make gifts of any of my property to anyone for any reason.

To lend money or other property of mine on any terms.

For any real, personal, or other property I own now or in the future, the power to lease, sublease, release, manage in any way, protect, insure, maintain, destroy, alter, grant easements upon, subdivide, develop, dedicate to the public, change boundaries or plats, collect rents and profits, and the power to do all acts that I could do regarding said property.

For any business in which I have an interest now or in the future, the power to operate said business and do anything regarding said business that I would be able to do.

With respect to my physical care, the power to do anything that I could do, including providing for my food, shelter, medical care, hospitalization, clothing, transportation, nursing home or similar institutional care, travel and recreational activities, religious needs, funeral and burial arrangements, making anatomical gifts, having access to medical records and other personal information, having the power to admit me to medical facilities, to hire and fire medical personnel, to give or withhold consent to medical and psychiatric treatment, including surgical procedures, and to grant releases to medical personnel.

I hereby authorize all persons or entities to release any medical or other information my agent requests regarding me to my agent, and I release said persons or entities from any liability for doing so.

If I revoke or amend this power of attorney, I release from any liability and will hold harmless from any loss any person or institution acting under instructions from my agent before such person or institution receives actual notice of the revocation or amendment.

This power of attorney shall not be affected by the subsequent disability or incapacity of the principal.

If any part of this power of attorney is invalid under any law, such invalidity shall not affect the remainder of this instrument.

This power of attorney shall be governed under the laws of the State of

_____
(3)

If this power of attorney is governed by a community property state, and the agent appointed under this power of attorney is the spouse of the principal, the agent's authority under this power of attorney only applies to the principal's separate property and the principal's one-half of community property, and is to be exercised only for the principal's benefit.

Additional provisions: _____
(4)

_____

_____

_____

_____

THIS POWER OF ATTORNEY IS A LEGAL DOCUMENT. IT PROVIDES THE PERSON DESIGNATED AS ATTORNEY-IN-FACT WITH BROAD POWERS OVER THE PRINCIPAL'S PROPERTY. THE POWERS EXIST FOR AN INDEFINITE PERIOD UNLESS OTHERWISE LIMITED, AND THE PRINCIPAL MAY REVOKE OR TERMINATE THE POWER OF ATTORNEY AT ANY TIME.

Fig. 15-6. (Cont'd). *Page 3 of 4* **283**

IN WITNESS WHEREOF, I have executed this power of attorney on

_____.
(5)

_____,

Principal   (6)

I, the undersigned agent, hereby accept the duties and obligations of the above appointment as attorney-in-fact for the above principal.

_____

Agent   (7)

We hereby declare that on _____,
(8)
we witnessed _____,
(9)
as principal, sign the above power of attorney in our presence, that the principal declared and published it to us as his or her power of attorney, that we know the principal personally and believe he/she is of sound mind and that he/she signed said power of attorney freely and voluntarily, and that we witnessed said principal sign said power of attorney at his/her request and signed this statement at his/her request.

Dated this _____ day of _____, _____.
(10)   (11)   (12)

_____

, Witness   (13)

_____

_____

_____

_____

, Witness   (14)

_____

_____

_____

STATE OF _____)
(15)

) ss.

COUNTY OF _____)
(16)

I, _____,
(17)

a resident of and notary public in and for the state and county named above, who am duly commissioned and sworn and legally authorized to administer oaths and

affirmations, hereby certify that on _____,
(18)

_____
(19)

who is known to me personally to be the principal in the above power of attorney, appeared before me, acknowledged signing the above power of attorney, and, after being first duly sworn by me under penalty of perjury, swore on his/her oath to the truth of the facts in the above power of attorney, declared said document to be a power of attorney that he/she gave to the above agent, signed it freely and voluntarily, and signed it in my presence and for the purposes explained in said power of attorney.

Subscribed and sworn to before me this _____ day of
(20)

_____ , _____ .
(21)   (22)

_____
(23)
Notary Public

My Commission expires:_____
(24)

(SEAL)
(25)

I, the spouse of the above principal, hereby approve the above power of attorney, and waive any dower, curtesy, homestead, community property, and other rights I have in property affected by the above power of attorney.

Dated this _____ day of _____, _____ .
(26)   (27)   (28)

_____
,Spouse   (29)

This instrument was prepared by _____
(30)

_____, whose address is _____
(31)

_____ .

After Recording Return To:

_____
(32)

_____

_____

Fig. 15-7. Special Durable Power of Attorney(Blank). *Page 1 of 4* **285**

Special Durable Power of Attorney

I, _____, as principal,
(1)

hereby appoint _____ as my agent,
(2)

to be my attorney-in-fact, and give my agent the power to do the following only:

_____
(3)

_____

_____

_____

_____

_____

   If I revoke or amend this power of attorney, I release from liability and will hold harmless from any loss any person or institution acting under instructions from my agent before such person or institution receives actual notice of the revocation or amendment.

   This power of attorney shall not be affected by the subsequent disability or incapacity of the principal.

   If any part of this power of attorney is invalid under any law, such invalidity shall not affect the remainder of this instrument.

   This power of attorney shall be governed under the laws of the State of

_____ .
(4)

   If this power of attorney is governed by a community property state, and the agent appointed under this power of the attorney is the spouse of the principal, the agent's authority under this power of attorney only applies to the principal's separate property and the principal's one-half of community property, and is to be exercised only for the principal's benefit.

   THIS POWER OF ATTORNEY IS A LEGAL DOCUMENT. IT MAY PROVIDE THE PERSON DESIGNATED AS ATTORNEY-IN-FACT WITH BROAD POWERS OVER THE PRINCIPAL'S PROPERTY. THE POWERS EXIST FOR AN INDEFINITE PERIOD UNLESS OTHERWISE LIMITED, AND THE PRINCIPAL MAY REVOKE OR TERMINATE THE POWER OF ATTORNEY AT ANY TIME.

   IN WITNESS WHEREOF, I have executed this power of attorney on

_____ .
(5)

_____
,Principal (6)

I, the undersigned agent, hereby accept the duties and obligations of the above appointment as attorney-in-fact for the above principal.

_____

, Agent (7)

We hereby declare that on _____(8)_____,

we witnessed _____(9)_____,

as principal, sign the above power of attorney in our presence, that the principal declared and published it to us as his or her power of attorney, that we know the principal personally and believe he/she is of sound mind and that he/she signed said power of attorney freely and voluntarily, and that we witnessed said principal sign said power of attorney at his/her request and signed this statement at his/her request.

Dated this _____ day of _____(11)_____, _____(12).
(10)

_____

, Witness (13)

_____

_____

_____

_____

, Witness (14)

_____

Fig. 15-7. (Cont'd). *Page 3 of 4*   **287**

STATE OF _____)
                    (15)
) ss.

COUNTY OF _____)
                    (16)

I, _____,
a resident of and notary public in and for the state and county named above, who
am duly commissioned and sworn and legally authorized to administer oaths and

affirmations, hereby certify that on _____,
                                                    (18)
_____,
                                    (19)
who is known to me personally to be the principal in the above power of attorney,
appeared before me, acknowledged signing the above power of attorney, and,
after being first duly sworn by me under penalty of perjury, swore on his/her oath
to the truth of the facts in the above power of attorney, declared said document to
be a power of attorney that he/she gave to the above agent, signed it freely and
voluntarily, and signed it in my presence and for the purposes explained in said
power of attorney.

Subscribed and sworn to before me this _____ day of
                                                 (20)
_____, _____.
         (21)   (22)

_____
                                                     (23)
Notary Public
My Commission expires:_____
                                              (24)
(SEAL)
(25)

I, the spouse of the above principal, hereby approve the above power of
attorney, and waive any dower, curtesy, homestead, community property, and other rights I have in property affected by the above power of attorney.

Dated this _____ day of _____, _____.
                    (26)   (27)   (28)

_____
                                               ,Spouse   (29)

This instrument was prepared by _____,
                                                              (30)

whose address is _____
                                              (31)

_____.

After Recording Return To: _____

_____
              (32)

_____

_____

Blank Affidavit of Agent (FIG. 15-8)   The following numbered instructions match the numbers under the blanks in FIG. 15-8.

(1) Enter the name of the state where the agent signs the affidavit.

(2) Enter the name of the county where the agent signs the affidavit.

(3) Enter the full name of the agent.

(4) Enter the full name of the principal. Staple a copy of the original power of attorney to the affidavit.

(5) Enter the full name of the principal.

(6) Enter the reason why the agent is preparing this affidavit. For instance, explain that the agent is providing this affidavit to a particular bank to ensure the bank that the agent has the power to act with regard to a principal's bank account, if that is the reason the agent prepared the affidavit.

(7) Enter the name of the person or institution that will be relying upon this affidavit.

(8) Enter the date that the agent signed the affidavit.

(9) The agent should sign his or her full name on this line in the presence of a notary public for the state where the agent signed the power. Under the signature of the agent, print or type the name of the agent.

Items 10–18 should be completed by a notary public:

(10) Enter the name of the notary public.

(11) Enter the date that the agent signed the affidavit.

(12) Enter the name of the agent who signed the affidavit.

(13,14,15) Enter the day, month, and year that the agent signed the affidavit.

(16) The notary public should sign his or her name on this line. Under the signature of the notary public, print or type the name of the notary public.

(17) Enter the date that the notary public's commission expires.

(18) The notary public should affix his or her seal to the affidavit to the left of his or her signature.

(19) Enter the name of the person who prepared the affidavit.

(20) Enter the address of the person who prepared the affidavit.

After completing the affidavit, make several copies of it. The agent should keep several copies of the affidavit. The agent should give the original affidavit to the person or institution for whom the agent prepared the affidavit.

Fig. 15-8. Affidavit of Agent (Blank). *Page 1 of 2* **291**

Affidavit of Agent

COMMONWEALTH OF _____)

(1)

)

COUNTY OF _____)

(2)

I, _____ ,

(3)

being first duly sworn, upon my oath and under penalty of perjury declare that:

_____

(4)

_____, appointed me as his/her attorney-in-fact by signing a power of attorney, a true copy of which I have attached to this affidavit and incorporate herein by this reference.

_____

(5)

____ is still alive and has not revoked or amended the attached power of attorney, and said power of attorney is still in effect.

I make this affidavit for the purpose of: _____

(6)

_____

_____

_____.

I understand that _____

(7)

is relying on this affidavit and the attached power of attorney in honoring the power of attorney and any actions under it.

IN WITNESS WHEREOF, I have signed this affidavit on _____

(8)

_____.

_____

(9)

, Agent

I, _____ ,
(10)

a resident of and notary public for the state and county named above, who am
duly commissioned and sworn and legally authorized to administer oaths and

affirmations, hereby certify that on _____ ,
(11)

_____ , who is
(12)

known to me personally to be the signer of the above affidavit, appeared before
me and, after being first duly sworn by me under penalty of perjury, swore on his
or her oath to the truth of the facts in the above affidavit, and signed and
acknowledged said affidavit in my presence, of his or her own free will and for the
purposes explained in said affidavit.

Subscribed and sworn to before me this _____ day of
(13)

_____ , _____ .
(14)   (15)

_____
(16)

Notary Public

(SEAL)
(18)

My Commission expires:_____
(17)

This instrument was prepared by _____
(19)

_____ , whose address is _____
(20)

_____ .

Blank Revocation of Power of Attorney (FIG. 15-9)   The following numbered instructions match the numbers under the blanks in FIG. 15-9:

(1) Enter the full name of the principal who is revoking the power of attorney.

(2) Enter the principal's state of residence.

(3) Enter the full name of the agent in the original power of attorney.

(4) Enter the date that the principal signed the original power of attorney.

(5) Enter the dates the original power of attorney was recorded in each county where it was recorded. If it was not recorded, put "none" here. Staple a copy of the original power of attorney to the revocation. Mark "Exhibit A" at the top of the copy. Mark "REVOKED" in large letters across each page of the original power of attorney.

(6) Enter the names of the counties where the principal or agent recorded the original power of attorney. If it was not recorded, put "none" here.

(7) Enter the recorder's fee numbers where the original power of attorney was recorded. If a recorder's office uses book and page numbers instead of fee numbers, enter the book and page numbers here. If the power of attorney was not recorded, put "none" here.

(8) Enter the name of the agent in the original power of attorney.

(9,10,11) Enter the day, month, and year that the principal signs the revocation.

(12) The principal should sign his or her name above this line in the presence of two witnesses and a notary public. Under the signature of the principal, print or type his or her name. The principal, witnesses, and notary should go through the following ritual when signing the revocation:

   a. The principal, witnesses, and notary should assemble.

   b. The principal should sign the revocation.

   c. The principal should tell the witnesses and the notary that the document he or she signed is a revocation of a power of attorney that he or she gave to the agent named in the revocation, and that he or she signed it voluntarily. The principal should then ask the witnesses to witness the revocation and to sign their names as witnesses.

   d. The witnesses should each sign the revocation as witnesses on Lines 18 and 19 as described below.

   e. The notary public should administer an oath to the principal, asking whether the principal solemnly swears upon his or her oath and under penalty of perjury to tell the truth regarding the revocation. The principal should raise his or her right hand and declare under oath to the notary that he or she swears to tell the truth regarding the power of attorney, that he or she is the person that the revocation names as principal, that the document he or she signed is a revocation of a power of attorney that he or she gave to the agent named in the revocation, that he or she signed it voluntarily in the presence of the witnesses, and that he or she asked the witnesses to witness the revocation and to sign their names to the revocation as witnesses.

(13) Enter the date that the principal signed the revocation.

(14) Enter the name of the principal.

(15,16,17) Enter the day, month, and year that the witnesses and principal sign the revocation.

(18) The first witness should sign his or her name on this line. Under the signature, print or type the name of the first witness. Put the witness's address on the lines below.

(19) Do the same for the second witness.

Items 20-30 should be completed by a notary public:

    (20) Enter the state where the notary public is authorized to notarize documents.

    (21) Enter the county where the notary public is authorized to notarize documents.

    (22) Enter the name of the notary public.

    (23) Enter the date the principal signed the revocation.

    (24) Enter the name of the principal.

    (25,26,27) Enter the day, month, and year that the principal signed the revocation.

    (28) The notary public should sign on this line. Under the signature of the notary public, print or type the name of the notary public.

    (29) Enter the date that the notary public's commission expires.

    (30) The notary public should affix his or her seal next to his or her signature.

    (31) Enter the name of the person who prepared the revocation.

    (32) Enter the address of the person who prepared the revocation.

    (33) Enter the name and address of the principal. The principal wants the recorder to return the original revocation to the principal after recording.

After completing the form, make several copies of it. The principal should keep the original revocation and several copies. The principal should send at least one copy of the revocation to the agent, by certified mail, return receipt requested. The principal should record the revocation of the power of attorney at the recorders' offices in the county where the principal lives, in any county where the principal owns real property, in any county where the original power of attorney was recorded, and in any county where the agent may attempt to use or already used the original power of attorney. The principal should give copies of the revocation of the power to attorney to any person, bank, or institution where the agent may attempt to use or already used the original power of attorney.

Fig. 15-9. Revocation of Power of Attorney (Blank). *Page 1 of 2* **295**

Revocation of Power of Attorney

I, _____,
(1)

a resident of the State of _____, appointed
(2)

_____ as my agent
(3)

by a written power of attorney dated _____,
(4)

a copy of which power of attorney I have attached hereto, marked Exhibit "A", marked "REVOKED", and incorporate herein by this reference, which power of attorney was recorded on the following dates in the following counties as the following recorder's fee numbers or in the following books and pages:

Date Recorded	County Where Recorded	Recorder's Fee No. or Deed/Book Page No.
_____ (5)	_____ (6)	_____ (7)
_____ (5)	_____ (6)	_____ (7)
_____ (5)	_____ (6)	_____ (7)
_____ (5)	_____ (6)	_____ (7)

I hereby revoke the above power of attorney given to _____
(8)

_____, and said power of

attorney is hereby null and void.

Dated this _____ day of _____, _____.
(9)   (10)   (11)

_____, Principal (12)

We hereby declare that on _____,
(13)

we witnessed _____,
(14)

as principal, sign the above revocation of a power of attorney in our presence, that the principal declared and published it as his/her revocation of a power of attorney, that we know the principal personally and believe he/she is of sound mind and that he/she signed said revocation freely and voluntarily, and that we witnessed said principal sign said revocation at his/her request and signed this statement at his/her request.

Dated this _____ day of _____, _____.
(15)   (16)   (17)

_____, Witness (18)

_____, Witness (19)

STATE OF _____)
(20)

)

COUNTY OF _____)
(21)

I, _____,
(22)

a resident of and notary public in and for the state and county named above, who
am duly commissioned and sworn and legally authorized to administer oaths and

affirmations, hereby certify that on _____,
(23)

_____,
(24)

who is known to me personally to be the principal in the above revocation of a
power of attorney, appeared before me, acknowledged signing the above
revocation, and, after being first duly sworn by me under penalty of perjury, swore
on his/her oath to the truth of the facts in the above revocation of a power of
attorney, declared said document to be a revocation of a power of attorney that
he/she gave to the above agent, signed it freely and voluntarily, and signed it in
my presence and for the purposes explained in said revocation.

Subscribed and sworn to before me this _____ day of
(25)

_____, _____.
(26)   (27)

_____
(28)
Notary Public
My Commission expires:_____
(29)

(SEAL)
(30)

This instrument was prepared by _____
(31)

_____, whose address is _____
(32)

_____.

After Recording Return To:
_____
(33)

_____

Glossary

acceleration clause—A clause in a promissory note, mortgage, or other contract, which provides that if the maker of the note or buyer under the contract fails to live up to any of the terms of the agreement, the entire unpaid balance of principal and interest becomes immediately due and payable.

administrator—Someone appointed by a court to manage a deceased person's affairs, or someone in charge of an institution, such as a hospital.

affiant—A person who signs an affidavit.

affidavit—Any voluntary written statement sworn to before a person legally authorized to administer an oath.

agent—A person who acts for and represents another person.

alternate beneficiary—A person who is named in a will or insurance policy to receive property if the primary beneficiary dies before the person who makes the will or before the insured.

appurtenances—Anything belonging to, and a part of, land, such as an easement for a road across property.

as is—A sale in which the seller makes no representations or warranties regarding the condition of the property sold.

assign—To transfer to someone else. Also used synonymously with *assignee* below.

assignee—One who receives an assignment from someone else. Also called an *assign*.

assignment—A transferring of something to someone else. In the context of landlord/tenant relations, an assignment is an agreement in which a tenant transfers all of the tenant's rights in a rental agreement to someone else.

assignor—One who assigns something to someone else.

attaching a bank account—Seizing a bank account for collection of a debt or judgment.

attestation—Witnessing the signing of a document and signing one's name as a witness to the document.

attestation clause—In a will, a clause which recites that the will was signed in compliance with all the requirements of the law. Otherwise, a clause which recites that a document was witnessed.

attorney-in-fact—An agent appointed under a power of attorney to act for a principal.

bargain-and-sale deed—A deed that contains some, but not all, warranties of title.

beneficiary—A person who receives a benefit, such as a gift.

bid—A proposal by someone to do something for someone else.

bill of sale—A document that transfers ownership of personal property from one person to another.

bond—When used for a trustee, executor, or executrix, a document which provides that the person or company issuing the bond will pay a certain amount of money if the trustee, executor, or executrix misuses the assets of a trust or estate.

breach of contract—A failure without legal excuse to perform any promise contained in a contract.

breaching the peace—When used in the context of a seller trying to repossess property sold to a buyer (or a landlord trying to repossess property rented to a tenant), any repossession by the seller (or landlord) in the presence of the buyer (or tenant) without the buyer's (or tenant's) consent, or any repossession that breaks an enclosure, such as a gate.

certificate of title—A document that shows who owns personal property.

chain of title—The links between the past and present owners of property.

cleaning deposit—A nonrefundable fee charged by a landlord to a tenant for cleaning up rented property before the tenant moves in or after the tenant moves out.

codicil—An addition to or amendment of a will, signed and witnessed after the testator or testatrix signed the original will.

collateral—Property someone gives another person to secure the performance of any contract or other agreement.

collision insurance—The type of insurance that pays for damage to the insured's vehicle in the event of a collision.

community property—A system of property rights affecting husbands and wives, the basis of which is that the earnings of either spouse belong to both spouses. There are nine community property states; Arizona, California, Idaho, Louisiana, Nevada, New Mexico, Texas, Washington, and Wisconsin.

comprehensive insurance—A policy of insurance which covers a number of different risks.

consent to release information or records—A document in which one person authorizes another to release information or records to that person, or to a third person.

consideration—In a contract, the money, property, or promise that is given in return for other money, property, or for another promise.

consumer—Someone who seeks credit or buys property for personal, family, or household purposes.

contingent beneficiary—Same as *alternate beneficiary* above.

contractor—Someone who agrees to perform a certain job for someone else, but who will control the details of the work.

convey—To transfer title from one person to another.

cost-plus—A payment arrangement with a contractor in which the person hiring the contractor pays for the costs of materials, the cost of the contractor's employees and subcontractors, plus an additional percentage of those total costs.

covenant—A promise to do or not do something, or a promise that certain facts do or do not exist.

credit agency—A company that collects financial information about people or other companies.

creditor—Someone who is owed something by someone else.

curtesy—A husband's rights in his wife's property.

custodian of records—The person responsible for maintaining the records of an institution, organization, or business.

debtor—Someone who owes something to someone else.

declarant—Someone who makes a statement, such as someone who makes a living will.

deed—A document transferring an interest in real property.

default—The failure to perform a duty or obligation.

deficiency judgment—A judgment against a debtor which equals the difference between what the debtor owes a creditor and the sums the creditor recovered upon foreclosure and sale of the collateral given to secure the debt.

demand—A request to perform an obligation.

dower—A wife's rights in her husband's property.

durable power of attorney—A document in which a principal gives an agent power to perform certain acts for the principal, and which remains in effect despite the principal's disability or incapacity.

earnest money—Money given by a buyer to a seller to bind the sale of real estate.

easement—A right to do something on land owned by someone else.

eminent domain—The power of the government to take private property without consent of the property owner.

employee—Someone who works for someone else, but who does not have control of the details of the work he or she performs.

encumbrance—A right to (or an interest in) land that reduces the value of real property.

escrow agreement—A document deposited by a person with a third party (escrow agent), to be kept until the performance of some condition, and upon the happening of the condition, to be delivered over to some other person.

estate—The property left by a deceased person.

estate in land—An interest in land.

executor—A man named by the maker of a will to carry out the directions in the will.

executrix—A woman named by the maker of a will to carry out the directions in the will.

Fair Credit Reporting Act—A federal law which requires consumer reporting agencies to be fair to consumers in investigating and reporting on a consumer's credit.

financing statement—A document that a creditor files to give notice to other creditors that the creditor has a security interest in certain collateral.

firm bid—A proposal that a contractor cannot change once an owner accepts it.

fixture—Something attached to real property which becomes part of the real property.

foreclosure—The enforcement of a lien, contract, trust deed, or mortgage in any manner provided by law.

garnishment—A creditor's action to satisfy a debt by seizing some property of the debtor that is held by some third person, such as wages the third person owes the debtor.

general power of attorney—A document in which a principal gives an agent broad powers to perform acts for the principal.

grant deed—A deed which contains some, but not all, warranties of title.

grantee—In a deed, the party to whom the grantor transfers the property.

grantor—In a deed, the party who transfers the property to the grantee.

guarantor—A person who promises (or the act of making a promise) to answer for the debt of another.

guarantee—A promise (or the act of making a promise) to answer for the debt of another.

guaranty—Same as to *guarantee*.

guardian—A person who has the custody and control of another person.

habitable—Fit for living in.

heir—One who succeeds to the property of someone who has died without a will.

hereditaments—Anything capable of being inherited, whether real property, personal property, or both.

hold harmless—To protect from any loss.

homestead rights—Rights which protect a person's home from creditors.

imminent—About to happen.

indemnify—To repay someone for a loss suffered by that person.

independent contractor—Someone who is in business for himself or herself and who controls the details of work he or she performs for other people.

intestate succession—The laws governing who is to receive property when someone dies without a will.

joint tenants—Two or more people who own property with right of survivorship, which means that when one of the joint tenants dies, the property automatically belongs to the other joint tenant(s).

joint property affidavit—An affidavit signed by joint owners of property declaring that they own property jointly with right of survivorship.

judgment—A court's final decision as to the rights of the parties in a lawsuit.

lease—An agreement in which an owner of property allows a lessee or renter to use that property temporarily, for a fee.

lease/option agreement—A lease in which the lessee or renter has the right to buy the property that he or she is renting.

legal description—A description of land by precise measurement, usually by metes and bounds.

liability insurance—The type of insurance that protects a person if they cause injury to some other person or damage to some other person's property.

lien—A charge upon property for the payment of a debt.

listing agreement—A contract in which the owner of real property employs a broker to find a buyer for the property.

living will—A document which expresses a person's desire to be allowed to die a natural death.

loss payee—The person in an insurance policy who is to receive the proceeds of the insurance policy in the event of a loss.

metes and bounds—A description of the boundary lines and marks of a piece of land.

month-to-month tenancy—A tenancy in which there is no definite duration of the tenancy and in which the rent is due monthly.

mortgage—A conveyance of property to secure the payment of a debt by making real property collateral for the debt.

natural death act—A law state legislatures pass to allow a person to die a natural death.

notarize—To certify to the authenticity of a signature on a document.

notice of nonpayment—Notice that a payment is past due, given by a creditor to a debtor.

notice of protest—Notice, given by a creditor to a debtor, of a bank or other official certification of nonpayment of a sum that the debtor owes the creditor.

null—Having no effect. Not binding on anyone.

personal property—Money, goods, and movable objects.

personal property sales contract—An agreement in which the seller of personal property finances the buyer's purchase of the property.

power of attorney—A document in which one person gives another person the power to perform certain acts for the person who gives the power.

presentment for payment—A demand for payment.

principal—In an agency relationship, the person for whom another acts. In finance, the amount of the original debt as distinguished from interest accruing on that debt.

probate—To prove that a will is genuine and was properly signed. The court process of managing a deceased person's affairs.

promissory note—A document in which the signer promises to pay the holder a certain amount of money on certain terms.

prorate—To divide proportionately.

protest—To obtain a bank or other official certification of nonpayment.

publish a will—A statement, made by the maker of a will to the witnesses when they witness the will, that the instrument they are witnessing shall take effect as the maker's will.

quitclaim deed—A deed in which the grantor transfers his or her interest in property to someone else, without any warranties of title.

real estate contract—A contract in which one party agrees to sell, and another party agrees to buy, real estate.

real property—Land, and things that are permanent, fixed, and immovable.

receipt—A document evidencing that someone received something from someone else.

recording a document—To file a document in the proper office established for records of documents.

rental agreement—An agreement in which a landlord allows a renter to temporarily use the landlord's property for a fee.

repossession—Taking back property after it is given or sold to someone else.

request for credit information—A document asking a credit agency or other creditor for information that the agency or creditor has in its file on a person.

request for explanation of denial of a credit application—A document asking a lender to explain why they denied a credit application, or granted the application but required a higher interest rate.

residuary estate—The part of the estate of a deceased person which remains after paying all debts, claims against the estate, and after making any specific gifts listed in the deceased person's will.

revocable trust—A trust that can be revoked or amended by the creator at any time.

revocation—A cancellation of something already done.

revocation of living will—A cancellation of a signed living will.

revocation of a power of attorney—A cancellation of a signed power of attorney.

right of survivorship—A condition of joint ownership whereby joint property automatically belongs to the surviving joint owner when another joint owner dies.

royalty—The right of an author, composer, or inventor to a portion of the money received from the sale of a literary work, musical composition, or invention.

seal—An impression, made by an instrument or device, which is a symbol of the genuineness of a document or of the signatures to a document.

secured party—A person who has a security interest in collateral.

secured transaction—An obligation secured by a mortgage or other lien.

security agreement—An agreement which creates or provides for a security interest.

security deposit—In the landlord/tenant context, a refundable sum of money given by the tenant to the landlord to be used by the landlord to repair any damage done by the tenant.

security interest—An interest in personal property which secures payment or performance of an obligation.

seisin—Ownership of an interest in land.

signature card—A card at a bank or other institution signed by whoever is authorized to deposit money into or withdraw money from an account, or to enter a safe deposit box.

special power of attorney—A power of attorney in which a principal gives an agent the power to do only certain acts.

special warranty deed—A deed in which a grantor conveys real property to a grantee, and the grantor claims that he or she owns the property, has the right to transfer the property to the grantee, that there are no liens or encumbrances against the property, and that the grantor will defend any actions brought against the grantee by anyone claiming an interest in the property, so long as the claim is based on something that the grantor did before the grantor signed a contract with the grantee for sale of the property.

subcontractor—Someone who performs part of a job that a contractor has agreed to perform.

sublease—An agreement in which a renter transfers less than all of the renter's rights in a rental agreement to someone else.

successor—One who follows another.

successor trustee—A trustee who replaces another trustee.

surety—Someone who agrees to be responsible for losses suffered because someone else failed to perform as he or she agreed to perform.

surety bond—An agreement by a surety to be responsible for losses suffered because someone failed to perform as he or she agreed to perform.

tenancy in common—Joint ownership in which, when one joint owner dies, his or her interest in the joint property does not automatically belong to the other joint owner(s).

tenements—Houses or buildings on real property.

terminal illness—An illness that will surely result in death.

testator—A man who died leaving a valid will.

testatrix—A woman who died leaving a valid will.

title—The legal ownership of property.

title search—A search of the chain of title of property to discover the past and present owners of property and any encumbrances against property.

trust agreement—A document in which one person, called a trustor or creator, appoints another person, called a trustee, to manage property for the benefit of another person, called a beneficiary.

trust deed—A deed that secures a debt by making real property collateral for the debt.

trustee—The person in a trust who manages property for a beneficiary.

trustor—The person who creates a trust.

undivided ownership—Ownership of all of something.

Uniform Commercial Code—A set of uniform commercial laws adopted by most states.

United States Code—The laws passed by the U.S. Congress in Washington, D.C.

usury—Charging more than the legal rate of interest.

void—Having no effect. Not binding on anyone.

waiver—The giving up of a right or claim.

warranty—A promise to do or not do something, or a promise that certain facts do or do not exist.

warranty deed—A deed in which a grantor transfers real property to a grantee, and the grantor claims that he or she owns the property, that he or she has the right to transfer the property to the grantee, that there are no liens or other encumbrances against the property, and that the grantor will defend any actions brought against the grantee by anyone claiming an interest in the property.

will—A document which contains a person's instructions for his or her property and other affairs after death.

workmanlike manner—The usual way of doing something in the area where it is being done.

Index

Forms Index